Shannon Miller

MY CHILD, MY HERO

by Claudia Miller

with Gayle White

FOREWORD BY SHANNON MILLER

UNIVERSITY OF OKLAHOMA PRESS
Norman

FRONTISPIECE: *Shannon Miller competing in the World Championships in Australia. Courtesy Felipe Monsivais.*

Quotations in this book are taken from the following sources:
Atlanta Journal-Constitution, June 14, 1992; April 25, 1993; February 5, 1995;
    July 22, 1996; July 30, 1996
Daily Oklahoman, August 4, 1992
Edmond Evening Sun, March 19, 1997
New York Times, July 22, 1996
USA Today, June 28, 1996; July 20, 1996

Library of Congress Cataloging-in-Publication Data
Miller, Claudia Ann, 1948–
    Shannon Miller : my child, my hero / by Claudia Miller ; foreword by
    Shannon Miller.
        p.   cm.
    ISBN 0–8061–3110–1 (alk. paper)
    1. Miller, Shannon, 1977–   . 2. Gymnasts—United States—Biography.
    I. Title
GV460.2.M55M55   1999
796.44'092—dc21
[B]   98–39127
                                                                                                    CIP

APR 2 0 2000

Text design by Trina Stahl

The paper in this book meets the guidelines for permanence and
durability of the Committee on Production Guidelines for Book
Longevity of the Council on Library Resources, Inc.

1 2 3 4 5 6 7 8 9 10

I wish to dedicate this book to my family: to Shannon, who worked so very long and hard to achieve her success; to my other two children, Tessa, who lovingly and patiently assisted Shannon whenever she could, and Troy, who never complained about going to gymnastics meets and always found ways to help the family; and, of course, to my husband, Ron. Without his help, I never would have finished this book. As we discussed our many memories and researched facts, Ron reminded me that this project was meaningful not only to Shannon and our family, but also to the parents and children who will follow many of the same roads we have traveled.

I also want to thank Gayle White for her infinite patience and wonderfully perceptive advice as we worked to polish my manuscript.

CONTENTS

LIST OF ILLUSTRATIONS

Photos are from the Miller family collection, unless otherwise noted.

FOREWORD

BY SHANNON MILLER

A T TWENTY-ONE, I now have an opportunity to take a breath and look back contentedly on a gymnastics career that has spanned more than fifteen years and continues today. There have been numerous ups and downs in my life and career throughout the years, but there has always been one very important constant: the support of my coaches, my community, and, most of all, the support of my family. I hope this book, so lovingly written by my mother, will provide a little insight into the world I have grown up in and will help readers understand the many roles my parents have had to play in order to give me opportunities to excel in every way possible.

The greatest lesson my parents have taught me is never to set limits on what I can do. They have helped me learn many life lessons that not only paved the way for my athletic achievements but will prepare me, I know, for whatever lies ahead.

My parents and I are frequently asked about the many sacrifices that we have had to make. But to me there really were no sacrifices. I love being in the gym and I enjoy pushing myself to be the best I can in every way. I believe my parents have always felt the same way. I think that in writing this book, Mom has made it clear that she and Dad have loved every minute spent helping me accomplish my goals. Certainly my life, both inside and outside the gym, hasn't been all fun and games, but with my parents' guidance I've always known that I can trust in God to see me through the tough times.

As I look back on the years I've spent in the gym, on the many memories of training, traveling, and competing; the friendships I've found; the places I've seen and cultures I've experienced; and the wonderful crowds for which I've performed, I cannot help feeling that I have been very blessed. I am honored to have had such loyal fans and such an extraordinary community, and I know how fortunate I am to have had knowledgeable, dedicated coaches and such supportive and loving parents. My parents have always been there for me—in times of trial or of triumph.

Shannon Miller

*If you believe in yourself and have dedication and pride—
and never quit, you'll be a winner. The price of victory
is high—but so are the rewards.*

PAUL "BEAR" BRYANT

Prologue

I GAZED IN NEAR-disbelief as my daughter Shannon sat stunned on a blue mat on the floor of the cavernous Georgia Dome with more than thirty thousand fans gasping in the stands and millions more watching on television. She had landed there while attempting a vault she had completed successfully hundreds of times. I felt numb. My husband, Ron, and I had watched from the stands high above as she charged down the runway for her second vault in this individual event competition, but the fall happened so quickly I did not know what went wrong. Thoughts and emotions crowded my brain. Foremost was the question, Is Shannon hurt? When I realized she wasn't—at least physically—I began to wonder what had happened.

The answer came on a giant screen as Shannon appeared in slow-motion replay approaching the vaulting horse. I cringed as I saw one of her hands miss the apparatus, then stared helplessly as she struggled for control. I knew the embarrassment and frustration she must be feeling. Shannon had competed through pain and injury during her career because she never wanted to disappoint a crowd. Now she felt she had let down every fan. She said later she wanted to stand up and scream, "I can do the vault!"

This was a low point in these roller-coaster Olympic Games, held in Atlanta and touted as the "world's largest peacetime event." Shannon was already an Olympic star, with five medals—the most of any American athlete—from the 1992 Games to prove it. In Barcelona she had outscored every other gymnast from the world's elite as she led the American women to a bronze team medal. Here in Atlanta she had been the top-scoring American woman in team competition as the young women who became known as the "Magnificent Seven" won the gold medal in a field of gymnasts from a record number of competing countries.

That had been a moment of a lifetime. Seven friends, fiercely competitive in national events but functioning as a unit in world competition, had sealed a place in history and set a standard for hundreds of thousands of girls who would follow them. The heart-bursting joy of that night seemed far away now. First Shannon had been disappointed in her performance in competition for the all-around medal. Now she had fallen on vault.

Ron and I knew vault was not Shannon's strongest event, but she had proven over the years that she was capable of winning on any gymnastics apparatus. She had seemed to be in a good mood tonight. As we watched her warm up, we could tell that she was focused and ready. She hit every vault without a hitch. In competition that changed. She took a small step on her first vault of the evening. As soon as she hit the springboard for her second vault, she said later, she felt something was wrong.

In the USA Gymnastics suite after the competition, Steve Nunno, her coach, met Ron and me with a plea: "Talk to her—please. She needs to pull herself together. She still has beam tomorrow." He did not need to remind us. We were well aware that the next day Shannon would have to climb onto a four-inch-wide beam forty-seven and a half inches above the floor and once again represent her country in a field of the world's best. She had to believe in herself again as she went into what could be her last Olympic event.

CHAPTER ONE

In the Beginning

WITH THE PRECISION required of an Olympic athlete, Shannon Lee Miller arrived in the world—in Rolla, Missouri, to be specific—on exactly the day she was due: March 10, 1977. She weighed in at only five pounds, six ounces, but her pediatrician, Barbara Russell, assured me she was healthy. "After all," said Dr. Russell, "great things come in small packages." The doctor had no idea that her statement was prophetic.

When Shannon was about four months old Dr. Russell noticed a problem that would make some of Shannon's later achievements seem even more remarkable. Her legs were turning in much more than was normal. At first the doctor advised Ron and me to try therapy each day at home, but after a month she determined that Shannon needed more.

At about this time our family was moving from Rolla to Edmond, Oklahoma. Ron and I were both from San Antonio, Texas, and had met in college at Trinity University there. When we graduated I went to law school at Washington University in St. Louis and Ron went to graduate school at the University of Missouri at Rolla, about one hundred miles away. That lasted only a year before we married on June 19, 1971. Shannon's sister, Tessa, was born four years later, about two years before Shannon. Ron completed a doctorate in physics and accepted a position on the faculty of Central State University, later renamed the University of Central Oklahoma, in Edmond. I took a job at a bank there.

Dr. Russell contacted an orthopedic specialist in Edmond, Dr. Rick Beller, and he shared Dr. Russell's concern. He explained that the problem could be corrected by having Shannon wear specially designed toeless baby shoes, attached to a metal bar. The bar would keep her legs turned out so that they would not continue to grow inward. We were worried about how Shannon would adapt to this apparatus, especially when Dr. Beller explained further that she might need to wear this brace for as long as a year. It should not be removed except to bathe her. Frequent removal could delay or even prevent correction of the problem.

Needless to say, Shannon was not happy about her new

1. Shannon Miller, age 1. Courtesy Olan Mills Portrait Studios.

shoes. A baby who rarely fussed now screamed her objections to us day and night. But we adhered to the doctor's advice, even having her sleep in the offensive shoes. Before long Shannon decided to make the best of the situation. And contrary to Dr. Beller's prediction that she would probably crawl and walk more slowly because of this impediment to her activity, she was crawling everywhere by eight months and walking before her first birthday, almost the exact schedule Tessa had followed. Shannon couldn't afford to be slowed down; she had an older sister to keep up with.

Shannon was getting about so well, in fact, that she nearly frightened me out of my wits on a shopping trip. Not long after she learned to walk I sat her down with Tessa while I looked through children's clothes in a local J. C. Penney's store. A few minutes later, when I looked around for the girls, they were gone. I found Tessa on the other side of a rack of clothes, but not Shannon. I wasn't too worried as it had been only a few minutes since I put the girls down, and Shannon never strayed far from Tessa. But Tessa didn't know where she was, so I took her hand and began calling for Shannon.

When we had not found her after a five-minute search, I became desperate. I asked every sales clerk I could find whether they had seen her. People brought me two other children, but not Shannon. She still had not turned up after ten minutes, and my panic was building. I was terrified that she had found her way out of the store and that someone had taken her. Both Tessa and I were crying as we combed the store for Shannon.

After fifteen minutes that seemed to last forever an older gentleman asked me if I was looking for a blond curly-headed little girl in a blue outfit. I screamed "Yes." Before I could say anything else he asked me to come with him. He thought I should see for myself where she was.

There was Shannon in the men's shoe department with a pair of big black shoes on her feet. Ironically, to this day Shannon has a shoe fixation. We tease her that her obsession with shoes started that day in J. C. Penney's. Of course, her taste has improved somewhat.

Shannon would develop many role models over the years, including some of the world's greatest athletes. The first and most enduring was her big sister, Tessa. From the earliest days Shannon wanted to dress like Tessa, go where Tessa went, say whatever Tessa said.

When Shannon was about eighteen months old and Tessa was almost three and a half, we bought the girls an old jungle gym at a garage sale. Tessa quickly learned to climb to the top, stand on the platform, and declare herself queen of the backyard. One day when I had run into the house for a minute while the girls were playing in the fenced yard, I returned to see Shannon near the top of the jungle gym. She was not about to be left on the ground. Now there were co-queens of the backyard.

It was a pattern Shannon would follow whenever she watched Tessa venture out. At six Tessa was eager to take

2. *Shannon and Tessa, 1979.*

3. Shannon, age 4, preparing to be a leopard in a beginning dance recital.

dance lessons with some of her friends. A couple of times a week Tessa went blissfully off to her ballet and jazz classes while Shannon stayed home. Ron and I had not enrolled Shannon because money was tight and she was only four. Shannon decided this arrangement would not do. The next time my mother, Rosemary Murff, called from San Antonio Shannon poured out her sad story. Of course, Grandma Murff immediately agreed to pick up the tab, and off Shannon went to dance class.

Shannon loved those dance classes and being a part of the December dance recital. In fact, she loved her leopard recital costume so much that she wore it around the house and for several years as a Halloween costume. When she outgrew her costume, she wore Tessa's.

Both girls were doing well at dance, but after a little over a year Tessa decided she was ready to move on to other things. She talked it over with Shannon, and the two of them announced that they would not be attending dance anymore.

Although I secretly harbored a hope that as they got older the girls would again want to take dance, I had to admit that not having to drive them to lessons twice a week was a blessing. Troy, the girls' baby brother, arrived in mid-December 1980. Both girls had been eagerly anticipating the baby's arrival. Tessa was prepared to mother the new arrival; Shannon envisioned a big, moving, noise-making doll. So I was not surprised to find Shannon wheeling Troy around the house in her doll carriage.

CHAPTER TWO

Trampoline Tricks

HANNON'S ROAD TO the Olympics began in our back-yard the Christmas before the girls quit dance lessons. Shannon, then four, decided to ask Santa for a trampoline. At first we tried to dissuade her, but rather than become discouraged, she simply enlisted the help of her big sister.

Ron and I were worried that a trampoline would be dangerous and, even though I found a good used one, too expensive. I was afraid if I spent all our Christmas money on this one gift the girls would not understand why there weren't any other gifts under the tree. But I knew how much they—especially Shannon—counted on getting the trampoline. They knew Santa always rewarded good girls, and they were sure they had been *very* good. I discussed my dilemma with my mother, and she volunteered to help pay for the trampoline. She didn't want her granddaughters to be disappointed.

The girls were thrilled with their discovery on Christmas morning. Shannon declared that Santa had brought the trampoline to her, but she would be glad to share. There was one problem: the temperature outside was 9 degrees, and the trampoline had to be assembled. We had hidden it in a friend's garage and Ron had not had a chance to put it together. Now Shannon was adamant that Santa would want her to jump on it right away. My parents and brother had come from San Antonio for Christmas, so my brother and father donned their coats and braved the weather to help Ron put up the trampoline.

Shannon and Tessa were so enthralled with their gift that they hardly noticed the freezing weather. In the days after Christmas they spent hours jumping on the trampoline. In fact, this addition to the backyard may have had something to do with the loss of interest in dance. After only a few weeks Shannon effortlessly executed a series of front flips. Her dad and I were astounded. Soon Tessa was also doing flips. Ron and I decided we needed to channel the girls' energy before one of them was hurt. I asked them whether they would like to take gymnastics. The girls eagerly agreed that they would like to try gymnastics, especially if they would learn to do more types of flips on or off the trampoline.

People who have Olympic ambitions for their little girls ask me today how we found a gym, assuming I have some great formula. The truth is that I left messages at three different gyms listed in the Yellow Pages, but only one returned my call. That's where the girls went. It was near our house and offered classes for their age group, and both girls could be in the same class. They bounded off eagerly once a week.

As summer began, their coach and the owner of the gym, Jerry Clavier, asked us to let the girls come for an hour a day, five days a week. He said he thought they both showed some potential for competing, and he wanted to get them into his "pre-team" group. I was a little hesitant. I was worried that they would get burned out and quit, just as they had with their dance lessons. They were having so much fun that I hated to see it become work for them.

Tessa was not enthusiastic about the proposal. Always eager to develop new talents and conquer new areas, she decided to quit gymnastics to take art classes. In the past

Shannon had always been quick to follow her older sister's lead. Now she was establishing her own destiny and interest. She didn't flinch. Instead she begged us to let her participate in the more intensive program with or without her sister. As a college professor Ron has a flexible schedule in the summer, so he agreed to drive her.

When Shannon started school she was no longer required to go to the gym daily. She went three days a week, including Saturday, but for about two and a half hours at a time. Now, instead of working at the sport five hours a week, she was actually practicing gymnastics seven and a half hours a week. Ron and I thought that was too intensive for a six-year-old, but Shannon's coach kept telling us she had the potential to accomplish more than she was doing. Since she seemed far more advanced than the other girls her age, he volunteered to give her free private weekly lessons. Each Saturday she stayed an extra hour to work on more difficult skills.

Soon Jerry said he wanted to put Shannon in the workouts with his Class II and III team gymnasts. At that time there were five levels of gymnasts, ranging in skill from the

4. At Jerry Clavier's gym, age 6.

5. First ski trip, age 6. Courtesy Summit Photography, Dillon, Colo.

beginners of IV to the skilled practitioners of I and, beyond, the "elite," the best of the best. I went to watch the first class and tried hard not to laugh as Shannon, small for her age, strode out onto the floor with girls that were twelve to fifteen years old. To their credit (I will always be very grateful to these loving and patient girls), they accepted her and treated her with respect.

People often mistake Shannon's quiet demeanor for shyness. But she frequently showed a brave, feisty streak even as a child. For example, shortly after her sixth birthday the family went to Denver to visit Ron's brother, Roger. The girls entertained themselves by tumbling around his apartment, an activity that threatened the expensive souvenirs from his military service in Europe. Tessa could be distracted by reading and drawing, but Shannon was more physically active. To allow the girls to let off some steam, we decided to take them skiing. I also decided to put Shannon in a class in a nearby gym. Shannon was excited, but the coach in the office refused to take a child for just a few days. I tried to explain that she had been taking gymnastics for a year and was familiar with the basic skills. When he still said no, Shannon informed him that she could already do a back handspring on the floor and a back walkover on the high beam.

The coach finally let Shannon into the gym to show him what she could do. Shannon quickly executed a back handspring, and then another. The surprised coach asked how old she was. Shannon replied that she had just turned six. He commented that he had one or two six-year-olds who could do back handsprings but not with the exceptionally good form Shannon showed.

By then Shannon was climbing up on a high beam. It was at this moment that I realized I had never seen her do a back walkover on the beam, and for an instant I thought about stopping her. Before I could say anything she had already finished her back walkover. The coach was so impressed he went to get three other coaches, saying, "Wait till you see this!" After Shannon performed again all four crowded around to tell me what a gifted child I had and that I should enroll her in their "special" class immediately. It took a while for me to convince them that we lived in Oklahoma so I could not possibly enroll Shannon full-time in their gym. Unfortunately, while her performance brought oohs and aahs, it did not get her into any classes on a short-term basis.

Within less than a year Shannon was able to keep up with or even surpass most of the girls on Jerry's gymnastics teams. Since she wasn't having to learn routines or go to meets, she grew bored when the older girls were involved in preparing for competition. At about this time Jerry heard about the United States Association of Independent Gymnastics Clubs (USAIGC) testing program, designed to identify talented younger gymnasts and give them the opportunity to attend training camps with other gymnasts of similar age and skill level.

Jerry thought this program might be good for Shannon.

He had few details but found out that a test was being given in Waco, Texas, in May. At his request Ron and I agreed that I would drive Shannon and Jerry to Waco. Shannon was excited about the trip.

We all got a big surprise that day. Only a few other girls showed up to take the test, and they were all well prepared. Shannon did not even know the names of some of the strength and flexibility skills she was asked to do. Seventy was passing, and Shannon scored a little over 50. While the other girls scored closer to 70, no one passed the test that day.

I was somewhat discouraged for Shannon, but Gary Goodson, who was giving the test, came over to say he thought she had done remarkably well for her age, size, and experience. He gave us a detailed copy of the strength and flexibility skills and explained that once she passed this part of the test, she would be eligible to take part two. We hadn't even realized there was a part two—apparatus skills—that had to be completed successfully within six months of passing part one.

Jerry immediately began training Shannon to retake the strength and flexibility portion of the test, and when time permitted they began to work on the skills for part two. At first Shannon enjoyed working on strength and flexibility. She hadn't liked failing that test. But working press to handstands soon got boring. In this exercise a gymnast sits with her legs apart and her hands between her legs a few inches in front of her, presses her palms flat on the floor, then shifts her weight from her seat to her hands. Gradually rolling her hips over her shoulders, she lifts her legs, ending in a handstand.

By the end of July Shannon still hadn't mastered this skill, which had to be performed on floor, vaulting horse, beam, low bar, and high bar. Jerry asked us to have her work on it every evening before she went to bed. Needless to say, if she was bored doing the exercise at the gym, she certainly didn't want to do it at home. We decided to find a way to make these presses a little more exciting.

At the time Shannon very much wanted a Cabbage Patch doll. They were being advertised and all the kids had heard of them, but no shipments had yet arrived in our area of Oklahoma. Ron and I promised Shannon that if she would work on her presses every night with no complaints, as soon as she could do one by herself we would find a way to get her a Cabbage Patch doll. We figured we had another month or two, by which time these dolls should be in the stores. A few days later Shannon was doing presses completely by herself and asking how soon we would be bringing the doll home. Fortunately, we had heard just that week that a local department store was expecting a shipment of dolls, but it seemed the whole world wanted them. It would be first come, first serve. Although the store didn't open until 10:00 A.M., at 7:00 A.M. the employees would begin handing out tickets to potential customers for the right to come back later and buy a doll. My husband got up at 5 o'clock to get in line for one of those precious tickets. He gave the ticket to me, and I took my lunch break from work at 10 o'clock to stand in line for my chance to get into the store and pick out a doll. I brought home a bald-headed baby boy, one of the few dolls left when I got in. Shannon was ecstatic. To this day she remembers his name: Oscar.

After that first test in Waco other parents began to hear of Jerry's program and wanted their daughters in the group preparing for the USAIGC test. Jerry held his own test of sorts and formed a new pre-team group with Shannon and five others about the same age, all talented and competitive.

The night before the test the girls were jittery and had trouble completing the required moves. Jerry was not optimistic that any of them would pass. But when show time came Jerry saw he had real competitors. Each girl tossed aside her fears and did what she had to do. When the test was over and the scores tabulated, all five of Jerry's girls had passed. Shannon had scored the highest with an 86.

Now the real work began. They all had just six months to

pass part two of the test if they were going to become part of the USAIGC junior elite program and attend the special training camps. They pushed and encouraged each other. Jerry increased the workout time.

All this work at the gym was eating into Shannon's precious TV viewing, so she decided she needed to find a way to save time. She began to surreptitiously put on her leotard at night under her pajamas and wear it to school under her clothes so that she could just pull off her school clothes and be ready for gym. Presto—a few more minutes of TV time. After a couple of months we discovered her trick when her school pictures came back and the sleeve of her maroon leotard was sticking out from under her peach-colored dress. This should have been our first indication that Shannon would later become a master at conserving time and using it efficiently and wisely.

The strenuous workouts did take their toll on Shannon, now seven. Shannon and Tessa rode the bus to and from school each day. Two stops were about equidistant from our

6. Shannon, age 6. The leotard that she secretly wore to school under her dress is showing below the lacy right sleeve in this school photo.

house, so, depending on which friends they were with, the girls might get off at different stops but always arrived home within a few minutes of each other. Ron generally got home from the university soon after the girls. One day he and Tessa realized Shannon was overdue. Tessa ran outdoors to look for her; Ron headed for the telephone to call the school. Before he could complete the call the school bus lumbered up in front of our house (usually the kids were dropped off a block or two away). Out stepped Shannon wiping sleep and a few tears from her eyes. She had been so tired she had fallen asleep on the noisy bus, and, because she was so small and near the back, the driver didn't realize he still had a passenger until he arrived back at the bus barn and Shannon woke up and, startled to find herself alone in a strange place, began to cry. The driver felt so sorry for her that he drove her right to her front door. Not long after this incident Ron began to pick up the girls at school some days so that they avoided the nearly hourlong bus ride. The school was only a ten-minute drive from our house, but we were almost the last stop on the route.

Jerry continued to press the girls to work very hard. He and all five girls knew they had the potential to pass part two of the USAIGC test, but the six-month training period seemed to fly by. Even a week before the test Jerry suggested to the parents that we rethink the testing. He had stayed to watch the second part of the test when his girls had taken the first part. He had seen that although the girls being tested looked very good, few had managed to pass. But who would tell our girls to quit now? The parents wouldn't. We felt the girls had worked too hard and deserved a chance. Jerry agreed he would take them.

Once again the five young girls surprised their coach. They were allowed two attempts to pass each skill on each of the four women's gymnastics apparatuses: vaulting horse, uneven parallel bars, balance beam, and floor. They took to each one fearlessly and proved their determination.

Shannon did things that day she had never done in the

gym at home. For the first time she performed a giant swing—a 360-degree swing around the high bar with her body stretched totally out from her hands to her toes. Because bars were closer together then than now, she had to bend, or pike, her hips at just the right time to avoid crashing into the low bar. If she piked too soon, she lost momentum and couldn't go all the way around; if she piked too late, she hit the bar.

Shannon was again the high scorer, but all five girls earned the right to join the USAIGC junior elite that day. The parents were proud; the coach was awed. He was starting to realize he had five exceptionally talented gymnasts who knew how to compete.

By now all the girls were about eight years old. Jerry was as eager to learn as his little gymnasts were. He heard about a camp run by the legendary gymnastics coach Bela Karolyi in Houston. Working with other talented girls from all over the United States at the Karolyi camp would be a great morale booster, and Jerry was enthusiastic about watching more experienced coaches at work. He presented his idea at the next meeting of the parents' club we had formed. Girls and parents immediately approved.

Bela was a former national champion hammer thrower in Romania who met his wife and partner, Martha, an accomplished gymnast, when they were students at the Physical Education University in Bucharest. As the story goes, he discovered the legendary Nadia Comaneci on a school playground in a town in the foothills of the Carpathian Mountains. As her fame rose, so did his. In the 1976 Olympics in Montreal, she scored the first perfect 10 in Olympic history for a routine on the uneven parallel bars, then went on to receive six more 10s before the games ended.

While in the United States for an exhibition in March 1981, Bela, Martha, and their choreographer, Geza Pozar, defected. After working at menial jobs in Los Angeles, he moved to Houston and opened a gym that went on to train many of America's top gymnasts, including Mary Lou

Retton. Bela was known as a tough taskmaster, an almost mil-
itaristic leader who controlled every aspect of his gymnasts'
lives and had no patience for girls who could not live up to his
demands. However, he was also seen as a teddy bear of a
coach who enveloped his tiny gymnasts in huge hugs after
they competed.

While Shannon made her packing list, Ron and I reviewed finances. I would be able to afford to go with
Shannon. I looked forward to the chance to be with Shannon
and to learn more about gymnastics. Since I had recently
become a gymnastic judge, I was eager to learn everything I
could.

When Jerry said he wanted to put the girls in meets, I
realized I did not have a clue about gymnastics as a competitive sport. I didn't know the names of the moves, and I didn't
understand how the value of the routines was determined.
When Shannon wanted me to spot her or help her through an
exercise, I had to trust her to tell me what to do. I couldn't find
a book to explain anything. Jerry suggested I take a judges
course to learn how gymnastics works. We met once a week
for five weeks, then took a test. I passed. I never really intended to judge professionally, but the next thing I knew I got
a contract in the mail.

I enjoyed judging for almost ten years, starting in late
October of every year and continuing sometimes into June.
After a couple of years off I am now judging again. The most
difficult part is recognizing all the skills and their values and
getting them down on paper. Competitions usually include
compulsories, in which each gymnast is required to do the
same moves, and optionals, in which the gymnasts have a lot
more freedom of selection and artistic expression.

In compulsory routines gymnasts must perform prescribed movements, and there is a specific deduction for
everything they do, from the way they stand to the way they
hold their hands. Optionals are harder to judge because
gymnasts put together their own routines. A judge has to be

familiar with the specific requirements for each level and recognize each move, know its value, and understand exactly how it is supposed to be performed. Since a series of connected moves are counted differently than separate moves, a judge has to be able to tell a series from several separate moves. This can be harder than it sounds since the gymnasts are moving so quickly. Furthermore, a judge also has to be able to do math quickly because everyone is waiting for the score.

Today gymnasts can work their way up through ten levels, with the newest, greenest students at Level 1 and the experienced girls who often qualify for college scholarships at Levels 9 and 10. The elite gymnasts are still in a class by themselves. Judges can qualify for various competitive levels by passing tests at those levels. Elite judges usually have years of experience and are invited to a special course.

Judging requires constant study. Gymnastics is different from most other sports because officials change the rules every four years and make additional smaller adjustments every year. Skills may be upgraded and given more value, or, more likely, downgraded and devalued as the skill levels of gymnasts rise. I knew that I could hone my ability as a judge by watching the girls at Bela's camp.

We wondered whether the great Bela really attended the camp, but he was there the very first day. He divided the girls into groups based on their tumbling skill level. Shannon was the only girl in Jerry's group who had mastered a full twisting back somersault, so she ended up in one of the more advanced groups without any of her buddies. She was not happy about this, but after a day or two she settled in and began to enjoy herself. She especially liked the beam coach, who also seemed to like her. One day when Bela strolled through the gym the coach motioned him over to watch Shannon as she connected two flip-flops. Bela was impressed and picked her up to hug her. Shannon was awed and worked harder than ever. She hoped to get his attention again.

Shannon knew Bela was important because he was

associated with Mary Lou. Like thousands of young girls Shannon had thought Mary Lou Retton was wonderful in the 1984 Olympics. She was thrilled at the opportunity to work in the same gym where Mary Lou had trained.

One day a rumor spread through camp that Mary Lou was there. Hundreds of gymnasts and their parents milled in the parking lot waiting for a glimpse and staring at the car that was reported to be hers. After a while someone came out of the office and told us Mary Lou was gone. She had slipped out a back way. Shannon and the other girls were crushed.

Now, years later, when Shannon is approached for autographs in grocery stores and restaurants—even while buying underwear at the mall—she remembers her disappointment and tries to be gracious. Shannon now counts Mary Lou as a good friend and still sees her as a great role model.

At the end of the camp Bela asked his coaches to pick out a few gymnasts for bar and tumbling exhibitions. Out of

7. Shannon and her best friend, Lisa Heckel, form the front row at Bela Karolyi's summer camp in Houston.

about three hundred gymnasts at the camp, Shannon was chosen for both bars and floor. She was ecstatic and scared by the thought that Bela was going to coach her personally. He did, in fact, spend time working with about six girls on each of these events for about forty-five minutes. Shannon was so excited that she begged me to take her picture with Bela, and I did.

I figured if she could get her picture with him, so could I. Another mother and I decided we would ask him to have his picture taken with us. He graciously agreed and handed the camera to his secretary, who took the picture. When it was developed at the one-hour photo service, the other mother and I, who are both short, looked great, but the much taller Bela was headless. I decided there was only one thing to do— drive back to the gym, see whether Bela was still there, and ask for another picture. The other mother was horrified, but I was driving. I marched into his office, showed him the picture, and begged for another chance. He had a good laugh and then asked a different person in his office to take the photo. It turned out great.

Jerry's girls came back from the Karolyi camp very excited, but since they were still too young to compete, gym became boring again after a few months. Jerry wondered how to motivate them. An answer came the following spring, just before Shannon's ninth birthday, in the form of an invitation from the USAIGC's Gary Goodson to participate in a delegation with Canadian gymnasts who would train for two weeks in the Soviet Union. No one had previously been allowed to train with the Soviets there, and this would give a handful of American gymnasts and their coaches a chance to observe Soviet training techniques up close.

Jerry was tremendously excited, but the parents were somewhat daunted. Most of our daughters were barely nine, too young to send to a foreign country without a parent along, which increased the expense significantly. We all mulled it over for several weeks while the girls begged to go.

Finally we decided to give our consent if we could raise money for the trip.

We organized a car wash and several bake sales; but we needed something bigger. We decided to put on a gymnastic show and let people in the community see what our girls could do. My husband's university allowed us to use one of their facilities. Mothers sewed costumes, and the coaches helped the girls select music and choreograph routines. Other gymnasts asked to be part of the program. We worked hard and raised some money to help with expenses, but Ron and I still had to take out a loan for the trip. We had a good time, and the girls discovered they loved performing.

Around this time, as president of the parents' club, I was headed to the gym for a meeting on an afternoon in May when I noticed that the sky was getting black. As thunderstorms were not unusual at that time of year, I paid little attention. The meeting had just gotten under way when the lights went out and we heard children screaming in the gym. I ran to the back door and was mesmerized by what I saw: a tornado heading straight for the gym. There was hardly time to think. We gathered the kids together and ended up in a nearby ditch. The wind was blowing ferociously, and it was raining so hard we could hardly see where we were walking. As we waited for the tornado to make its way to us, I anxiously tried to figure out where everyone in my family was. Ron should be home with Shannon and Troy, but our home was near the tornado's path. Tessa was at a friend's house in the direction of the tornado. I was in agony.

Abruptly the winds let up, but the rain did not. We realized the tornado must have skipped over us. I raced to the gym with several kids and tried to call home, but, of course, the lines were all down. I needed to find out how my family was. Although we lived only lived two miles from the gym, it took some time to make it through the onslaught of water. Once home, I found Shannon and Troy crawling out of the hall closet in the center of our house. We waited to see whether the other parents brought Tessa home. After a while I insisted we try to get to her, but the tornado had wiped out many homes in the neighborhood across from us and a large area had been cordoned off so we couldn't get out. Soon Tessa arrived home. She and her friend had crouched in the bathtub with blankets on top of them, but fortunately the tornado had missed their house.

Across the world and much nearer the girls' destination, another disaster was occurring. On April 26, 1986, a nuclear reactor went out of control at Chernobyl, a town in north central Ukraine. Radiation spread across Europe as far as Great Britain. More than 100,000 Soviet citizens were evacuated for more than a year, and at least 31 people died as a result of the accident.

Seven weeks later Jerry and our five girls, each accompanied by one parent, boarded the plane for Moscow. No calamities would deter them. For a little over two weeks the girls caught a bus to the gymnastics facility each morning at 8 o'clock and worked until 5 o'clock, with a short break for lunch. Our girls actually worked out with the Soviet gymnasts on only a few occasions, but at least some of the Soviets were usually in the gym training at the same time. The Soviets worked very hard, seldom laughing or kidding with each other. Our girls adopted the same work ethic. They wanted the Soviets to see they were not "soft" Americans and Canadians but capable athletes. The girls spent a good portion of each day in dance training, something that had not been stressed at home.

The Soviets allowed some of their best coaches to work with our gymnasts. They were used to gymnasts following strict commands, giving 100 percent regardless of how many times they were required to perform a skill, and showing eagerness to try something more difficult. When an American or Canadian gymnast was prepared to adhere to this same work ethic, the Soviet coaches were prepared to give her all their expertise. Shannon thought she should be able to do everything the coaches asked, and they asked a lot. The better the gymnast performed, the more they expected. Shannon couldn't always rise to the occasion, and when she failed to master a skill she sometimes became frustrated to the point of tears. The Soviets were remarkably patient.

When the camp was over the Soviet coaches asked for a meeting with all the American and Canadian coaches to evaluate the training. As a gymnastics judge, I was invited to attend. About forty gymnasts had participated in the camp. The Soviets were very candid. They strongly recommended recreational gymnastics for most, but they identified three girls they felt should be placed in a program that could take them to an elite level. I was astonished when Dr. Vladirmir Zaglada, one of the top Soviet coaches, named Shannon as one of the three. Jerry was equally astounded. Shannon had spent part of each day crying and often seemed to be struggling, but the Soviets had noted physical prowess, a competitive spirit, and a willingness to be coached.

Just before we left Moscow a picture of Shannon and some of the other gymnasts appeared in *Pravda,* an important Soviet newspaper. We did not imagine at the time that Shannon would eventually become much more involved with the Soviet gymnasts. Shannon now counts Svetlana Boginskaya as a good friend, toured for months with Tatiana Gutsu, and performed exhibitions with Tatiana Lysenko, Lilia Podkopayeva, and other Soviet gymnasts.

CHAPTER THREE

Competition Kickoff

THE GIRLS RETURNED to Oklahoma eager for the competitive season and finally old enough under the rules of the time to take part in it. Rather than overwhelm her, Shannon's experience in the Soviet Union had inspired her to be a great gymnast. She wanted to get started.

Jerry, however, had been overwhelmed. The Soviets spent all day every day in the gym. They didn't go to public school. Their training and competition were state funded. Jerry worked nights as a nurse in a local hospital to make ends meet. He didn't have the time or the experience to take these girls to the level they were capable of reaching. He had five extremely talented girls and didn't know what to do with them. He realized that although they had impressive raw skills, they were not fully prepared for competition. They had little finesse and had not developed full routines on any of the equipment. He wanted them to spend another year training before he exposed them to competition.

Shannon was devastated. She had been training about a year longer than most of the other girls and was ready to take on new challenges. All year she had been thinking about competing. She had loved taking the USAIGC test and performing in the exhibition. She wanted an audience. The trip to the Soviet Union had only intensified these feelings. She complained to us, so we talked to Jerry. He agreed she could begin to compete but said he could not be her coach because he would be spending his time preparing the remaining girls and a few new students for the next competitive season.

Shannon and her best friend, Lisa Heckel, who had also gone on the trip to the Soviet Union, began working with another coach who worked for Jerry. After only a month Shannon realized she was not making the necessary progress. We were frank with her. If she still wanted to compete, we would support her, but she would probably need to move to another gym.

We had found Shannon's first gym by chance. Finding a new program was a more serious undertaking. There were two logical possibilities, one in north Oklahoma City and one in Norman. Shannon decided to try out at both, compare their programs, talk to the coaches, and choose one. She settled on Steve Nunno, who called his program Dynamo Gymnastics.

Steve is a former gymnast born in New York State and raised in Burlington, Massachusetts. He has a graduate degree in sports administration from the University of Massachusetts. He had operated his own gym in the past, worked for a year in Houston as assistant to the legendary Bela Karolyi, and assisted the University of Oklahoma women's gymnastics team. When Shannon signed on with him he was renting space in a gym in Norman, about thirty miles from Edmond, owned by 1984 Olympic gold medalist Bart Conner. Steve had only nine or ten girls on his team, all at either Class II or Class I, and three of them were about Shannon's age and ability.

Shannon had met Steve on the trip to the Soviet Union. Steve had not taken any gymnasts with him but had gone to improve his coaching techniques. Like Shannon, he came back fired up and determined to compete on a level with the

Soviets. Steve had watched Shannon in the Soviet Union. He knew she was talented and competitive, but he also knew he'd have his work cut out for him. He had seen how easily the tears flowed when she was frustrated, and he did not like tears.

Tessa was competing Class III at Jerry's gym at the time, and when Shannon left, Jerry said Tessa had to go too. She moved with Shannon to Bart Conner's gym and several times a week spent about an hour waiting for her sister to finish her sessions with Steve. Lisa, Shannon's training partner at Jerry's, also moved to Steve's program. Within the year two more of Jerry's kids from Shannon's group also made the move to Dynamo.

Shannon's competitive career did not start out as she planned. Steve left her at home while the girls he had trained longer went off to their first meet. But by the second meet he was ready to include her. Shannon's first meet would be in Dallas. She would have to be away from home for a couple of

8. *Shannon, now a dynamo, age 9.*

days. We didn't know if she was ready for this. We soon learned it was her parents who weren't ready.

I drove to Dallas with some of the other parents. Our children were not allowed to stay with us. In fact, Steve insisted we stay completely in the background and not even talk to the girls. While this restriction was hard on me, it didn't seem to bother Shannon. She regarded the experience as a great new adventure.

Shannon's first event was beam, already her best. She promptly fell attempting a side aerial, a move that involves rotating through the air without using one's hands. She moved to the floor where in warm-ups she had trouble getting her new double twist-around, but she nailed it solidly in the meet and earned what we thought was a great score, an 8.3. She headed to the bars, struggled in warm-ups, and missed her giant swing between the bars. Not a great score. Vault went fine, but she was only doing a half-on, half-off. (On leaving the springboard the gymnast does a half-twist in the air and lands on the vaulting horse; as she pushes off with her hands, she again performs a half-twist in the air.) I think she barely crested a 31 all-around score, but Steve seemed pleased with her first outing. I had been judging compulsory meets and was unfamiliar with optionals. I was delighted she had survived her first competition. And she seemed pleased with herself.

Steve believed in going to lots of competitions, so Shannon headed off to a meet almost every weekend. When she mastered a new skill on one event, she seemed to lose one on another event. Her worst meet of the season occurred right before Christmas. She fell twice on beam and at least once on every event after that. Steve kept telling us she was a terrific gymnast and would someday be an elite. We wondered whether he remembered which girl was ours.

In early January Steve informed us he was taking Shannon and some of the other girls to a big international meet in Reno, Nevada. Shannon had never been that far from home without Ron or me, but we couldn't afford to fly to all the meets with her. Shannon didn't seem to be fazed. She hopped on the plane with barely a look back at us.

She had a good meet—not as good as Steve felt she was capable of, but she was starting to fulfill some of her potential. She really enjoyed the Circus Circus Hotel, where they stayed. She came home with a bag full of stuffed animals. When I asked how she had gotten all those animals, she first said, "Gambling." Then she giggled and told me that as she and some of the other girls were walking through the hotel, a man came up to her and asked if she liked stuffed animals. She said "Sure," so he handed her a bunch he had just won. We had a discussion about accepting gifts from strangers, but it was hard to be upset because she was so delighted with her treasures. This was the start of a huge collection of stuffed animals.

Back in the gym, Steve had begun "kicking out" gymnasts he thought were not giving him their full attention. He would send them to the lobby for a while as he continued to work with other gymnasts. I knew this was going on but did not realize to what extent until Shannon's tenth birthday.

Planning a little after-workout party, I blissfully walked into the lobby of the gym with a birthday cake-sized cookie. To my surprise, although the girls were scheduled for at least another half hour in the gym, ten of Steve's eleven gymnasts—including Shannon—were sitting in the lobby. I looked at my watch, thinking I had miscalculated the time, but they told me Steve had booted them out, one by one.

When Steve and the surviving gymnast came out he was furious to see the other ten eating the cookie and having a great time when they were supposed to be being punished. I felt guilty until it occurred to me that if ten of eleven girls had been kicked out of the gym, maybe it was the coach who had a problem. I cut a big slice of cookie and headed to Steve's office. He glared at me as I walked in. "You need a little sweetening up," I told him, offering the hunk of cookie. He was not amused. But as he talked to me, he began to realize the situation looked a little ridiculous. Steve seldom stayed angry very long.

Shannon had been competing at the Class II level, and the Class II state meet was fast approaching. After a poor work-out one day Steve told her she was capable of being as good as Shelly Pendley or Tracy Cole, two of his Class I gymnasts Shannon greatly admired, but she had to stop the tears and stay focused. That day Shannon decided Steve was right. She could be the best if she really wanted to. She announced to us that she would be winning her next meet in Ardmore.

While we laughed to ourselves about her announcement, Ron and I always tried to show complete belief in her ability. Among the many things we have learned over the years is that parents often limit their children without even realizing it by making excuses for them, by allowing them to blame circum-stances or other people for their mistakes, or even by not set-ting high enough goals. This is a lesson Ron and I would have to relearn several times. Shannon is not going to limit herself, so we had better not limit her either.

After the meet Shannon marched into the house with the first-place trophy and her first 9 on beam. Now she set her sights on the state meet, which would be held in Altus, a two-and-a-half-hour drive from Edmond. The girls were divided into age groups: 9–11, 12–14, and 15 and over. All of Steve's Class II's fell in the 9–11 age group, making it doubtful the team could bring home the first-place trophy; but Steve had high hopes for several of his students in the individual com-petition. The girls competed in compulsories the first day and optionals the second day, then both scores were added together to determine their final all-around standing.

After the compulsory session Shannon was in the lead by a fraction. Two other girls on the Dynamo team, Whitney Kopas and Jill Perryman, were right behind her, followed by Lisa Heckel and Susan Coles. In optionals Shannon did a great floor routine but did not score as high on vault as she knew she could. She had thrown what was a relatively new vault for her, a piked Tsuk, named after the famed Japanese gymnast Mitsuo Tsukahara and involving half a turn onto the vault and then a back flip. She was glad to have performed it reasonably well. Uneven bars went exceptionally well, and after that event Shannon still held a slim lead over Whitney, who was also having a terrific meet.

Beam was Shannon's best event and her favorite, although most gymnasts dreaded it. At barely ten years of age she was already elegant on this apparatus. She had scored a 9.4 on her compulsory beam routine, at least half a point higher than anyone else in the meet. Her optional beam routine was packed with difficult moves for her level of competition—a round-off back handspring connection in which she would flip from feet to hands and back to feet, an aerial, a switch leap, a press to handstand mount, and a double full dismount with one complete somersault and two twists. Today she would also attempt a back handspring into a lay-out, stepout, back flip, a new skill no one else in the meet was doing on beam.

The layout came early in her routine, and she missed it. In an instant she was on the floor, but just as quickly she was back up on the beam. The Shannon of a few months before would have been rattled and would have held back on the rest of her routine for fear of falling again. The more confident Shannon knew that with a 0.5 deduction for the fall, she had to squeeze everything else she could out of this routine. The rest of the routine was almost flawless, with great extension, good rhythm, and excellent execution. The judges were impressed and deducted very little except for the fall. Her score was 9.2.

Shannon, who so recently had won a meet for the first time, was the new Class II state champion. She had learned some lessons from this meet that she would carry with her throughout the rest of her gymnastic career: never give up, and believe in yourself. Shannon and her teammates of nine-to eleven-year-olds also brought home the first-place team trophy from the meet, outscoring all other age groups, including older, more experienced girls.

Shannon attempted more new skills at the regional competition, where she competed against Bela Karolyi's team, but she missed her dismounts on both the uneven bars and the beam. Steve's solution was for her to train harder. He did not like to back off skills just because a girl missed one. He was planning a meet in a few weeks at the Dynamo gym and fully expected Shannon to throw a double back dismount off bars and a double back tumbling pass on floor—and make them. Ron and I were excited but a little scared. We had never seen her do a double back on floor other than into a foam pit. The execution might not have been the best, but she hit everything.

Steve was once again thoroughly excited and making plans. He had entered a team from Dynamo in the national USAIGC meet to be held in Delaware in June. Six girls would compete on this team. Steve had five Class I gymnasts, his best gymnasts, but he would need to round out the team with one of the Class II girls. He had a little over a month to make this decision. It would probably be a close battle.

Shannon knew one spot was open, and she wanted it. She put everything she had into her workouts. By the time the girls were ready to go to Delaware, Steve had made the decision. Shannon would be the sixth team member, but he had entered the other girls in the individual competition so everyone would be going to the meet. The team portion of the meet would be televised. All twelve teams entered would compete the first day, then the top four teams would move into the final round the next day.

The Dynamos all competed well in the team meet. The lowest of the six scores in each event was thrown out, leaving the other five to count toward the overall team score. Shannon was ecstatic when she realized she performed well enough that all her scores counted for the team. The Dynamos finished in the top four and would be in the televised final competition.

Shannon was not really nervous, but she was excited because she had never been on television. When she hit a great bar routine, the announcers began to take notice. On beam Shannon had problems with her layout. Although she had hit it perfectly the day before, this time she found herself on the floor. She climbed back up and completed her routine with grace and style but melted into tears after landing her dismount. For once Steve was not upset with her tears. He wanted her to be displeased when she fell, but he now had to pull her back up emotionally for the remaining two events. This would test how good a competitor she really was.

Shannon performed an outstanding floor routine and earned the top score for the team. Then she went on to score a 9 on her piked Tsuk vault, a new high for her. Steve was so amazed at the powerful vault that he encouraged her to try a layout Tsuk for her second vault. She had excellent execution in the air but pulled it around a little too slowly and ended short. Nevertheless, now both she and Steve knew she was ready to move on to a more difficult vault.

The Dynamos ended the meet with a bronze medal, a truly exhilarating achievement. Steve quickly returned to planning. He asked Ron and me to meet with him to make some decisions about the direction of Shannon's career. We had assumed Shannon would move up to Class I now, and we were excited about our ten-year-old competing at this level. Steve had bigger plans. He wanted to bypass Class I and work at moving her into the elite ranks. We were surprised, but we trusted him. He certainly knew more about Shannon's gymnastic ability than we did, and he also understood the system. Shannon was also enthusiastic about trying to be an elite. Wasn't this what the Soviets had talked about? It sounded good to her.

The first step toward the elite ranks for Shannon involved Steve getting his own gym. As the number of gymnasts under him had grown rapidly after his success at the state meet, he needed more room. He also wanted Shannon and some of the other girls in the gym longer hours. He knew I had seen first-hand how long the Soviets trained, and he knew that with public school those hours were not possible at the time. But during the summer he wanted the small group of girls he had identified as potential elites to stay later several afternoons a week and train more difficult skills, such as release moves on bars and a Yurchenko vault. The vault, named after the Soviet gymnast Natalia Yurchenko, starts with a round-off—a cartwheel-like move that ends with both feet together—onto the springboard and into a back handspring onto the vaulting horse. Shannon was more than prepared to put in the hours.

Steve found a large warehouse for rent in Oklahoma City and moved his gym. We were very happy to now have a twenty-minute drive one way instead of a thirty-five-minute drive one way. Ron spent many hours during this summer of 1987 helping Steve build offices and otherwise get the facility ready.

With fall came the beginning of a new meet season. The season opener for the Dynamo gymnasts every year was their own Halloween meet. Steve did not believe in eating candy, but he was willing to let the girls indulge once a year. Gymnasts, coaches, and judges all wore costumes, and Steve gave generous candy prizes to the gymnasts whose outfits were most impressive. I judged the meet several times, showing up as everything from a pumpkin to a witch.

Shannon had been a ghost her first year at Dynamo but decided that she needed something unusual. She was handicapped in the costume department by a mother who is not very creative artistically and has trouble sewing on a button. Despite my limitations, I knew it was my duty to help her come up with a good costume. For a couple of weeks I mulled over possibilities, but inspiration came in the grocery store. Shannon could go as a bag of groceries. She was so small that a grocery sack would easily fit over her (no sewing for me). We could save egg cartons, cereal boxes, and other packages and glue them so that they stuck out around the edge. To top things off, literally, Shannon could wear an empty potato chip bag with holes for her eyes and nose (no sewing there, either). Her little bare brown legs would stick out the bottom and she could go barefoot.

Shannon did not share my enthusiasm for the idea. Being a bag of groceries was dumb, in her opinion, so we continued to brainstorm. A few nights before the meet she walked into the kitchen and accepted her fate. She couldn't think of anything else, and all my other ideas were at least as bad.

As she got into her contraption the day of the meet, Shannon considered backing out but decided that having no costume was even worse than wearing a grocery sack. The

9. The infamous Halloween costume.

gymnasts lined up for the contest, and the audience clapped their approval. The field narrowed to six and then to one—Shannon. While I like to think the audience was impressed with the originality of the costume, I have to admit they were probably amused by the skinny legs poking out of the bottom of the sack and the potato chip bag over her head.

Soon it was on to much heavier competition. Steve wanted to face the big guns head-on, so he signed the girls up for a big meet in Houston. Shannon now had a round-off entry layout vault as well as a release move on bars, and she was ready to give these new skills a try. Right after the state meet she had learned a double back on floor, and Steve was feeling so confident that he wanted her to close with this skill.

The first blow in that meet came on vault. Since Shannon was not yet an elite, she was not allowed to do the Yurchenko vault, the vault she had been training all summer. Her true competitor colors surfaced once again, and she quickly adapted and threw a Tsuk layout instead. On bars she went for a reverse hecht—swinging around the bar, letting go with her legs facing the ceiling, then straddling as she flies backward over the bar before grabbing it again. She just missed her hands and fell hard onto the floor below. (To this day her dad uses video of this fall to teach certain physics theories to his class at the university. Of course, he always laughs and says it's in his contract with her that if he shows her falling, before the class leaves he has to show a video of a good routine in which she makes all the skills.) Beam was great, and floor started out wonderfully, but Shannon ran out of gas and put her hands down on the final double back tumbling pass. Steve was not worried. She had gone for all of her new skills. Next time she would make them.

After a series of meets close to home, in March 1988 Steve informed us he was taking his Dynamo team to San Antonio for the Alamo Classic, a meet to which Bela Karolyi usually took his best gymnasts. Here was another opportunity for Shannon and her teammates to test themselves.

I couldn't take vacation time from work, but Ron was able to go with Shannon. Both sets of Shannon's grandparents and many other relatives still lived in San Antonio, where both Ron and I had grown up. Most family members were unaware of how deep Shannon's interest in gymnastics ran or of her apparent talent. Her grandparents planned to come, just as they watched their other grandchildren's Little League games, but they certainly had no expectations of any medals.

Shannon didn't ask what family members would be coming to watch. We wondered whether knowing might make her nervous. In retrospect, I don't think that once she started competing she ever thought about who was there.

Many of Shannon's skills were still relatively new for her—two release moves on bars, a double pike dismount off bars, a double back closing on floor, and a layout-layout on beam—so Ron and I were eager to see how she handled all of these routines. Since she was competing against a field that was older, including such greats as Wendy Bruce and Sandy Woolsey, not to mention some good Karolyi seniors and juniors such as Tina Snowden, Kim Zmeskal, and Erica Stokes, we had no delusions about her winning. We just hoped she would hit all her skills (or at least most of them).

I was surprised and delighted when Ron called to tell me Shannon had finished second in the all-around right behind Wendy Bruce and had made three event finals. But that wasn't the real news. Ron was calling from the arena while he was waiting for Shannon to finish signing autographs. When he tried to get to Shannon to talk to her, the other parents were incensed to think he was cutting in line. This was a new experience for Shannon, and, of course, for Ron too. We laughed for a long time at the thought of Shannon, barely eleven, signing autographs.

Shannon gradually started to bring home first-place trophies. Spring arrived, and Steve now had another hot gymnast, Gina Jackson. He decided to take Shannon and Gina to the practice meet for elites, where a committee would determine whether they were ready to try to become elite gymnasts. Both Shannon and Gina had had a great meet season so far, and Steve had no doubts both girls were ready.

At the meet Shannon watched as one of the more experienced girls from another gym fell several times during warm-ups but nailed her routine perfectly during the competition. Up to that time if Shannon had a bad warm-up, she usually performed poorly during the meet. As she watched the other gymnast Shannon realized she did not have to concede an event just because of a bad warm-up. The lesson stayed with her. Since then I've watched her take some bad spills during warm-ups and come back to perform an outstanding routine during the meet. A year later at the U.S. Classic Shannon fell during the thirty-second warm-up, hit her head on the beam standard, and sat dazed for a minute before being helped up by her coach, Peggy Liddick. A few minutes later she mounted the beam and earned a 9.8, the highest score of the meet. Now one of her trademarks is her ability to recover after a mishap.

Both Shannon and Gina had rough performances at the practice meet, but the judges recognized their potential and authorized them to prepare for the Junior B division at the 1988 American Classic to be held in about a month. This was a qualifying meet for elite status. At this important meet both girls qualified for the Junior B elite team. Shannon finished in second place after making only a few small mistakes that kept her from winning first.

Steve planned to take Shannon and Gina to another upcoming qualifying meet even though they had already made the team. He wanted both to improve their standings. The year was 1988, and the Summer Olympics in Seoul, South Korea, were approaching. Kenny Rogers was planning to sing the theme song for the gymnastics portion of the competition. The second classic meet was being held near his home in Atlanta, so he invited the winners of the meet to his home for lunch.

Shannon not only won this competition but at barely eleven she threw a full twisting double back as her opening floor pass. Steve was a happy coach. He packed his videocamera and headed for Kenny Rogers's house. Steve had instructed Shannon to wear a nice dress. He thought Shannon looked cute in her little pink dress and dirty tennis shoes. Steve suddenly realized Shannon didn't have on her dress shoes. It seems she forgot to pack them. So Steve took a detour to the shoe store and bought her a new pair. The group had a great time. Steve brought back a video of the entire experience, including Shannon's ride with Kenny in his golf cart around his estate.

With Olympic Trials coming up and all the top gymnasts training too hard to travel to international meets, Shannon and other Junior B gymnasts were invited to attend the Junior Pan American Games in Ponce, Puerto Rico. One coach was named by the gymnastics federation to travel to the meet and coach the entire team at the meet. Steve had not had elite gymnasts before so he was not selected as the team coach.

This was a difficult time for Shannon. Her dream of being an elite was coming true, but while the other girls at the gym got the traditional week off, she had to continue training by herself because she had a meet in the middle of summer. She didn't know the coach she would be working with, or any of the other girls. She was feeling sorry for herself when Steve had an idea. He knew Kelly Garrison was training by herself at the University of Oklahoma for Olympic Trials. Steve also knew how much Shannon admired Kelly, who is now a good friend. When Shannon was seven, Jerry Clavier had taken his girls to a clinic in Kelly's hometown and Kelly had stopped in. While Kelly leaned up against a beam, Shannon had scrambled up on it and then onto Kelly's back. Kelly had patiently carried her around. When Kelly had to leave, Shannon, believing Kelly would want to hear from her, begged for her telephone number. Steve knew that if

Shannon could see Kelly working hard all by herself, it would make an impression.

Steve also said he would go to Puerto Rico with Shannon if we could pay half his expenses. We readily agreed because we did not want Shannon to have to go through the Miami airport and change planes alone, and we knew she would be much happier at the meet with Steve there.

So Shannon and Steve went to Puerto Rico for her first international meet representing the U.S. She had a good meet, if not a great one. Her legs were very sore, and the coach in charge decided she should not try the full twisting double back. Shannon had learned a Yurchenko full twist in a tuck position and had thrown it successfully at several meets, but the team coach felt it was a much too difficult vault for such a young competitor and had her do a piked Tsuk instead. The decision frustrated Shannon and infuriated Steve, who afterward started a crusade to allow a gymnast's personal coach to be on the floor during competition. Even so, Shannon ended up second in the all-around and second on bars, a nice finish for this important meet.

Shannon came home happy. She had fun with the other American girls and met gymnasts from other countries. She especially liked Louisa Portocuerra, a Guatemalan gymnast who later moved to Canada to train and whom Shannon would continue to see at meets long after the 1992 Olympics.

Now Steve set his sights on the 1989 U.S. Olympic Sports Festival to be held in Oklahoma City. The festival, which showcases athletes in many Olympic sports, has been held in non-Olympic years since 1978. Shannon would be competing before a hometown crowd. The top junior gymnasts would not have to share the limelight with the seniors here. The U.S. Gymnastics Federation had decided to use the Sports Festival, which would be televised, as a Junior A competition since there was a high probability that the next Olympic team would come from the ranks of the Junior A's. Steve's girls,

Gina and Shannon, would be going head to head with the Karolyi kids.

Shannon continued to add more difficult skills to her repertoire on all events. Each time she became comfortable with one, Steve demanded something harder. If Shannon was going to be ready to compete successfully in the 1989 Sports Festival, Steve wanted her in the gym more. She was prepared to stay later in the evening but refused to sacrifice school. Not only did she insist on attending full time, she was determined to make all A's. Steve extended the evening hours. She trained from 4:00 to 9:00 P.M. Monday through Friday and from 8:00 A.M. to 1:00 P.M. on Saturday. If an important meet was coming up, she trained on Sunday.

At home life was becoming a little more complicated. With Tessa, Shannon, and Troy, Ron and I sometimes felt like we lived in our cars. I was working as a bank vice president, Ron was teaching, and we were busy keeping up with the children's crowded schedules. Before the children came I played a lot of tennis and rode in horse shows. Now my life was so full of children's activities that there was little time to enjoy such pastimes.

Shannon stayed with gymnastics. Tessa wanted to try everything—art, gymnastics, tennis, swimming, track. As Troy got older he became interested in karate and for a time also took gymnastics.

One Thursday night Ron came home exhausted. When he calculated his time he realized he had spent four hours in the car: take Shannon, come home, take Troy, take Tessa, pick up Shannon, pick up Troy. When we saw that we just couldn't do it anymore, Steve changed Troy's gym schedule so that Ron could take Shannon and her brother at the same time.

All our children had to make their beds and clean their rooms. We developed a routine. I cooked, and Ron cleaned up afterward. Sometimes I would prepare something the night before which could be popped in the oven or on the stove. On really long nights we ate take-out hamburgers or pizza, a special favorite of Shannon's. We had a rule that I would prepare one meal and everybody would have to take at least one or two bites of everything. Tessa and Troy would immediately take bites of foods they didn't like to get them over with; Shannon would wait until the last possible minute.

Shannon never got any special privileges. In fact, she was good about helping with dinner when she was home. Once I had a lot to do and had to take cookies to work the next day. When I came down from working upstairs, she had made the cookies.

Tessa was an excellent student, and Shannon was determined to keep up with her academically. She was thought of by some teachers as "Tessa's sister." Shannon didn't discuss gymnastics at school; that was another world, and she liked it that way. At school she was Shannon the student, not Shannon the gymnast. When she was out of town for meets we picked up her homework assignments. The teachers were usually impressed with how quickly she got caught up, but they seemed to give little thought to the demands of her sport. In the summer of 1989 her teachers and classmates were about to get a surprise.

CHAPTER FOUR

Infiltrating the Six-Pack

THE EXTRA TRAINING paid off. Shannon was winning invitational meets regularly. She pulled her left hamstring right before the zone meet, but Steve ingrained in her the need to work through some pain. As parents, we had to get used to this idea. My natural inclination as a mother was to let her take a break every time she was injured, but Steve pushed the girls and Shannon wanted to compete. At the zone qualifier Shannon captured first in the all-around, an auspicious start to the elite season.

Shannon, Gina, and Steve went to California for the 1989 American Classic. Shannon easily won the all-around and three event finals. The Karolyi gymnasts were not there. Nevertheless, we thought winning a classic as a new Junior A was a heady achievement.

The U.S. Classic was being held in San Antonio. Ron and I planned to drive there for the meet and spend some time with our families. As at the Alamo Classic, we were again somewhat concerned that Shannon might feel a lot of extra pressure with so many relatives in attendance. It wasn't family that was the problem. Shannon's pulled hamstring had been getting progressively worse since she had not been able to ease up on training. Now she was struggling. She was distracted by her injury and failed to perform as well in compulsories as she usually did. Shannon had been building a reputation on beam and bars, but she had to take an extra swing on compulsory bars and fell on her beam mount. Although optionals went better, she still had some errors and ended up in sixth place overall. All but one of the Karolyi gymnasts outscored her.

Steve felt Shannon could not afford to take any time off to let her hamstring heal. He was convinced Shannon was the best junior gymnast. Shannon had been invited to a meet in Australia, but Steve turned it down to concentrate on the 1989 Sports Festival where he planned for Shannon to begin making a name for herself. Steve was not about to let her miss this meet.

Of course, the Karolyi gymnasts were also very talented and much more experienced. Most had already been Junior A's for a year, had been to a number of international meets, and had good reputations. B's were the youngest elites; the A class were twelve- to fourteen-year-olds. In the world of gymnastics, expectations can sometimes influence outcome. If a gymnast is known as a star, she is more likely than a newcomer to get high scores. Shannon would have to have more difficult moves and even better execution to catch the judges' attention.

Steve told Shannon she must finish in the top five at the Sports Festival to be invited to meets critical to her career during the next year. Shannon began to get worried. She always wanted to do her best and really loved winning, but none of the meets so far had seemed so very important. What would happen if she didn't make the top five? Would her career be over? What if she humiliated herself in front of the hometown crowd that would include a lot of her friends? Shannon was starting to feel real pressure. At least Gina would be suffering through this ordeal with her.

When Shannon started to feel overwhelmed at the need to

finish in the top five, we reminded her that the top sixteen girls from this meet made the team. It had been twelve in the past, but there were so many Junior A's this year that the federation had expanded the team. While Ron and I never doubted she had the ability to be in the top five, we thought just making the team in her first attempt at Junior A would be pretty darn good. With the pressure eased a little, Shannon set off for the University of Oklahoma dorm where she would stay for the meet.

Looking back on that meet now, Shannon says, "I remember the 'six-pack.' When Bela was at a meet, there was a whole aura about it. Watching his girls stand in a line, they were focused and precise, kind of what I wanted to be like. I wanted to be that good."

Despite her admiration for Bela and his gymnasts, Shannon didn't consider going to Houston to train with him. She lived at home, attended public school, and had as normal a childhood and adolescence as possible. We knew Shannon's gymnastics training was important, but we thought her home life and our family were more important. She stayed in Edmond and faced the six-pack from afar.

Shannon performed outstanding compulsory routines but was in fifth place after the first meet. Being a judge, I had a very good idea of what to look for in the compulsory routines, and, of course, also being somewhat prejudiced, I was frustrated that Shannon had not earned better scores. I felt she had performed excellent routines. However, she was still in the coveted top five and we were happy about that.

Shannon was raring to go in optionals. She wanted to hang on to fifth place and please Steve. She hit a great vault and bar set and a beautiful beam routine. Floor was her last event. She had been performing well on floor at recent meets, but her hamstring bothered her most on tumbling and floor leaps. When after an impressive sequence she landed short on a double back flip and found herself on her elbows, there were no tears. As she rolled her eyes, the camera caught her expression, which clearly said, "Oh great . . . and I was doing so well."

She had given it her best and refused to feel bad. Kim Zmeskal, Bela's star gymnast who was a year older than Shannon, had a good lead. Even without the fall Shannon would not have won the gold, but she would have captured the silver. In spite of the fall she found herself on the podium accepting the bronze medal while Erica Stokes, who also trained with Karolyi in Houston, slipped into the second spot. Shannon had finished better than fifth and was happy. First place was starting to seem possible.

The next day Shannon performed an outstanding uneven bars routine and won the gold. She had also made floor and beam finals but did not win a medal in either.

Overall, the 1989 Sports Festival was a great success. Besides her individual achievements, Shannon led her team to second place in front of the hometown fans. Suddenly all of Oklahoma knew who Shannon Miller was. They had watched and cheered for her for three days. Her teachers and school-mates looked at her a little differently. Shannon didn't just enjoy gymnastics, she was really good at it. Oklahomans were beginning to think she might be someone to watch—maybe even a future Olympian.

The judges had also taken note. Shannon had infiltrated the Karolyi six-pack. Two of Karolyi's girls had beaten her, one by only a hair, and four had finished below her.

Soon after the Sports Festival Peggy Liddick, an elegant gymnast from the University of Nebraska, joined Steve's staff. Peggy was in charge of beam and floor choreography. Shannon had a lot of natural elegance, but she still needed refining. Peggy was the person to do it. Peggy was also an exceptionally good compulsories coach, a real stickler for every detail, and while Shannon handled the compulsory skills exceptionally well, the routines were not particularly polished. Peggy would soon correct this.

Immediately after the Sports Festival Shannon and Gina,

who had finished eighth at the meet, were invited along with one of the Karolyi gymnasts to go to a prestigious junior meet in Japan. This was exactly what Steve wanted. He eagerly accepted, forgetting Shannon's hamstring, which hurt more each day. Although Shannon cried when she was angry or frustrated with herself, she seldom complained about physical pain. Now she was making some noise about her injury, and Steve began to get worried.

If she could just tough it out a few more weeks and get through the Japanese meet, he assured her, she would be able to give her hamstring a rest. She agreed. She really did want to make this trip. Going to Japan, especially with her friend Gina, would be fun. So Shannon packed for the second big international meet of her career.

By now her dad and I realized Shannon was going to be taking quite a few trips inside and outside the United States. We didn't want her forgetting her dress shoes again, so we developed a standard packing list and put it on the computer. Whenever she had to start packing for a meet, she checked off the items as she packed them. Shannon used these lists for years, gradually changing them as her requirements changed. Makeup and hair spray hadn't been on those early lists.

Shannon had fun in Japan. She and her teammates, Gina Jackson and Kelly Pitzen, discovered the adventure of tossing water balloons, that is, until the American judge who accompanied them discovered what they were up to. While she couldn't bring herself to reprimand them, she did advise a little more caution in their exuberance. Shannon also learned a little more of what it means to be a celebrity. The Japanese were enthralled with the American gymnasts and mobbed them every time they left the arena. Steve started sneaking them out a back way and literally running for the hotel.

Shannon had a good meet. She finished sixth in the all-around, an admirable feat since some impressive gymnasts from the Soviet Union and Romania were there. Tatiana Lysenko and Gina Gogean both competed. Tatiana won the

10. *Kelly Pitzen, Shannon, and Gina Jackson made up the team for the 1989 Junior Elite meet in Japan.*

meet, and Gina edged out Shannon for fifth. Shannon qualified for all four event finals and had sound routines. She did not win a medal, but she and Steve arrived home pleased with her performance.

Now Steve was plotting to have Shannon invited to be part of an exhibition by the 1988 Olympic team scheduled for November in Oklahoma City. She received the invitation, but Steve had neglected to ask Shannon how she felt about it. She knew it was another great opportunity, but her hamstring was causing her a lot of pain. She had been working on a pulled hamstring with no relief since April. Now, in September, Steve was asking her to stay in top shape until early November. When was she ever going to allow the leg to heal? Shannon plodded along for another month rarely complaining.

At the end of October Shannon walked into the house, came directly to me, and asked if it would be okay if she just did recreational gymnastics. I was stunned but tried to remain calm and objective. I sat her down and asked what was bothering her. She insisted she loved doing gymnastics but was really tired of the pain. If competing meant one always had to work in pain, she wasn't sure she wanted to continue to compete. We did not want to push Shannon to give so much time and energy to competing if that's not what she wanted. However, we weren't sure she was ready to give it up. We wanted to make sure she didn't act too hastily.

"You can make your own decision," I told her, "but, in fairness, you need to tell Steve what you're planning." She reluctantly agreed, and her dad and I scheduled an appointment with Steve. Shannon carefully explained that she didn't think she could work with the pulled hamstring any longer. While we had tried to hide our surprise, Steve let her know he was shocked.

"You have a great future in gymnastics," Steve said. "The great times are just beginning." He assured Shannon he would find someone with expertise to help with her hamstring. We had taken her to a doctor and to a trainer, but the solution they prescribed was to rest the hamstring and there had never been time to do that. Now Steve vowed to do whatever was needed. He also promised her that she would not have to work in pain the rest of her gymnastic career. (Oh, what promises we make!) "Let me get some help for your leg, and then if you still want to quit, we'll talk again," Steve suggested.

True to his word, Steve immediately sought help. He contacted his longtime friend Bart Conner and asked about the trainer who had worked with him before the 1988 Olympics. If he was going to get help, it would be the best. Bart would soon be flying to his second home in Las Vegas and invited Steve and Shannon to stay at his house and see his trainer, Keith Klevin.

Off they went. Keith prescribed a variety of therapeutic exercises, stressed the importance of doing them faithfully, and also said Shannon absolutely had to get off the leg for a while. How long? Optimally four months. Steve, always the horse trader, negotiated for three.

Shannon practically gave up vaulting as well as floor and beam tumbling; however, she did perform a watered-down beam routine in the exhibition. Gradually, the hamstring began to feel better.

At the end of December Steve was once again tempted. The gymnastics federation invited Shannon to compete in the American Cup. Juniors had not previously been invited to this meet, the only international invitational sponsored by the U.S. Gymnastics Federation (now USA Gymnastics). Steve was wild with excitement. He suggested they cut the three-month rest of the hamstring by a couple of weeks. After all, wasn't it feeling much better? The meet was at the beginning of March. If they started training hard in mid-January, he felt sure he could have her ready.

Shannon was tired of watching the other kids work on new skills and go off to meets while she took it easy. She wanted to be back in the real gymnastic scene, so she readily agreed with Steve. They would prepare for the American Cup.

CHAPTER FIVE

Going National

MOST OF SHANNON'S skills came back quickly. Vault took a little longer. Her timing on the Yurchenko was way off. Steve opted to prepare a Yurchenko full twist but in the easier tuck position. This vault would be scored at a maximum of 9.9.

The American Cup was a huge success for Shannon, although she did not make finals. Only two gymnasts from each country could advance, and Sandy Woolsey and Kim Zmeskal outscored her. But she executed all her routines well and placed sixth overall in an international field filled with experienced senior gymnasts.

Now that Shannon was back in regular training Steve was enthusiastically looking toward the U.S. Championships. He intended to have Shannon compete as a senior. Making the Junior National team had partially opened the door. Making the senior team would open it the rest of the way. Once on the senior team Shannon would be invited to international meets in Europe, where she needed to be exposed to international judges—crucial if she was going to be a serious competitor in the next Olympics. Steve was sure she could be not only a U.S. team member but also a significant factor in the next

Games. Shannon, however, was just starting to think seriously about being a part of the 1992 Olympics.

She accepted an invitation to participate in the Toronto Cup in Canada, where she would be the only American. She felt lonely just thinking about the trip. It occurred to me that it wouldn't be too costly for Tessa and me to attend this meet and spend some time sightseeing. Tessa, a top student, often helped Shannon with homework and had always been supportive of her gymnastic endeavors. Tessa would love an opportunity to see Canada and cheer for her sister. Shannon was thrilled to have her family there. We left a few days after Shannon and arrived the night before the meet. We stayed at a different hotel.

Steve had not pressed Shannon too hard in training just before the meet. He didn't want to risk redamaging the hamstring. Vault was still coming back slowly, but Steve felt Shannon was prepared. She would be doing a Yurchenko layout full twist this time.

Shannon had a rough meet. She made her vault, but it was not particularly good. Bars were lackluster, and she fell on floor. On beam, after a fall, she realized she would not only take a deduction for the fall but also would lose her series bonus, so she made up another series on the spot and inserted it. Although she finished the meet in ninth place, she discovered she could think on her feet—literally. Steve remained calm, and Shannon was not too disturbed. She was looking forward to a postmeet party at the Hard Rock Cafe and to sightseeing with Tessa and me. We all learned a little something from this experience. Shannon had been so focused on activities after the meet that she hadn't really been up for the meet itself. She was determined not to make that mistake again.

A month later Shannon was asked to join the team that would compete in the 1990 Pyramid Challenge, a dual meet against Germany. She fell on beam and on floor and finished a disappointing seventh, although the American team beat the

German team. Her performance made Steve realize he had his work cut out for him if she was going to make the senior team. She was only thirteen, and at first the federation argued she was too young to compete in the senior category, but Steve got out the rulebook and found a loophole. Now he had to make sure she was well prepared for the competition.

Shannon's compulsories were improving, and she had more difficult optional routines than most of the seniors. She just had to hit the routines as effectively in competition as she did in the gym every day. She began working at least ten beam routines daily, five or six bar sets, two or three floor sets (although not always with full tumbling), and as many as ten compulsory and ten optional vaults. Needless to say, Steve had again increased the workout time. He brought in clinicians to look at her compulsory and optional routines; they praised both.

At the 1990 U.S. Championships Shannon performed compulsories very well, even catching the release move on compulsory bars that tended to give her problems. She was in seventh place after compulsories, a good start considering the quality of the competition. Steve was pleased, but he expected Shannon to move up in the rankings after optionals. He knew she had great routines and had been hitting them solidly in workouts.

In her optional beam routine, Shannon was the only American who competed with a full twisting double back dismount—a double back somersault with a twist in the first somersault. She nailed it and scored well. With a successful floor routine, she moved to sixth in the standings. She executed a laid-out full twisting Yurchenko vault, and Steve was riding high. Only bars was left, and she was the reigning junior champion on this event. But, with a slight loss in concentration, she fell on an easy move and slipped into eighth place.

When Ron called from the meet and said Shannon placed eighth, I was thrilled. She had actually made the Senior National team at thirteen. Only later did we realize that

without the fall, she would have been fourth or fifth—a stag-
gering thought. We knew one of these days Shannon would
pull everything together. Then where would she place?

There was no one moment or single event that made us
aware that our daughter had a special talent. The realization
crept up as we saw her excel among larger and larger groups
of competitors. In the same way, expenses gradually multi-
plied. We were paying for gymnastics lessons and buying leotards. Then there were meet fees and more leotards and
warm-up suits. At first for out-of-town competitions there
were driving expenses and hotel rooms, then airline tickets.
We not only paid the coaches—now there were two—we
paid at least a share of their expenses on trips. If other gymnasts were going, we split the cost; if only Shannon qualified
for a meet, we paid everything. If Ron or I went to a meet,
there were more costs. When choreographers or other spe-
cialists were called in, expenses rose even higher. We never
considered any of the time or money we spent on Shannon's

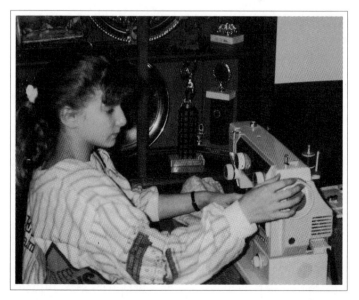

11. *For a year or two, in 1991 and early 1992, Shannon made her own workout leotards.*

gymnastics to be a sacrifice. If you want to do this for your child, how is that a sacrifice? But the expenses did mount, and we did have other children.

With Shannon's new national ranking, Shannon, Ron, and I had a difficult decision to make. She had placed high enough to earn the right to receive training funds to pay some of her gymnastics expenses. If she accepted the money, she would be disqualified from competing in college. At thirteen it would be difficult to rule out the possibility of a college scholarship later, but we had used up most of our savings. If Shannon did not accept the financial assistance, our funds might well run out before 1992.

We asked a good friend, Paul Ziert, Bart Conner's former coach and current manager, for advice. Paul suggested we take the money rather than risk Shannon's gymnastic career. Even if she didn't make the Olympic team—and he felt she had a very good chance—after so many years of gymnastics, she might not be interested in competing in college. Shannon agreed with Paul. She wanted to make sure she had an opportunity to try for the 1992 team, and she also thought she might well be tired of gymnastics by the time she reached college. So we accepted the training funds and, fortunately, have never regretted that decision.

The only somewhat disappointing result of Shannon's fall at Championships was that she did not qualify for the Goodwill Games to be held in Seattle later in the summer. These games, held every four years between Olympics, were founded by Soviet leaders and the American media mogul Ted Turner in 1986 after Americans boycotted the 1980 Olympics and the Soviets refused to compete in Los Angeles in 1984. When Shannon went to Moscow in 1986 the first Goodwill Games were just getting started, and we had watched the participants practice for opening ceremonies. As an alternate to the 1990 U.S. Goodwill Games team, Shannon was invited to San Jose for a dual meet against the Soviets.

The gym became a battlefield, with Steve pressing Shannon harder than ever and Shannon beginning to show some resistance. She hit flawless routines daily in the gym. Steve was tired of the falls at meets and told her that if she fell at the meet in San Jose, he was through with her.

Shannon was terrified. Workouts got worse instead of better, she was coming home in tears every day, and Steve was getting angrier. After a few nights of hearing Shannon cry herself to sleep, I knew I had to do something or she might give up. It was clear to me that Shannon needed much greater help than Ron or I or any person could provide.

When the children were very young, I had taken them to church regularly, but as our schedules got busier and Shannon was frequently gone on Sundays, religion had taken something of a backseat in our family. We still firmly believed in God's guidance, but we forgot to actively turn to Him with our problems or remember to express gratitude for all that He had given us. That was going to change.

My husband was raised as a Baptist and I as a Christian Scientist. Before we got married we had set aside these formal affiliations and talked about how we really felt about Christ and God. Christian Scientists, members of the Church of Christ, Scientist, believe that healing can come through prayer and spiritual communion with God. Christian Scientists often turn to a "practitioner" for assistance in getting our thoughts on the right track rather than to a doctor. Ron respected my decision to use a practitioner for myself and the children. If the situation was so severe that he wanted a doctor to see one of the children, I willingly acceded to his wishes. Now I told him I would like Shannon to talk with a Christian Science practitioner.

Ron didn't object, but Shannon hesitated. She had never talked with a practitioner before, didn't really understand how one could help, and was a little embarrassed at the thought. I explained this to the practitioner, Kittie Burris, and she suggested we come to her house. Shannon agreed to go. Kittie was very outgoing and understanding, and Shannon found it easy to talk with her. Kittie lovingly told Shannon about Jesus and other biblical figures and how they overcame fear with love and trust in God's goodness, his omnipotence, omnipresence, and omniscience. She made sure that Shannon understood what she was saying and then asked her to go home and read some passages from the Bible and from *Science and Health with Key to the Scriptures*, by Christian Science founder Mary Baker Eddy, which is used in our church to help explain the Bible.

Shannon soon approached gym with a much calmer and more positive attitude. She no longer feared Steve. Shannon visited Kittie several more times and called her on the telephone when she had a question or was feeling low.

Shannon and I spent time every evening just before she went to sleep talking about what she was learning. Tessa had accompanied us to see Kittie several times and wanted to broaden her knowledge of God. I bought a children's book at a local Christian bookstore and began to read Bible stories with all three children each evening.

Shannon was much happier, but Steve was still a little crazy. I finally decided I had to talk to him. Many of the parents were afraid to question Steve, but I knew there were times when, for Shannon's sake, he needed to hear what I had to say and I needed to understand where he was coming from. Sometimes I would see that he had good reasons for what he was doing which I may not have considered. Other times, he might even come to agree with me or might not have realized how Shannon was being affected. Since Steve was a master at directing the conversation, I discovered it was wise to bring in a list of topics I wanted to cover, so when the discussion began to get sidetracked I could get back to the issues at hand.

I explained how pressured Shannon had been feeling and told him that she was visiting a practitioner but didn't go into much detail. I told him Shannon really did want to do her best for him and that I only asked that he back off a little and give her some breathing room.

As her coach, Steve had more credibility with Shannon about her ability and her performance than Ron or I did. Positive reinforcement from Steve when she was frustrated in the gym had more impact than our reassurances. Steve reacted wonderfully. He said he realized how tough he had been on her. After that day he was more supportive and patient in the gym.

Shannon had a terrific meet in San Jose. In a field of very experienced American and Soviet gymnasts, including the acclaimed Svetlana Boginskaya and the up-and-coming Tatiana Gutsu, she finished sixth overall and was the number two American behind Kim Zmeskal. Life was looking up in more ways than one. Shannon had renewed confidence in her abilities and discovered a new source of strength in God.

The immediate pressure was off, and no other meets were imminent. In these situations Steve usually applied a little pressure of his own. He was not about to let his gymnasts get lazy, so when he thought they were not living up to their full potential, he continued his policy of kicking them out of the gym. Shannon was vying for the dubious title "Most Kicked Out." She had a stubborn streak and Steve had his bad days, so sometimes clashes were inevitable.

Steve didn't give Shannon much of a rest. He took her to the U.S. Classic in the fall where she finished second behind Elizabeth Crandall of the Desert Devils. Her placement qualified her for the 1991 U.S. Championships and earned her an invitation to the Catania Cup in Sicily along with Agina Simpkins. Steve is Italian and still has many relatives in Italy, so he was elated. He promised Shannon that after the meet his relatives would take them to see some of the interesting sights.

The United States had been entering a gymnast in the Catania Cup for several years, but no American had yet won it or even received a medal in the all-around. All the

European countries, as well as other countries such as Japan, sent their best youngsters (usually fifteen and under). At thirteen Shannon would still be one of the youngest gymnasts in the meet. The Catania Cup was a particularly exciting meet because of the interesting prizes—a gold ring, a fur coat, and marvelous trophies.

Shannon hit all her routines beautifully, walked away with the all-around title, and qualified for all four event finals. With all his relatives in the crowd, Steve was a very proud coach. Shannon could hardly believe the bounty she received for the win. She returned the next day for event finals. Her vaulting had suffered because of the pulled hamstring, and she had had little opportunity to work a second vault, which would be required. Steve considered withdrawing her but at the last minute decided to let her enter with her full twisting Yurchenko and a front somersault. She hit both solidly and captured the vaulting gold—surprising both herself and her coach. She executed a great bar set and earned the silver. On the beam she again won gold and finished up with a gold on floor. By now the Italians were calling her Queen Yankee. After the meet she and Steve were mobbed. Steve lifted her on his shoulders to keep her from getting trampled, but Shannon loved it. The Italians loved her, and she loved them.

Steve, Shannon, and Agina and her coach spent a day in Rome sightseeing. They saw the Coliseum and the Vatican, but what impressed Shannon most was watching some street urchins attempt to pick a man's wallet. She held tightly to her purse after that.

When she boarded the plane for home, Shannon found that winning so many trophies could be a liability rather than an asset. The trophies had big marble bases and were well over a foot tall, and she had five of them, plus the fur coat. Steve had received a guitar and various other gifts. Now the airport personnel were telling them they had too much baggage. Steve argued vehemently with them, "Your country gave us these things. Should we repay their generosity by leaving them behind?" The authorities decided they could bring all the items but they would have to carry most of them on the plane with them. Shannon shared her seat with her large trophies, but she wasn't complaining.

Winning this meet was more important than Shannon realized. World Championship competition was coming up next fall and Steve wanted Shannon on the U.S. team so that she would have a good shot at the 1992 Olympic team. Winning in Italy was the first step.

Shannon enjoyed the trip to Italy but was happy to be home. She always got a little homesick on longer trips. Christmas was coming up and Shannon loved decorating, wrapping gifts, and helping with the Christmas cooking. Of our three children, she most enjoyed picking out the Christmas tree. Shannon loved everything about Christmas, so with her usual creativity she decided to squeeze the absolute most out of the holidays.

12. Shannon playing Santa Claus, age 8.

For Easter, the tradition at our house had been to hide all the eggs the night before along with a small gift for each child. The children were always up early on Sunday morning searching for the eggs and gifts. Even as they got older and realized there was no Easter bunny, they still liked hiding and finding the eggs. Shannon figured this could be fun for Christmas too. Several years earlier she had hinted to me, not too subtly, that Santa should hide a little gift on Christmas Eve for them to find the next morning. Just think, she said, while they looked for these gifts and dumped out their stockings (and surely Santa would want to include a little gift in the stocking), Mom and Dad could sleep a few extra minutes. It made sense to me! If Santa chose the hiding places well, I could get at least fifteen minutes more sleep on Christmas morning. Then Shannon mentioned part two of the master plan. The kids might need some guidance in locating these gifts, so perhaps Santa could leave a poem that would give them some hints. For fifteen more minutes of sleep I could become a poet. To this day I'm still writing those poems. I'm either a great poet or a really lousy one because I've never gotten more than seven or eight minutes of extra sleep.

Shannon thoroughly enjoyed Christmas 1990. She was healthy and eager to learn new skills. School was going well, even though she had missed quite a bit. After the Sports Festival in 1989 her teachers made every effort to help her keep up. She took all her tests and did all her homework, even the extra credit.

CHAPTER SIX

Taking on the Big Guns

THE 1991 MEET season promised to be very exciting. Shannon was again invited to the American Cup, and she wanted very much to make finals. She trained hard and competed even harder, hitting excellent routines. When Ron called home and said she had finished third I was thrilled and assumed she had succeeded in making finals, but I was wrong. Only two gymnasts per country could move on, and Kim Zmeskal and Betty Okino had placed first and second.

Steve was even more disappointed than we were. He argued with the federation that Shannon deserved to be in the finals, but he had to live with the rules. Shannon wasn't too upset. She knew she had had a good meet.

Back in the gym, Steve was already looking forward to the next competition when Shannon was to compete in a dual meet against Romania—or so he thought. She was finally getting close to the top, and he desperately wanted her to climb up that last notch or two. Then Steve learned she was not actually on the team but had been invited along with several other gymnasts to vie for spots. He was furious. Shannon had placed second at the U.S. Classic, won the Catania Cup, and was third at the American Cup. Why did she have to "try out"? To make matters worse, the trials were to be held at Karolyi's ranch, which seemed like an unfair home-court advantage for his five gymnasts who were also trying for a spot. After a while Steve calmed down and decided they would simply have to beat Karolyi in spite of the advantage. He and Shannon left for Houston. In the preliminary competition, Shannon came in second to Kerri Strug, who was then training with Karolyi, and earned a place on the team.

The trials at Karolyi's ranch were closed to spectators, but I traveled to Houston to watch the actual competition and sat excitedly in the stands, not really sure what to expect. I didn't travel to too many of Shannon's meets, but this was relatively close to home. I had heard Shannon had done well in preliminaries and Kim had faltered a little, but I knew what a tough competitor she and all the Karolyi kids were, and the Romanians were fantastic.

Shannon hit a good vault and got a mediocre score. I felt that it deserved a higher score but had to admit I'd seen her vault better. On bars she was wonderful, hitting two big release moves and a full twisting double back dismount. While the score was good, it was not great. Then came beam, which she executed flawlessly with a difficult routine that included a flip-flop to two layouts and another connected flip-flop, a front aerial, and a full twisting double back dismount. This time she got the score her mother felt she should, a 9.95, and tied with Christina Bontas of Romania for first place on beam. She hit a beautiful floor routine, closing with a full twisting double back. Her combined scores earned her a third-place tie (with Hilary Grivich) for all-around.

Kim won the meet, and a Romanian finished second. Shannon, Steve, and I were thrilled with her third-place finish. Shannon was continuing to serve notice that she fully intended to be a force in Barcelona.

In what seemed like no time, U.S. Championships were approaching. Shannon had finished eighth the year before in her first try as a senior. Steve expected her to be in the top

13. Shannon performing a dive roll in the floor exercise at the U.S. Championships, spring 1991. Photo courtesy Steve Lange.

three this time, and in a great position to make the 1991 World Championship team.

Compulsories were great. Shannon had a few bobbles during optional floor, but bars were the big disappointment. She fell on a jam to the high bar. Because of the pulled hamstring, Shannon had not tried this move until recently. A jam, transitioning from the low bar to the high bar, involves grabbing the low bar, gliding out to full-body extension almost horizontally, then keeping the knees straight while pulling the legs back to the low bar and ending almost in a sitting position on the low bar with legs still straight. Momentum from the move is supposed to carry the gymnast forward to the high bar.

It should have been an easy move. Shannon wasn't sure what happened, but she didn't make it all the way to the high bar. She had been in contention for a top spot, and a portion of these scores carried over to World Championship Trials if she was among the top twelve who were allowed to compete.

Shannon put the fall behind her and concentrated solely on beam, which she had to nail to still have a good chance at making the team. She performed a superb routine that moved her into seventh place. She still had a good chance to make the World Championship team.

Training was harder than ever. Shannon was the only gymnast from Dynamo to qualify for Trials. In the middle of the summer, a time to be outdoors having fun, going to movies, or cruising the mall with friends, Shannon was spending four hours at the gym every morning and going back in the late afternoon for three hours.

Then something wonderful happened. Erica Stokes, who had been training at Karolyi's, moved to Dynamo. She had suffered some injuries and had not competed much for the last year. Since she hadn't been to Nationals, she was not eligible to compete at World Championship Trials unless her coach could petition to have her included. Karolyi had not made the effort since he felt there was little chance of her petition being accepted.

Steve was excited to have Erica. He knew she was a great gymnast and would be a great training partner for Shannon and a real asset to his gym. The federation, at Steve's insistent urging, finally agreed to send a qualified judge to take a look at Erica. If she appeared ready, she could compete at Trials.

Now Erica and Shannon trained harder than ever, but Shannon was elated to have someone training—and suffering—with her. She also knew she would have a friend to room with on trips. Life just got better.

Sharon Weber, a brevet judge qualified to judge international meets, came to check out Erica. By the time Sharon arrived, Erica was looking great. Shannon, however, was showing signs of stress. She had been training at this very intense and hard level longer than Erica and was starting to get worn out. While Sharon watched, Shannon made entirely too many mistakes. She was already qualified for Trials, but this was not the impression Steve wanted to leave with an important judge. He was furious with Shannon, and she was soon in tears. When I arrived to pick her up Sharon came out and spoke to me briefly, mentioning Steve was not happy but that she knew Shannon was capable of doing better. She felt sure Shannon would turn everything on in the meet. I told Shannon what Sharon had said and her spirits were lifted, just a little.

All too quickly the two girls and Steve headed to Indianapolis for the meet. While Shannon had to finish only in the top six to be on the team, Erica was required to place in the top four since she had been petitioned into the meet. Erica finished third and Shannon fourth in compulsories.

The optional portion of the meet had a different format than standard competition. Rather than have gymnasts on different equipment at the same time, the competitors went one at a time, dragging the meet out. After two events everyone broke for dinner and then resumed competition. The gymnasts spent long periods waiting to compete, which broke their concentration and focus. Nevertheless, Shannon and Erica were on a roll. Both scored well on vault, bars, and beam. Going into floor, Shannon was in about fourth place and Erica about fifth. Erica had only one event left to move up into at least fourth place as required for her to make the team. Steve had a plan to increase her chances, but his idea scared even him. He posed the idea to Paul Ziert, who strongly recommended he forget it. Then he questioned Jackie Fie, the top elite judge, about what the consequences would be. She cautioned him to think his proposal through carefully. She didn't like it.

What was Steve planning? Shannon was in a great position to make the team even if she made some mistakes on floor. So what if he took out some difficulty so that her routine did not score as high? She would probably still get a pretty good score and be on the team, but she might slip a little in the standings to fifth or sixth. Then if Erica did well—and she had been doing great—she should move ahead of Shannon into fourth, thus qualifying for the team.

Shannon was scheduled to go on the floor before Erica. As she prepared, Steve told her what he planned to do and why. He was sure she would understand. She didn't. She didn't say a word, but the look she gave him while her eyes filled with tears told him exactly what she was thinking. In that instant he knew he couldn't go through with his plan. "Forget what I said," he told her. "Just go out and hit your floor routine." With a sigh of relief, Shannon stepped on the floor and aced her routine, completing the meet in fourth (with the scores from Championships added in). Erica ended up struggling on her floor routine, falling twice. Even at that she finished in sixth place, but too low to qualify for the team.

Steve realized what a dreadful mistake he had almost made. Had he followed through with his plan, Shannon would probably have slipped to fifth, but Erica wouldn't have moved into fourth. Now Shannon held onto a good spot.

It was only a few weeks until World Championships, which were also being held in Indianapolis. In the meantime school had started, but Steve had convinced Shannon that she had to continue to be in the gym long hours if she was to do well at this critical meet. Her dad retrieved her homework daily, and she did her best to keep up. At fourteen she was now a freshman in high school and grades were more important than ever. Shannon planned to go to a good college and knew that meant she needed good grades in high school. Besides, Tessa was well on her way to becoming class valedictorian and Shannon wanted to keep up with big sister.

By the time Shannon and Steve left for Indianapolis, she had recovered from those days of potential burnout during the summer and was eager for the meet to start. She called home just before the compulsory sessions were to begin. The format for the compulsory session was for each country to have two gymnasts in each session. Kerri Strug and Hilary

Grivich would go first, Kim Zmeskal and Betty Okino second, and Shannon and Michelle Campi last. Shannon was delighted. The last session is usually considered the best position because early in an event judges seem to be more cautious about granting high scores, reserving the top marks in case someone better comes along. We were happy for her, but off the telephone we had some questions. Why would Kim and Betty be going in the second session? Was it because that session was on Sunday evening when everyone could come to watch? There wouldn't be a big crowd to cheer Shannon and Michelle on Monday morning when all the youngest fans were back in school. We felt rotten for harboring these thoughts and pushed them away to revel in the knowledge that our little girl was really going to compete in the World Championships.

Ron had gone to Trials and U.S. Championships, so I was going to World Championships. I was looking forward to the trip. As a judge, I could attend Congress, the meetings and classes for coaches and judges held at this time. I would see a lot of my judging friends, and Ron's parents, Mabel and Charles Miller, were planning to be there to watch their granddaughter.

I faithfully went to every competitive session whether or not American team members were in it. I loved it all. Even compulsories were exciting. Seeing so many fantastic and famous gymnasts was mind-boggling. I had made no effort to keep up with the scores, so I sat stunned and transfixed as the scores came up for the compulsory round. I knew Shannon had done well, but I had no idea she was in second place. In the world! She was actually tied with the Romanian gymnast Chistina Bontas for second, while the renowned Svetlana Boginskaya held first. To say I was awed is an understatement. I didn't even try to contain my excitement. I wanted to shout to the world, My daughter can really compete with the big guns.

Optional competition was almost as wonderful. Shannon

finished a more than respectable fourth overall and was the top performer for the Americans. More amazing, she was one of only a few gymnasts and the only American to qualify for all four event finals in addition to the all-around. In fact, no American had ever qualified for all four event finals at World Championships. Only three gymnasts per country could advance to the all-around, and only two gymnasts per country could make each event final. The U.S. team had won the silver medal, edging out the Romanians, a real coup for this very young team.

The all-around competition was sobering. The scores tightened up, and although Shannon once again performed well, she came in sixth. Previously, the best an American had done was seventh, so sixth looked pretty darn good.

Kim won the meet, so no one noticed that Shannon had done remarkably well too—no one but her family, her coach, and most of Oklahoma. My fellow employees at the bank were bringing TVs to work every day and cutting out newspaper articles. Until now coverage of Shannon's gymnastic successes had been largely confined to the Community section of the newspaper. Now she had graduated to the Sports page.

Event finals sent me soaring. Shannon hit some good vaults but didn't medal. When she landed a solid dismount on bars I was out of my seat cheering. She tied Tatiana Gutsu for the silver medal, behind a Korean gymnast who had a perfect 10 but was later disqualified because of a discrepancy in her age records. This disqualification did not change the medal that Shannon received, but that really didn't matter. We were unbelievably excited that Shannon had won a medal at World Championships.

Shannon went on to hit a nice beam routine but took some steps on her dismount and finished out of the medals. She then headed to floor, did a solid routine, and finished Worlds with a fourth place on this event. What a week!

Shannon had competed day after day, hitting all of her routines. Regardless of placement or medals, this was a feat. She had not fallen or had any major breaks in her routines during four days of competition. Steve was positive Shannon would not only be in Barcelona, she would be known in Barcelona!

Shannon came home a tired but very happy girl until the reality of school hit. Silver medals didn't buy grades at Edmond North High School or earn homework waivers. Shannon had about three weeks of homework to make up and quite a few tests to take.

Actually, Shannon was glad to be back in school. She enjoyed being with her friends and thinking about something other than gymnastics. Steve rolled back workout hours so she had a little more time to get caught up. She thought school was going well, but when grade cards came out, Shannon got a surprise. A B in geometry stared back at her after a high school career of all A's. Shannon couldn't believe it. She enjoyed geometry, and if she had trouble understanding a concept, her dad, a physicist, was always there to help.

Shannon rarely questioned a teacher, but she was truly disturbed. She went to see Darrell Allen after school. He told her she had not done the homework properly.

"I thought I got all the problems right," she said. "My dad even checked them for me, and I got them right on all the tests."

Mr. Allen agreed. "But," he said, "I told the class to write out each homework problem on the paper before working it. You didn't."

Shannon countered with, "But I wasn't in class when you explained it, and I didn't know."

"It is your responsibility to find out what is required," Mr. Allen replied, and that was that.

Shannon came home distraught. Mr. Allen's position didn't seem fair to her. Ron offered to talk to him. After at first refusing to let him, she changed her mind. Ron went to the school the next morning and once again explained Shannon's position. Mr. Allen again explained his. The B stood. It was the only B Shannon received during her four years of high school. One thing was sure—she'd get all the homework directions in the future.

Other than this minor setback, Shannon was having a great year. It was nearing the end of 1991. Steve told her she needed to get ready for more competitions in Europe to be held in late November and early December. The bad news was that she would have to train hard and be gone on Thanksgiving weekend. The good news was that she wouldn't be going alone. Erica Stokes had also been invited to the Swiss Cup in St. Gallen, Switzerland, the Arthur Gander Memorial Meet in Montreux, Switzerland, and the DTB Cup in Stuttgart, Germany. Steve had secretly been praying that Shannon would have the opportunity to go to this series of meets, but several of the Karolyi gymnasts had been invited first. At the last minute Karolyi turned down the invitation for his gymnasts, and Shannon and Erica were invited.

Steve worked at pumping the girls up. These were terrific opportunities so close to the upcoming Olympics. Here was a chance for the girls to be seen in Europe and to improve their reputations. Both girls were training well in the gym, and Steve had high hopes for their success.

Three days before the girls and Steve were to leave for Switzerland Erica told him she did not want to go. Steve could hardly believe his ears. Shannon was stunned, but she was sure Steve would change Erica's mind. By the next day Erica was even more adamant. She would not go. Steve called the federation to let them know of Erica's decision, but it was too late to replace her. Shannon would be going to Europe by herself. We worried that she would be distressed, but mostly she was baffled.

On Thanksgiving morning we dropped Shannon at the gym so she and Steve could squeeze in one more workout before boarding the plane for Switzerland. As we left the gym we looked back at the wistful face of our little girl, knowing we were all going to Texas to spend the holidays with relatives while Shannon had many days of hard work and loneliness ahead of her. Our only consolation was knowing the decision was hers. No parent or coach can make an athlete give so much dedication to her sport. Such focus, determination, and sacrifice has to come from the heart of the athlete. Furthermore, we reminded her and ourselves that she was not alone, that God was always with her.

The Swiss Cup, the first meet, was for mixed pairs. Male and female gymnasts from each country were paired and their scores added together. Scott Keswick teamed up with Shannon. They were a great team and won the gold together. Shannon's stellar performance on beam earned her her first perfect 10.

At a reception after the meet the medalists were allowed to pick out their prizes from a large assortment on a table. Scott and Shannon got to choose first since they were the gold medalists. Shannon, remembering our videocamera had recently died, picked one out. Scott picked out the camera too.

We were delighted with her prize until we found out it recorded tapes in a European format that could not be played in an American VCR. Shannon was disappointed. The camera was a JVC, so I called a local dealership to ask whether we could work out a trade. They sent me to company headquarters where I told my story several more times. For months I kept in touch with the company, knowing that the European branch was separate and a trade looked unlikely. Then one day a representative of the American JVC called to tell me they were unable to work out a trade with the European company but would send us an American camera anyway. We're still using that camera and it still works perfectly. It has now recorded two Olympics. The camera also comes in handy when only one of us goes to a meet. The parent at home still gets to enjoy the meet! We long ago learned to ask Steve to bring home the results of meets neither of us attends because

Shannon pays so little attention to scores. She can tell you whether she felt good about her routine but is not likely to remember the marks she, or any other gymnast, received.

About six months after we received our American camera Shannon and I ran into Scott Keswick when we were using it at an event. He asked whether that was the camera Shannon won in Switzerland. I replied, "Well, sort of," and explained what had occurred. He still had his useless camera. I told him not to worry, and I gave him the name of the person at JVC who had been so helpful to me. About a week later I got a call from the company asking about Scott. I backed up his story.

"Is there anybody else I need to know about?" the woman asked me. I assured her that I knew of no other prize-winning gymnasts who would be calling her to trade in their European cameras. Scott later told me he had received an American camera from JVC and was very pleased.

Following the Swiss Cup, Shannon headed to the Arthur Gander Memorial. Once again she nailed all of her routines, won the all-around, scored another 10 on beam, and set a new all-around record for this meet at 39.875. Her score was the highest all-around score ever earned by an American gymnast.

After a trip to the top of a Swiss mountain for a view of the Alps and some hot chocolate, Steve and Shannon went to Stuttgart. Shannon wanted to see the remains of the Berlin wall, which had recently fallen, but Steve explained they were much too far away. Shannon tackled the DTB meet with the same determination she had exhibited in Switzerland. She performed very well in the all-around but was edged out by two outstanding young European gymnasts, Livinia Milosovici, who won the gold, and Tatiana Gutsu, who won the silver. Shannon was a very close bronze. Steve was happy.

Shannon came back in event finals to take the bronze on vault, the silver on bars, and the gold on floor. Steve knew she was in good position, and by Barcelona he expected her to be right up at the top.

A disappointment awaited Steve and Shannon when they returned. Erica had decided to quit gymnastics. Shannon was surprised and Steve was saddened by her decision.

Christmas was exciting as usual for Shannon. She appreciated even more just being home with her family after being gone so long. She helped bake sugar cookies. Shannon and Tessa liked decorating them. Troy liked eating the dough. On Christmas Eve the children picked out one present to open, but they opened all the other gifts on Christmas morning while Ron tuned the radio to Christmas music and our two cats crawled through the wrapping paper.

Once the excitement of seeing everyone's new treasures subsided, Ron and Troy straightened up the house while the girls helped me prepare the turkey, start the cornbread stuffing, make salad, sweet potatoes, green vegetables, and gravy, polish silver, and get out the good china. Our families could seldom come to Edmond for Christmas, but we always invited lots of friends. Steve usually stopped by, sometimes for dinner and sometimes just for dessert and coffee.

By the time all the guests had eaten, visited, and played a variety of games, we were all pleasantly worn out. But the fun was just beginning. The next day we would pack up and drive to San Antonio to visit for a week with relatives.

Steve was never thrilled when we decided to take a trip, but we were always careful to choose times when no meet was impending. We felt strongly that Shannon deserved a break now and then, so at least twice a year we took a week's vacation, usually out of town to escape the pressures of work, school, and gym. The mental as well as the physical relief of these short vacations helped keep Shannon from burning out. She always came back refreshed and ready to work hard again.

CHAPTER SEVEN

1992: Olympic Countdown

IT WAS NOW the beginning of that all-important year, 1992. Steve had a busy competitive season planned for Shannon. As always, he had her schedule carefully mapped out for the next several months.

First there was the Dynamo Classic at the end of January, an annual meet put on by Steve and his club. Teams from Mexico, Canada, and the United States attended. This meet was always a good warm-up for the competitive season, but it was nerve-racking for Shannon because so many friends and teachers came to watch. All too often she would end up falling on an event. This year she was determined to go to Barcelona, and she started her season by winning the all-around at the Dynamo Classic.

A few weeks later in Missouri she easily captured the all-around at the Dragon Invitational, outdistancing the rest of the field by two points. But after the meet, instead of being all smiles, she was fighting tears and limping noticeably. Steve checked her out and concluded she had again pulled a hamstring. In less than two weeks, Shannon was again entered in the American Cup, and Steve just knew she could make finals this year. Only now both she and Steve were wondering if she would even be competing.

Steve tried to take it easier on her in workouts, and Peggy did her best to work around the injury on beam and floor. By the time they arrived in Orlando for the meet Steve believed not only that Shannon would make finals but also that she would win; but warm-ups did not go well. The last few days before competition Steve had had to push Shannon hard and the leg was sore. She could hardly tumble on beam. Peggy was frustrated and suggested that perhaps Shannon should withdraw. Steve was not prepared to give up, and Shannon was adamant that she wanted to try. Steve decided to forgo the rest of beam warm-ups and prepare for vault and bars, which weren't as painful as beam and floor tumbling. He would do minimal floor warm-up and count on experience to pull her through.

Kim Zmeskal was also in the meet and in great shape. She and Shannon battled it out in preliminaries, but Shannon emerged the victor. She and Kim moved on to finals. Steve, Peggy, and Shannon were elated. Shannon had at last made event finals and was in a perfect position to win the next day, although scoring started over.

Once again warm-ups were very difficult, but Shannon had pulled it off the day before and Steve knew she could do it again. In the first three events Kim and Shannon were neck and neck. The last event, floor, would decide the winner. Kim was a powerful tumbler, but Shannon's routine had very difficult moves and she was very graceful.

Shannon was first up on floor. She ran hard into her first tumbling pass. Fearing she would not make it because she had warmed up so little, she put everything she had into the full twisting double back and overrotated it onto her seat and out of bounds. She jumped up stunned and headed into her second pass, almost putting her hands down again. The score was not good. Shannon dropped to third place. She was very disappointed and in a lot of pain. The tears flowed. She was hoping to compete in World Championships in France in April, but now the pulled hamstring might prevent her from going.

The next day the tears were forgotten as the gymnasts all relaxed at Disney World before preparing for the Mixed Pairs meet. Shannon had competed in this meet following the American Cup twice, but she had never made the finals. Once again she was paired with Scott Keswick, her partner from the Swiss Cup. Scott, too, had fallen short in the American Cup as Jarrod Hanks surpassed him for the win. Now both Shannon and Scott were hungry for gold. Both nailed their routines and found themselves in the final round. Shannon chose to do floor in the finals. It was time to redeem herself. She scored well. Scott also nailed his routine on high bar. The duo easily captured the gold. The date was March 10, a great day for the birthday girl. Shannon turned fifteen.

While the American Cup had not turned out as Steve and Shannon had hoped, they had ended on a high at the Mixed Pairs meet. The hamstring was still a problem, but Shannon and both her coaches were now confident they could work around it and have her ready for Worlds in April. Five Americans would be going to this event, Shannon, Kim, Betty Okino, Kerri Strug, and Dominique Dawes.

This was only an event meet, not an all-around competition. Most of the girls would do two or three events, but Steve was toying with the idea of having Shannon compete in all four. She had some new skills on almost every event he wanted her to try. Although Steve realized he would have to ease up on workouts for a while to alleviate the pain in her hamstring, he also knew this was another time she would have to get tough and work through some pain. They could take it easy after Worlds before gearing up for U.S. Championships.

Ron and I were excited that Shannon was again getting the opportunity to compete in a world championship. As we talked about it, it occurred to us that neither of us had been to a meet overseas. Even if Shannon made the Olympic team, we didn't know whether we would be able to arrange for the family to go. We had decided that if the whole family could not go to Barcelona, then no one would go. We had all worked too hard to help Shannon get where she was and we would either go together or stay home together and watch on television.

Shannon asked whether I could come to the meet in France. The idea appealed to both of us. I had noticed an ad in *International Gymnast* magazine for an inexpensive tour to Worlds. I called the number listed, but the deadline for signing up had been several weeks before. I was disappointed but knew that things usually work out for the best. I mentioned that I wanted to go because my daughter, Shannon, would be competing. The person on the other end became excited. "We've got to get you there," he said. "Give me a couple of days to see what I can do." A few days later he called back and said he had found someone I could room with on the trip and had been able to persuade the airlines to get me a ticket. I was going to Paris!

Just a few days later and about two weeks before Shannon was to leave for France, while I was cooking dinner and expecting Shannon home from gym in less than an hour, the telephone rang. It was Steve. He was in control but clearly upset. He told me Shannon had had an accident at the gym and he needed to take her to the hospital. Could we meet him there as soon as possible?

At the end of Shannon's bar workout, Steve decided she should do one more complete bar set simulating the feel of competition. Therefore, he removed the large soft crash mat and replaced it with a four-inch landing mat. He gave her a few last-minute instructions and then saluted her, indicating she should begin her routine. As she swung around the bar preparing for the dismount, a laid out back flip with a full twist, she clipped her toes on the bar, which forced her to curtail the dismount. Realizing she would not rotate around to her feet, Shannon instinctively threw out her arms to brace for the fall. She crashed to the mat, landing with her elbow in an unnatural position. It might be broken or just dislocated. Steve wasn't sure. Shannon felt sure it was just dislocated and begged Steve to "pop" it back into place. She didn't want to consider the possibility that there might be a more serious problem.

Ron and I remained relatively calm. I grabbed the book containing my Sunday School lesson and decided to read it on the way to the hospital. I needed to be in the right frame of mind when I saw Shannon. I believed in my heart that God would always take care of her and had the right plan for her. At church we learned that God is good and loves us no matter what, so He would never harm his child.

Shannon was very calm when we arrived. The doctor had looked at her arm and taken X-rays. While we waited I asked Shannon if she would like to call Kittie, the practitioner, who had moved with her husband from Oklahoma City to California. She immediately said "Yes." The nurses quickly arranged to bring a telephone to the emergency room. Shannon had started to get a little scared and weepy soon after we arrived, but after talking with Kittie she felt confident in God's protection.

Dr. David Holden showed us the X-ray, which showed a piece of bone had broken off the elbow and slid away when the elbow was dislocated. He strongly recommended surgery to screw the bone back in place as the quickest way to get it healed enough to allow Shannon to train again. Shannon preferred not to have surgery, and I was willing to abide by her wishes. But while Ron respected our religion and trusted in God, he also believed doctors performed a great service. Steve very much wanted Shannon to have the surgery. Kittie, anticipating this problem, had told Shannon she did not have to be in conflict with her coach or her dad. Whether she had surgery or not, God was there guiding, protecting, and healing her. So Shannon told her dad she would be willing to have the surgery if this was really what he wanted. He said it was. Dr. Holden wheeled her into surgery at about 11:00 P.M.

I stayed at the hospital, continuing to pray and study the weekly church lesson. Several hours later a smiling Dr. Holden emerged from surgery. He felt everything had gone very well. He would stop by in the morning and see how Shannon was doing and would arrange for me to have a bed in her room so I could stay the rest of the night with her. Shannon slept well, but a nurse kept coming in to wake her, make her go to the bathroom, and encourage her to take some pain medication, which she continued to refuse.

At eight o'clock the next morning Dr. Holden visited Shannon. Looking at her chart, he noticed she had not been given anything for pain and began to question the nurse, who explained Shannon would not take any. Shannon told him she was not in any pain. He looked doubtful, wrote out a prescription, and handed it to me. I put it in my purse and forgot about it. I never did get it filled.

Shannon was eager to go home, so Dr. Holden released her. Steve arrived and walked beside her as they wheeled her out to the car. The date was April 1, so as Shannon rose to get into the car, Steve said, "Okay, you've had your April Fool's joke, now get to the gym!" For an instant, Shannon thought he was serious and said she was trying to figure out how she was going to work out with her arm in a sling. Then Steve said, "Well, OK, you can take today off, but I'll see you tomorrow." This time she knew he was serious. It had not crossed her mind that she should take more than one day off.

Dr. Holden had decided not to put the arm in a cast, which would have made it stiffen. He predicted she would need the sling for about ten days and then she could remove it and slowly start to pull her arm straight and put pressure on it. It would take six to eight weeks before she could work out fully on it again. He told her to come back in about five days so he could keep a close watch on the progress.

Shannon continued to work with Kittie but did as Dr.

Holden requested. When he took a look at the elbow five days later he was impressed with the healing. Her arm had not bruised as much as he had expected, and it looked so good that he decided to remove the sling that day.

A few months after the 1992 Olympics the pin in Shannon's elbow began to cause some problems. Dr. Holden decided to remove it. He had originally said he expected it to be a number of years before it would need removal, if ever. Shannon saw this early occurrence as more proof of God's care. As the nurses prepared her for surgery to take out the pin, Dr. Holden mentioned to us that he had received quite a few calls from athletes and coaches requesting his procedure for getting Shannon's elbow healed so rapidly. He told them it was not his procedure but God's.

While the pin was in, Dr. Holden had given Steve explicit instructions on how to work with the elbow to regain full use without causing any further damage. Steve adhered strictly to his guidelines—for a while. As the weeks slipped by and U.S. Championships grew closer, Steve got more anxious. Shannon was making remarkable progress. If she couldn't use both arms to do a skill, then she would use one. She did one-armed back handsprings on floor and beam and vaulted with one arm. Bars were the biggest problem, but as her arm straightened she was doing more. Maybe, he thought, she could be ready for Championships, which were scheduled for just over five weeks after her injury. Sure the doctor had said she shouldn't train fully for at least six weeks, five if her injury improved more quickly than expected, and it was only about three weeks since the accident, but Shannon was ready to work hard and the arm was looking and feeling great. So Steve pushed the schedule up a bit.

Steve couldn't get her ready for Worlds in less than two weeks, but he rationalized that maybe it was for the best. He had been pushing her hard for quite some time. She had competed hard during the fall and was once again beginning a heavy schedule with only a few months until Olympic Trials. She had a painful pulled hamstring, and if he wasn't careful he could burn her out before she had the chance to try for the 1992 team. He remembered all too well the fall of 1989 when after months of working on a pulled hamstring, she had finally considered giving up gymnastics. He knew her heart was in this sport and she was every bit as eager as he to make the Olympic team, but they needed her body to cooperate. Rather than feel depressed about missing Worlds, he and Shannon would work at turning this event to their advantage. She would give the rest of her body some time off while the elbow recuperated. Steve let her know he still expected her to add all the new skills to her routines, but now they would add them at Nationals (or, if need be, at Trials).

While Steve and Shannon put together a plan of action for her, I was trying to figure out my own plan. Shannon wasn't going to Paris, but it appeared I was since I would forfeit about two-thirds of the cost if I canceled. I was a gymnastic judge and it would be a great experience. So I went to Paris for a little over a week. I had a great time, and it was very inspiring to watch the American gymnasts compete and do well. I also discovered I really loved chocolate and strawberry crepes. But I wished my child was competing and wondered how she was handling the injury. Would she still have a chance to be part of the team in the summer of 1992? (This was a major concern at this point.)

I shouldn't have wasted any time worrying about how Shannon was coping. By Nationals she was as hungry for competition as Steve had hoped she would be. They both felt she could do a good job in compulsories. Steve never believed in playing strictly by the rules, doctors' or anyone else's; he preferred to make the rules. In this case he figured Dr. Holden's guidelines might need to be altered somewhat. Shannon had other reasons for moving on more rapidly. She was still working with Kittie and felt God's presence in her life more strongly each day. We prayed together at night, not asking God for any concessions but rather knowing He was prepared to give us all the good we were willing to accept.

When Shannon had started traveling out of the country by herself I had wanted to give her something she could take with her to rely on each day. I prepared little note cards with Bible verses and quotes from *Science and Health,* which she could read daily to gain the spiritual strength to tackle the daily difficulties. One of Shannon's favorite verses is "with God all things are possible." Now, as she worked to get ready for U.S. Championships and to add all the new skills she needed in her routines, she kept this verse in mind.

Shannon had an outstanding compulsory meet, finishing in first place just ahead of Kim Zmeskal and astounding the crowd that had not expected her to be able to compete. Steve had to decide whether to have her compete in optionals the next day. Shannon was feeling great and wanted to do it, but Steve wasn't so sure. He felt confident she could get through all her routines without the new skills but was not sure he wanted the judges to see her doing routines without the added difficulty or the fine-tuning they needed. The scores would carry over to Trials, and while the compulsory scores were good, chances are the optional routines, without the new more difficult moves, might not score at the level he wanted. However, if she didn't finish the meet, none of the scores would carry forward. He would have to petition her to Trials, and they would risk relying entirely on her performance at a single meet. Her Trial scores would count 100 percent toward determining whether she made the team and where she would be placed on it.

Placement was definitely important. Where Shannon competed in the lineup on each event would be crucial to her opportunity to make the all-around and event finals at the Olympics. Steve and Shannon had learned this firsthand the previous fall at World Championships.

Shannon warmed up for the meet the next day, but just

before competition Steve made his call. Shannon would sit this one out. So Shannon watched from the sidelines and ached to be out on the apparatus. She reacted as Steve had hoped. She was itching to get back in the gym and get ready for Trials. Steve instituted long, hard workouts. Shannon was again going to the gym twice a day and putting in six to eight hours of work, but she headed off eagerly. Steve realized that missing Worlds might not have been so bad.

In what seemed like the blink of an eye to me, Shannon, Steve, Peggy, and Ron were leaving for Olympic Trials. Between Championships and Trials, less than a month, Peggy had decided Shannon needed better floor choreography and different music. After listening to hours of music she narrowed the choices to several pieces. Peggy and Shannon listened together and made a final selection, "Hungarian Rhapsody." While Shannon learned routines quickly, she was very stubborn about what types of moves she would and would not do. Peggy needed to find a choreographer who was not only skilled but also able to work well with Shannon. She chose Nancy Roach.

Shannon and Nancy hit it off immediately. Nancy had watched Shannon compete enough to have a good feel for her style, and she seemed to put the routine together almost effortlessly. Shannon liked the moves and picked them up rapidly. By Trials the routine was not perfect, but Peggy expected it to look much better by the Olympics.

Steve was more worried about vault, which was coming back slowly because it had been difficult to practice with an elbow injury. Shannon's timing was still a little off. She had recovered more quickly on bars and appeared to be in great shape on beam.

Shannon started the meet with a first-place finish in compulsories. She began optionals on vault, where she was a little weak, but earned a respectable score. Kim and Kerri Strug, both outstanding on this event, started the meet very strongly. On bars Shannon really showed the judges she planned to be on the team. She hit her reverse hecht, full over (while swinging into a handstand, releasing the bar, doing a full twist, and regrasping the bar), and Gienger (releasing the bar, doing a piked somersault, and regrasping the bar) solidly and stuck her full twisting double back dismount. Kim suffered a few problems on bars, and her score dropped slightly. Kerri had a good routine but less difficult than Shannon's. Betty Okino, another of Bela's top gymnasts, was sitting this meet out because of a back injury.

Shannon clung to one of the top positions. She was strong on beam and scored high. Kim again had a few wobbles and didn't earn quite as good a score. Kerri had a good routine but also scored under Shannon. Only floor was left.

Ron, in the stands, was hardly breathing. I had stayed home with our other two children, but a large group of parents from the gym reserved a room at a local restaurant, brought in a large TV, and asked me to join them. To be honest, I didn't want to go. My nerves were on edge, and I wanted to watch the live coverage alone in my own living room, but these were good friends and I knew I should accept their invitation—so I sat there in the restaurant, unable to eat, as Shannon took the floor.

I really loved watching this routine. I thought Shannon performed it beautifully, but I could hardly think about the lovely dance as I worked through every tumbling move with her. She went out of bounds on her first tumbling pass, which I knew would cost her a tenth of a point. Otherwise she hit all her skills, including the difficult last pass.

I was overjoyed. Even with her small error I knew she must have qualified for the Olympic team. As I began to breathe again, one of the parents came over and said, "I guess you know your daughter just won Trials." I gave him a puzzled look. Kim, who was usually excellent on the floor, hadn't even performed yet, and Shannon had a mediocre vault score and an error on floor. The man insisted that he had calculated the compulsory and optional scores and found that even if Kim got a 10 on floor, Shannon would win. I had my doubts but wasn't worried. If Shannon ended up in second or third, we would be thrilled beyond comprehension. It turned out that Kim's fantastic 9.95 on floor was not enough to overtake Shannon.

Ron told me later he had sat in the stands astounded. Our daughter had been the top scorer at U.S. Olympic Trials. The only slight disappointment was that the federation decided not to declare a winner. Rather than announce final placement, they simply announced the names of the seven gymnasts who were eligible to go on to the Olympic training camp where the team would then be chosen.

Things really heated up for us with Shannon's top placement. The "Today Show" contacted us to do a remote interview with Shannon. They also planned to interview Kim. This was pretty exciting stuff, and Shannon was looking forward to it, but on the Sunday evening before the Monday morning program a woman called to tell us that instead of interviewing Kim and Shannon, they would be interviewing Kim and Bela.

Bela was furious that Shannon had edged out Kim, and he was worried that it might affect Kim's position at the Olympics. He blamed everybody from the federation to the judges. "I think that's a crime," he told Karen Rosen of the *Atlanta Journal-Constitution*, adding that Kim had been "hunted down" and "pushed in the mud."

Kim, however, admitted that she had made some mistakes and said, "None of this is going to matter in a month. What people are going to remember is who won the Olympics, not who won the Trials."

When we watched Bela's interview the next morning, angry that Shannon had been excluded, we had a feeling that Bela had given the show an ultimatum. He wanted an opportunity to have his say. At the time we were hurt and irritated, but as Shannon's status in the gymnastic world grew over the next years, we understood Bela better. We had been naive about the politics in the world of international gymnastics competition. Bela understood the politics and wanted to use it to his advantage. I still don't totally agree with Bela, but I've come to see what he already knew—you really need some political clout going into a major meet if you intend to bring home gold. Rather than accept this situation, our family hoped to change it.

On the forty-minute drive from the airport with Ron and Shannon after the Olympic Trials, I suddenly realized our daughter was probably going to be competing in the Barcelona Olympics and we had no room reservations or airline tickets and no money to get them.

Ron and I were determined to stick to our old pact that if the whole family didn't go, none of us would. Tessa and Troy had put up with a lot over the years to accommodate Shannon. Her training had taken money that could have gone to some extras for them. Tessa helped Shannon with schoolwork and chauffeured her around when Ron or I couldn't. Troy had tagged along to nearby meets for years, packing his toys and playing quietly in the stands. Both had waited patiently for dinner at 9:30 P.M. so that we could eat as a family. They deserved a chance to go. We mulled over the possibilities but realized that even if we had the money, it was probably too late to make arrangements.

The telephone was ringing as we walked into the house. It was Pam Henry, the mother of a close school friend of Shannon's. She had anticipated our dilemma and made some telephone calls. An insurance company in her bank's building had bought some room and airline ticket packages and would sell us some for half-price. We were thrilled until we found out how much half-price was. We still couldn't afford it.

The next day at work my telephone began to ring. Some local banks, knowing I was a banker, wanted to know if they could chip in with my bank to raise funds for us to go to Spain. While everyone in my office had been trooping by with congratulations, no one had mentioned fund-raising. I thanked the callers and told them I would give them an answer later.

It turned out that the president of Equity Bank, where I worked, had already called our advertising agency to make some plans. They estimated that the cost to send the four of us to Barcelona, including lodging, transportation, food, and tickets, would be $25,000. To us, that seemed to be a staggering amount.

When the Alfred P. Murrah Federal Building was bombed in the spring of 1995, the rest of the world discovered what a caring, loving, resilient people Oklahomans are. We discovered all these qualities and more in the summer of 1992 when an entire state chipped in to send the Millers to Barcelona.

Equity Bank put a large advertisement in the newspaper to explain the fund-raising efforts. A local T-shirt company offered the bank shirts at a greatly reduced price to sell on behalf of the efforts. In no time people all over Oklahoma were sporting the shirts, which showed an Olympic torch encircled by the words, "I helped send the Millers to Barcelona." Several more shipments of shirts also sold out.

14. Shannon and Troy at the send-off reception given by Equity Bank, 1992.

Local radio and television stations promoted the effort and held a benefit softball game. A local amusement park sponsored a golf tournament. A Texaco station held a car wash. Grocery stores donated food for sale. People from all over the state sent checks. American Express, which provided my bank's travelers checks, even gave us travelers checks for spending money. Everybody, it seemed, wanted us to be in Barcelona to watch Shannon.

Even before our fund-raising was complete, Shannon, Steve, and Peggy had to leave for the training camp in Florida. A friend of Steve's had also heard about our efforts and asked Steve if he and Shannon could come to New York before going on to Florida. Steve Karavellas owned the Team USA gymnastics camp and worked on the Commodities Exchange. He was sure the brokers would want to help. So Shannon and Steve made the stop, and while Shannon signed autographs the brokers shouted "USA! USA!" and graciously donated to our cause.

In less than four weeks the fund-raising effort raised $35,000. Our trip cost $24,000, and we decided to donate the remaining $11,000 to the Oklahoma Special Olympics so that even more children and parents could benefit from Oklahoma's generosity.

Once in Florida at Brown's Gymnastics, Shannon and the other girls began intensive training. Michelle Campi had competed at U.S. Championships and done very well, but she had fallen on a tumbling pass in warm-ups for Trials and incurred an arm injury similar to Shannon's. Michelle and her coach learned from Shannon's experience and worked to get ready for the training camp. Betty Okino, who was doing much better physically, was also invited to be part of the camp. Eight girls were there. Seven would be chosen to go to Barcelona, six of whom would actually compete. The competitors would be chosen the day before the meet began.

The girls were all performing fairly well, although each had some problems to overcome. Shannon seemed pleased with her progress, and Steve was downright elated. He said she was more consistent than any of the other girls. The last night before the team prepared for their Olympic departure, the final seven girls were selected: Shannon, Kim Zmeskal, Kerri Strug, Dominique Dawes, Wendy Bruce, Michelle Campi, and Betty Okino. Kim Kelly was not chosen.

The decision raised some difficult questions and caused some real controversy. Shannon and Michelle had been able to petition to Trials under the rules. We were grateful, but we could see how even this might be frustrating to Kim who had withstood the competition at both Championships and Trials. In the end, Betty Okino, who had not competed at either of these meets, was chosen for Barcelona over Kim.

There were strong arguments on both sides. The coaches had to look at who was doing well at the time. Even though Betty had not competed in Championships or Trials because of injuries, she was now healthy and performing good routines. She had represented the United States admirably in many international meets. Surely she deserved this opportunity. Kim had also represented the United States on many occasions, had endured both Championships and Trials, and had emerged in the top five when both meet scores were added together. She and her coaches believed she was in good shape.

We were disappointed for Kim, but we would have felt bad for Betty also. There were no hard-and-fast rules to cover the situation because it had not come up before.

Most coaches, parents, and gymnasts agreed that the training camp was not a good idea. Whereas teams in some sports were chosen weeks or months before the Olympics, we were asking our girls to peak time and time again: at Championships, because the scores carried over; at Trials, to make the team; at training camp, when they would again be evaluated; and finally, at the Olympic Games. Before the next Olympics, the women's gymnastics team was named after Trials and the training camp was open only to the girls who would be competing and two designated alternates. There were to be seven girls on the team, and though all seven would get to compete, they would not all be able to perform in all four events.

The 1992 team trained in France for a week before continuing to Barcelona. The coaches hoped to set up a dual meet with the French team for practice, but this never took place. Shannon was glad not to have another competition since the training camp had seemed like having a meet every day.

France was boring for Shannon. She was homesick, disliked the food (I had loved the food, but I guess crepes weren't on their diet), and was nervous about the impending big event. She placed a distress call to us. She was hungry.

Peggy had not been allowed to stay in the Olympic village since she was not an official team coach. Steve and Bela stayed in the village but not, of course, with the girls. Bela's wife and partner, Martha, stayed with the gymnasts and was used to closely monitoring the diets of her girls.

There had been rumors of gymnasts starving themselves to achieve certain body types. In a 1995 book, *Little Girls in Pretty Boxes*, the San Francisco sports columnist Joan Ryan told the stories of former gymnasts who had developed eating disorders. I never believed Steve was unreasonable about food and would not have stood for it if he had been. One advantage of having Shannon living at home was being able to see that she was taking reasonable care of herself.

Steve had always cautioned Shannon not to overindulge in fattening foods, but he knew she was careful and he had worried little about her diet. Later, as other elite gymnasts came to his gym, Steve would institute more rules.

In Barcelona Martha felt responsible for Shannon and thought she should eat like her girls. From what Shannon could tell, Martha seemed to dictate what Kim, Kerri, and Betty ate. Shannon was not prepared for this. She wanted me to bring her a survival package. I took crackers, dried fruit snacks, and canned soup.

CHAPTER EIGHT

Barcelona Bounty

I T WAS FINALLY time for us to catch our plane. Although we were planning a stay of about two weeks, from the amount of luggage, it looked as if we were planning to be gone for two months. We gave our destination little thought. We were nervous wrecks, working constantly to stay calm.

When we arrived at the Oklahoma City airport we found a long line of anxious travelers. Our flight had been canceled, and the airline was trying to rebook everyone on other flights. We headed to the end of the line, realizing we were not going to make our connection in Dallas to New York and that we would probably miss our flight out of New York to Barcelona.

We were scheduled to arrive the afternoon before opening ceremonies. If we got there a day late, we wouldn't miss the compulsory competition, which started the first morning, but we would miss the opening ceremonies. At that time we assumed the gymnasts would be marching and did not want to lose the chance to see our daughter walking in with the other athletes behind the American flag.

We stood in line hoping things would work out, but Pam

Henry, who had taken us to the airport, was less patient. She marched up to the counter, informed the attendants that we needed to get to Dallas, and asked what the airline was going to do about it. It happened that an earlier flight to Dallas was boarded and ready to leave but had some empty seats. The ticket agent quickly got on his telephone, explained the situation, and asked the captain to hold the flight until we could get there. The pilot gave us five minutes.

People in line helped us get our baggage to the counter. While the clerks checked in our luggage, we literally ran for the gate. Our friends still laugh as they recall seeing news footage of us leaping over other people's baggage to get to the metal detector.

We made that flight, and we made it to Dallas in time for the flight to New York City, but that plane was delayed, first because it had been overbooked and then because of weather. While we again nervously wondered if we'd make our flight to Barcelona, the pilot got permission to take off. As we landed in New York our watches told us we were going to be very close. When we pulled up to the gate there was no one there to open it. Another delay. Precious time was slipping by.

When we finally emerged from the plane we were glad we were wearing our tennis shoes. It was time to run again. We got out to the area where the shuttles to the other terminal were departing, but several shuttles drove right past us. I flagged down an airport security officer driving by in a car, and he explained that the shuttle drivers were on strike. Now we were certain we would not make our flight.

I had nothing to lose, so I told the officer our story and asked for his help. He hesitated only a second before telling us all to hop in (a violation of airport rules). As he refused to take any money, we gave him an autographed picture of Shannon. We arrived at the terminal in time to get to our gate.

Out of breath but happy, we charged the gate counter, but Ron noticed there was no airplane. It turned out the flight out of New York was also late. After all our rushing we sat for more than two hours waiting for our plane to arrive.

Once in Barcelona, we watched as everyone else's bags drifted by and finally realized ours were not on the plane. We reported our lost luggage. The airline authorities assured us they would deliver it to us when it arrived. We caught the bus to Barcelona, stopping there before going on to Salou, the small town about sixty miles from Barcelona where we were staying. We had decided not to stay in the hotel with the other gymnasts' parents because USA Gymnastics could not guarantee us space for Tessa and Troy and because acceptance of a room from the gymnastics federation would obligate Shannon to a ten-city post-Olympic tour. We did not know how she would be feeling after the Games and wanted to leave her options open.

We thought our adventure was over, but Ron's big challenge was just beginning. The U.S. Olympic Committee (USOC) had our tickets to the competition and to opening ceremonies the next evening. We thought that would be no problem. The committee had an office just a few blocks from the AT&T hotel and reception area. We were part of an AT&T tour package even though our lodging was in Salou, so whenever we came into Barcelona we could go to this hotel to get out of the heat and get something to eat and drink.

We took a taxi to the USOC office to pick up our tickets. The office was a large structure with a window in the outside wall, which turned out to be where tickets were sold. It was in the middle of the afternoon and very hot, but there were only five people in line in front of us. These people, however, were trying to buy tickets, and the tickets were in small boxes scattered all over the room, where only one person was working. The clerk spent a long time going through all the boxes to try to find the tickets for each person to purchase. When we got to the head of the line, tired and hot, he told us Bela Karolyi had our tickets. We were not happy. Bela was staying in the athletes' village, and no one could visit or telephone into the village without an elaborate authorization process.

We walked back to the AT&T hotel. There I began asking questions. I found out how to get to the village. Someone also got me a telephone number. After several attempts I reached an American who was familiar with the gymnastics team and explained our problem. The man told me how to go about contacting someone with access to the gymnastics coaches once I was at the village. Then Bela could send our tickets out.

First we had to get to Salou, check into our hotel, and find out about our luggage. On the bus to Salou we learned it took a good two hours to make the sixty-mile drive. When we arrived we learned our luggage hadn't. We were able to obtain necessities such as toothbrushes and toothpaste from the hotel.

The next morning I decided to stay in Salou with Tessa and Troy to wait for the luggage and then catch a bus to Barcelona. Ron would take an earlier bus, go into Barcelona, and try to get our tickets. We would meet at the AT&T hotel about the time the bus was scheduled to depart for opening ceremonies.

My aunt, who had traveled to the games, was staying in a hotel in Salou with some of the team parents. Before leaving for Barcelona, Ron went by to see my aunt and ran into Bert Strug, Kerri's father, who was preparing to go to the USOC office in Barcelona to get his family's tickets. Ron explained that Bela now had the tickets, then headed back to our hotel to catch the bus.

In Barcelona, after figuring out the subway system to get to the village, he talked his way into the visitor's center and to a telephone. By now federation officials had realized that parents would have trouble getting the tickets from Bela, so they planned to have the tickets sent to Salou. When they learned no trains went to Salou they had the tickets taken back to an apartment used by the federation in Barcelona.

While Ron's contact was tracking down this information, Ron waited, not so patiently, in the village visitor's center from about 10:00 A.M. until 3:30 P.M.

At about 3:15 he heard some of the gymnasts were out on the sidewalk. When he stepped outside to get a look, there was Shannon. She was happy to know we had made it to Barcelona. Ron gave her a hug and our telephone number in Salou so that she could call us since we couldn't call her.

After the gymnasts boarded a bus to work out, Ron heard that our tickets were now at the federation apartment. He got directions and hailed a taxi. Finally he had the tickets in his hand. He grabbed an orange, the only food he had all day, and looked for the subway station.

Tessa, Troy, and I arrived at the AT&T hotel about 4:00 P.M. for the bus to opening ceremonies, which was scheduled to leave at 5:00. We expected Ron to be waiting for us at the hotel, since he had left early that morning. By 4:55 I was worried. I wasn't sure what to do. At 5 o'clock I boarded the bus with the children, thinking maybe he planned to meet us at opening ceremonies, although how we would find him, I didn't know. Just as the bus started to drive off, I saw Ron running toward it. I jumped up and headed for the door. The driver opened it and Ron boarded.

The wonderful opening ceremonies were definitely worth the effort, even though the gymnasts didn't participate as their coaches wanted to preserve their energy for the next morning's competition. We arrived back at the hotel about 2:30 A.M. We didn't want to miss one minute of the Olympics, at least of the gymnastics portion, so although Shannon did not compete until later in the day we arose a few hours later to catch a 6:00 A.M. bus into Barcelona for the 8:00 A.M. session.

The first four Americans competed well, hitting solid compulsory routines and laying a good foundation. Kim and Shannon were the last Americans to compete, in the next-to-last session. Shannon started on bars and Kim on beam. Shannon earned an excellent score with a superb routine. She

15. *Tessa, Troy, Ron, and I wait for the compulsory meet to get under way at the Barcelona 1992 Olympic Games.*

followed suit on beam and floor and finished with a meet high of 9.95 on vault. Steve was jubilant and astonished when he looked at the scoreboard. Shannon was in first place.

The Russians, now known as the Unified Team, still had Tatiana Gutsu and Svetlana Boginskaya competing in the last session with some other outstanding gymnasts, but Shannon's score held. We could scarcely believe she was still in first place at the conclusion of the compulsory meet at the Olympics. Her accomplishment was especially noteworthy since historically the Americans had trouble competing internationally because they were weak in compulsory competition. To bolster attention to compulsories, USA Gymnastics had instituted a scoring system for national competitions that counted compulsories 60 percent and optionals only 40 percent. Internationally, including at the Olympics, each part of the competition counted half. It was amazing that an American gymnast led the world in compulsories.

Kim had taken a fall on beam so the American team did not end up with as much of a lead as they had hoped, but they were still in second trailing the Unified Team. I lingered after the meet, hoping to get a chance to talk to Shannon, but the security guards let me know it was time to leave. I made one last effort, yelling Steve's name at the top of my lungs. He looked up and saw me hanging over the rail and strolled over to talk. I handed down the bag I had packed for Shannon.

"What's this?" he asked.

I told him about Shannon's telephone call begging for food and offered to let him look in the bag. Steve was disturbed. He realized Shannon was expending a lot of calories and wanted her to eat right. After that Peggy and Steve ate all their meals with her so that she could eat what she wanted without any criticism from another coach.

After a day's break following compulsories, we again arrived early on the day of team optionals competition. The top four teams from compulsories would compete in the prestigious final session. The day was long but exciting as we watched excellent gymnastics and prayed Shannon and the other girls would hit their routines.

The Unified Team started on vault, the Americans on bars, the Romanians on beam, and the Chinese on floor. Shannon was last up on bars for the team. Each girl hit a good routine, but none stuck the dismount. Shannon performed a flawless routine and then solidly stuck her full twisting double back.

The team moved to beam. The first two girls were a little shaky but turned in nice routines overall. The next two girls hit well. Kim performed a beautifully executed routine and received a big score. Shannon's routine was packed with difficulty—a flip-flop to a layout to two feet, a flip-flop to three layout step-outs in a row, a front aerial, and a full twisting double back dismount, not to mention an assortment of leaps and turns and a back handspring quarter turn to a handstand. Her performance, while very good, was not quite up to perfection. The judges gave her a 9.9.

Next for the team was floor. Although the Americans

were looking good, the Romanians had pulled ahead and were now in second place. All the Americans executed good floor routines. Shannon completed all her major tumbling with beautiful execution, again scoring a 9.9.

While the Americans were on floor, Tatiana Gutsu, one of the meet favorites, had fallen on her beam mount. It was doubtful, given the depth of the Unified Team, that she would qualify for the all-around competition. Only the top three gymnasts from a country were eligible to make the all-around cut.

The Americans concluded the meet on vault. The lowest score was a 9.9, but the high scores were not enough to pass the Romanians, who just edged the Americans for the silver medal. The Unified Team took the gold.

Kim had a terrific meet and pulled slightly ahead of Kerri Strug to make all-around finals along with Shannon and Betty Okino. Ron and I were so thrilled that Shannon would get the chance to compete in the all-around that we didn't at first feel

16. Shannon on the balance beam at the Barcelona Games. Photo courtesy Jerry Butler.

the impact of what she had accomplished. Not only had she qualified for the all-around competition at the Olympics, but she had done it in grand style. The scoreboard in the arena proudly displayed that the Americans won a bronze medal at the Olympic Games, a true accomplishment, and that Shannon was the number one gymnast in the world after team competition, a feat never before achieved by an American.

Again I stayed in the arena as security tried to remove me. I was determined to see Shannon as I had not been able to talk to her after compulsories. I didn't get to this time either. Peggy saw me and came over to say she and Steve had just learned that Shannon had qualified for all four event finals, another first for an American at an Olympic Games. Although Peggy seemed calm, I could tell from her eyes and her voice that she was bubbling with excitement. Shannon, who had been the first American ever to qualify for all four event finals at a world championships, was once again setting records.

Ron, Tessa, Troy, and I were euphoric on the long ride back to Salou. The evening meets started at 8:00, and by the time they ended and everyone walked down Montjuic to the Bull Ring where the buses parked, found the right bus, and then rode back, it was usually between 2:00 and 3:00 A.M. when we dragged into the hotel. We weren't dragging tonight regardless of the time. We wanted to shout to the world what our daughter had done. Even if she didn't finish high in any of the other events, she had already accomplished more than we had dared to dream. And she would always have an Olympic medal.

The gymnasts had the next day off. We stayed in Salou, splashing in the ocean, shopping for souvenirs, and having dinner with my aunt, who wanted to talk about how wonderful the meet had been. We didn't discourage her. It was a wonderful relaxing day, and we needed it.

Soon enough we were gearing up for the all-around competition. We had to get ourselves mentally prepared. The long bus ride in each morning gave me an opportunity to read my Sunday School lesson and do a little praying. More than winning a medal, we wanted Shannon to feel good about herself, leave the Olympics with pleasant memories, and remember to trust in God. One of Shannon's favorite quotes from Mary Baker Eddy was, "To those leaning on the Sustaining Infinite (God), today is big with blessings." We knew, and we were confident Shannon knew, that blessings come in many different forms, not always medals.

As always on the day of all-around competition we caught the early bus into Barcelona and watched the early rounds. Shannon would be competing in the evening rotation. Ron and I were too excited to worry about our appetites, but Tessa and Troy were as hungry as ever. We went to dinner with some friends from Puerto Rico whose daughter was training at Dynamo (and went on to compete in the 1996 Olympics for Puerto Rico). In their company, we were finally able to understand a Catalonian menu.

Back at the Palau Sant Jordi arena, we waited in a long line, a practice that was all too common for us by now. Tessa and Troy brought books to read. The atmosphere was electric. Movie stars and some of the Dream Team were there to watch.

For the first time in an Olympics a rule called "New Life" was in effect. Each girl now started from scratch in individual all-around competition. In previous Olympics scores from team competition were carried forward and added to the scores from the individual all-around to determine the overall medalists.

The change hurt Shannon, who had been the top scorer at the end of the team event, but it greatly benefited Tatiana Gutsu, who, despite her fall on beam in the team competition, now showed up in the individual competition for best all-around gymnast. The Unified Team coaches had complained that one of the other qualifiers, Roza Galieva, was injured and could not compete. Tatiana was next in line. (Four years later, during the 1996 Olympics, Roza and her coach would confess that she had not been injured, but the Unified Team officials thought Tatiana stood a better chance of winning.)

Shannon started on bars. We weren't surprised. She seemed always to start on this apparatus, and things had gone well so far. She did a great routine and stuck the landing but didn't score quite as high as in the team competition. She was the first gymnast to perform in the meet, and, as prejudiced parents, we wondered whether that had anything to do with the lower score. Tatiana Gutsu, who was in the same rotation of gymnasts, scored somewhat better. Both girls headed to beam. Both had balance checks while performing but scored well. This time Shannon came out slightly ahead.

Ron and I made no effort to keep track of overall scores. Our main focus was praying for Shannon to execute her routines well. We wanted her to do her best and knew the standings would take care of themselves.

Both Shannon and Tatiana did exceptional floor routines. Tatiana, who opened with an impressive double back in a laid-out position, earned the higher score this time.

As Shannon went into vault, we realized she was having a very good meet. Was it possible she could win a medal in the all-around? A look at the scoreboard showed us that Tatiana was in first place and Shannon was in fourth, with two excellent gymnasts between them. Vault was not traditionally Shannon's strongest event, so we doubted she was vying for a medal. But if she didn't slip out of fourth, she would set another record—the highest placement in all-around competition any American gymnast had ever recorded in a nonboy-cotted Olympics.

Shannon vaulted before Tatiana. As a judge, I could see that her first vault was stupendous, with great distance and repulsion—height and power coming off the horse—and a spectacular landing. When the scoreboard flashed a 9.975,

Ron and I were beside ourselves with joy. Her second vault was also exceptional, but the landing was not quite as good. It scored a 9.95. The higher score would count. The scoreboard wasn't showing the standings, but it seemed inevitable that Shannon would hang on to fourth.

Tatiana did not hit a particularly good first vault, but her second vault earned a great score. We assumed she was still in first. We had not kept track of Svetlana Boginskaya of the Unified Team or Livinia Milosovici of Romania who were both ahead of Shannon going into the final rotation. They were both outstanding gymnasts, so we assumed they had also held on to their positions.

When the meet was over the girls lined up to march out. As they neared the exit one of the Olympic authorities stepped forward and pulled Tatiana, Livinia, and Shannon out of the line. The scoreboard in the arena had not displayed the final standings, but when I saw the official pull her out along with the other two girls I realized she had probably won a medal. My heart started doing flip-flops. I turned to Ron. Had he seen? Yes, and he was thinking the same thing. The next minutes seemed like an eternity as we anxiously awaited the awards ceremony. It seemed too good to be true that our daughter might bring home an individual Olympic medal. We assumed it would be bronze.

Finally the three medalists marched out, Shannon among them. When the girls climbed up on the awards stand and the scoreboard flashed the results, we were astounded. Shannon had won the silver. We wouldn't need an airplane to fly home. Two Olympic medals. Not so long ago we had just hoped fervently she would make the team.

Shannon had received little media attention in the shadow of the Karolyi competitors before the Olympics. Kim had been on the cover of *Time* magazine the week before competition began. After Shannon finished first in the world in team competition, reports had focused on Kim's rebound to make the all-around finals. Bela Karolyi had also captured a share of the spotlight by declaring to the world via NBC television that he quit. "I can't cope with it," he said. "I can't go anywhere without being criticized." Some newspaper reports wondered whether he was "merely posturing, begging to be recognized, needing to be needed." And perhaps he was needed as his resignation from the sport was short-lived. However, if he was seeking attention, he certainly got it.

But tonight belonged to Shannon, and everyone had to take notice. Although some commentators seemed to suggest that Shannon had "lost" the gold, none of their remarks could wipe the smile off her face. She had earned two Olympic medals. She was happy, and her coaches were exuberant.

With four event finals to go, Ron and I were beginning to wonder whether we would hold up. We had never experienced so much excitement in such a short time. Tessa and Troy were telling everybody around them that Shannon was their sister. Those bus trips back to Salou were becoming more fun all the time.

There was another day of "rest" and then competition for all four apparatus finals on the same night. We learned later that early in Olympic competition Shannon's ankle had become quite sore from a small stress fracture. She didn't tell us that until we were all back home in Oklahoma. Shannon was not about to let a little pain get in her way at this stage of the game.

We were among the first spectators to arrive for event finals. I had brought a book from church and planned to do a little last-minute mental preparation. These meets were tough on parents. All we could do was watch, hope, and pray.

As the gymnasts warmed up Peggy spotted us and came over to talk for a few minutes. She told us Shannon would be second on vault, fourth on bars, second on beam, and first on floor. She was disappointed that Shannon was up so early in three events, lessening her chances for top scores. Ron and I started to get frustrated. Shannon had worked so hard, come so far, and done so well that it didn't seem fair. But we soon decided we'd do Shannon more good by not worrying but just expressing gratitude that she was able to compete in all four event finals.

We were a little amused that Shannon was in vault finals. She had struggled mightily with this event since injuring her elbow and hadn't even been able to work a second vault. She had begun learning a front somersault with a half twist just before the injury but was far from mastering it at the time of the accident. Now, she hadn't worked even a front somersault in four months. We wondered what Steve would do.

Shannon did her faithful Yurchenko full twist first but took a small hop on the landing. She still earned a good score. Now came the interesting part. Each vault is identified by a number, and when Shannon's number was flashed, as a judge, I immediately knew she would do the front somersault. This was not a big surprise. The surprise would be if she hit it.

She blasted down the runway and did a powerful vault, the best I had ever seen her do. Actually she had too much power, lost a little control on the landing, and took a big step. We were so happy that she had stood up both vaults that we couldn't be disappointed. When all the vaulters had finished we cheered wildly at Shannon's sixth-place finish. Sixth in the world on vault after an injury sounded fine to us.

We had higher hopes for uneven bars, which came next. Shannon had four release moves (taking both hands off the bars) and a difficult dismount. Her execution was usually perfect. She lived up to our hopes, but a Chinese gymnast, who had a fantastically original and difficult routine, also performed extraordinarily well. We couldn't complain about her great score. Tatiana also hit a very good routine and scored slightly higher than Shannon, although, as a mother and a judge, I questioned her score. However, we didn't care for very long because our little girl had just won her third Olympic medal and we were entirely too busy screaming our heads off.

Next came beam. Peggy took over as Shannon's coach.

She was very confident in Shannon's abilities, and we agreed with her that this could be Shannon's best event. The first girl up, Lu Li of China, executed an almost flawless routine. This was going to be really tough. Shannon performed an outstanding routine with a little more difficulty than the first gymnast but with one balance check (a pause to make sure her center of gravity was over the beam) and a slight wiggle on the landing. She earned the same score as the first gymnast. It was a good score, but with six gymnasts left to perform, we thought it would probably not hold up. To our surprise, after five more gymnasts Shannon and Lu Li still had the lead. With one to go, we knew Shannon would get at least a silver medal—maybe gold.

We barely moved as Tatiana Lysenko of the Unified Team mounted the beam. She had a spectacular routine packed with difficulty. She did it well and earned the score she deserved. The gold was hers. Shannon had another silver medal, her fourth medal of these Games. We thought we must be dreaming.

Shannon was first on floor, so we thought we would get relief from our anxiety early. Floor had never been Shannon's strongest event. Bars and beam were where we had placed our greatest hopes, and she had already come through on these two events. Now we just wanted her to successfully complete her floor routine and round out her joyous memories of these wonderful Games.

After performing a beautiful routine Shannon was obviously relieved and elated. She had competed in sixteen routines in this Olympics. Only Livinia Milosovici of Romania had competed in as many, and only Shannon had survived with no falls or major wobbles.

One by one the other gymnasts finished their routines. Shannon's score continued to stand in medal contention. We laughed to each other—what if she got a medal in floor after going first? She held on to bronze.

Shannon had set another record: the most gymnastics

medals ever won by an American in a nonboycotted Olympics. When the 1992 Olympic Games were over we learned she had won more medals than any other American there.

After the Games reporters insisted on asking Shannon whether she would trade her five medals for a single gold. The answer was an emphatic "No." She was proud of each one, regardless of the color.

The *Daily Oklahoman* called her "Miss Consistency" and pointed out that she was the true top performer of the 1992 Olympics. In sixteen events, with a high score of 9.975 and a low score of 9.837, she had averaged 9.916. In three-fourths of her events she had topped 9.9.

We had been ecstatic after the team competition knowing our daughter would be taking home an Olympic medal. I can't describe how we felt about five. Tessa and Troy could hardly comprehend what had happened, but they knew the crowd loved Shannon. Some sailors in the audience were holding an American flag and screaming her name. We began to understand that Shannon might be a bit of a celebrity.

As was now my habit I headed to the railing in the hope of seeing Shannon. This time Steve and Peggy were ready for me. They brought Shannon over and lifted her up, and we gave her a hug. We arranged to come to the Olympic Village and take her for some sightseeing the next day. Except for daily drives to work out, she had not seen any of Barcelona and she was ready.

We hardly noticed the trek down Montjuic and the bus ride back to Salou. That night Ron and I had no desire to sleep; we preferred to review the events of the last two weeks. Five medals! That was astounding, but not so remarkable as the manner in which Shannon had acquired them. In a full field of amazing athletes, she had had no hometown advantage or political clout. Our daughter was a terrific gymnast, a great competitor, and a determined individual. We had known all this for some time, but even as prejudiced parents we had never dreamed winning so many medals was possible on European soil with the weight of her country seeming to rest on her tiny shoulders. We were especially proud of the way she had conducted herself: focused and gracious, and yes, happy. Even the media hadn't seemed to notice. Shannon had displayed a maturity of which most of us only dream. Proud just wasn't a powerful enough word for how we felt.

With the women's gymnastics competition behind us, we were relaxed and content, but mostly excited to see Shannon. Except for those few brief moments the night before, we had not seen her in a month. Tessa and Troy wanted to see their sister but, to be honest, they were much more excited about seeing the other celebrated athletes.

We arrived relatively early in the morning, eager for a tour of the athletes' village and then sightseeing and shopping. Things wouldn't be so simple. We carefully explained that we were Shannon's parents and that we had come to take her out for a while. We had assumed they would get her, she would show us around, and off we'd go. Not so. We couldn't even get anyone to let her know we were there. She had no telephone in her room. Time was slipping by, and all of us were scheduled to leave for home the next morning.

After two hours of trying every tactic we could think of, I remembered that a Spanish gentleman sitting behind us during the all-around competition had told me he worked in the village. He had given me his name and told me to get in touch if we needed anything. I dug through my purse, found his name, and finally communicated that I wanted to talk to him. This seemed to impress a few of the workers and after a little while he showed up. He located Shannon, Steve, and Peggy and gave us rare visitors' passes.

We started with Shannon's room, which she shared with her teammate Dominique Dawes. The room was so small that the girls had to walk over their luggage to get to their beds. There was no air-conditioning, but they had a large window that opened toward the sea and allowed a nice breeze. We

17. Shannon with Carl Lewis in the Olympic Village in 1992.

then walked around the rest of the village and ended up at an athletes' gift shop where Shannon, Tessa, and Troy talked us into some purchases. As we left to show Shannon Barcelona, she was stopped several times by other athletes who wanted her autograph. We still found this amusing.

We had one last stop before we headed to La Rambla for shopping. Just outside the village people had pins displayed for trade. Shannon, who had been collecting pins since her Moscow trip in 1986, had had to walk by them every day without stopping. Now she wanted to trade. Tessa had also been collecting pins, so the two sat down on the sidewalk to do some tough negotiating. They both came away pleased.

We took the subway to La Rambla and strolled the entire length of it, not missing a shop. Lots of people back home would love a souvenir. Knowing little Spanish, we were unaware of the publicity Shannon had been getting, so we were surprised at how many people recognized her. At last we came to McDonald's, and all three kids begged for *real* American food. We all indulged.

During our time with Shannon she told us a story about the Dream Team, the professional basketball stars who were competing in the Olympics for the first time. They did not stay in the village but visited once. The other gymnasts found out and met many of the players, toured their bus, and traded gymnastics paraphernalia for basketball souvenirs. Shannon, who was taking her regular afternoon nap when they came, learned about the visit only after it was over, when the other gymnasts got back, each with a Dream Team pin, hat, or shirt. She was crushed.

Steve went into action. He made some inquiries and eventually spoke with John Tesh, who was working for NBC as an Olympic commentator, to ask whether there was any way for Shannon to meet some players. John responded with tickets to the game against Spain and an invitation for Shannon, Steve, and Peggy to come to the locker room afterward. Shannon sat raptly through the game but could hardly believe she was going to meet some of the players.

18. Shannon meeting Larry Bird and other members of the "Dream Team" in Barcelona, 1992.

Peggy had a videocamera and was determined to film the occasion so that Shannon would have a record of her momentous visit, but she was firmly informed that no cameras were allowed in the locker room. Realizing this was a once-in-a-lifetime event for Shannon, Peggy sneaked the camera in under her jacket and pulled it out at every opportunity. We still have that terrific film.

Shannon was able to meet most of the players, including her favorites, Magic Johnson, Michael Jordan, Larry Bird, and Charles Barkley. Magic hugged her and told her he had been to see the all-around competition and loved it.

Shannon had only one small regret. She had not been able to trade for any Dream Team attire. She heard through the village grapevine that a basketball trainer had some Dream Team apparel he would be willing to trade for some gymnastic apparel. She went in search of him early the evening after our sightseeing trip but couldn't find him. She was leaving the next day and was going to a farewell party that night, so her only chance to see him would be early the next morning.

She arose early, packed some gymnastic apparel to trade, and set out for where she had heard the trainer would be but was told he was unavailable. She waited as long as she could but soon had to leave for the airport. Somewhat dejected, she headed off, retrieved her bags, and went out with the other girls to wait for the bus. While she waited the trainer came running up. Someone had told him she had been looking for him. He brought his Dream Team items and was prepared to trade with her. In exchange for a workout leotard and a long-sleeve leotard, he offered her quite a haul—five Dream Team items, including a great shirt for her dad.

While Shannon was looking for the trainer after we dropped her off, we went to dinner and then the farewell party. Because we were all tired and thirsty and had so many bags from our shopping trip (especially from Shannon, who had to do all her souvenir buying in one day), we decided to splurge and take a taxi. As the taxi cruised by Montjuic on the way to the hotel for the party, we all breathed a sigh of relief that we did not have to hike up it any more.

In the hotel we immediately met some of the other parents and champion gymnasts. Nadia Comaneci and Bart Conner, who are now married, were also there. Nadia and Shannon shared the honor of cutting the big cake baked in the gymnasts' honor. During the party a huge cheer went up, and we learned that Trent Dimas of the American men's gymnastic team had won a gold medal on high bar. What a night to celebrate!

It was getting late and we had to get up very early the next morning to go to the airport, so we trooped off to the Bull Ring one last time to catch our bus to Salou. The last two weeks had been a tremendous emotional high, but we were ready to get back home to Oklahoma, to our family, friends, and jobs. School would be starting soon, and Tessa and Troy were already thinking about school supplies and seeing their friends again. We thought life would get back to normal.

CHAPTER NINE

Oklahoma—OK and More

AFTER ONLY A few hours sleep, we arose at 3:00 A.M. to get our luggage to the bus for the ride to the airport. The flight was pleasant but seemed much longer than our trip to Barcelona. Our flight out of New York City departed late, and by the time we arrived in Dallas our plane to Oklahoma City had left. Ron called our neighbors Debbie and John Donner, who were picking us up, to let them know we'd be arriving in Oklahoma City about midnight instead of 10:00 P.M. as planned. Debbie puzzled Ron by chattering about having to contact television stations, but he was so tired he didn't ask any questions.

On the plane he wondered aloud whether a television camera would be at the airport. Since Shannon was not with us, we shrugged off the possibility and fell asleep. When the plane landed we stretched out of our seats, happy to be home and eager for our own beds. As we exited the plane we suddenly realized what Debbie had been talking about. We faced cameras from almost all the local news outlets.

With my hair a mess, mascara smeared down my cheeks, sleep still in my eyes, and my clothes terribly wrinkled, I tried to smile. We couldn't believe so many photographers and reporters had come out at midnight. And that wasn't all. There were dozens of our friends and neighbors. My whole staff from work came in their pajamas and slippers (they claim they wanted me to recognize their sleep sacrifice). One message we got loud and clear: Oklahomans were very proud of the Millers (well, mostly Shannon). Sleep didn't seem very important.

The gathering at the airport was only a foreshadowing of things to come. Everyone was talking at once trying to tell us about all the coverage Shannon had been receiving and about all the activities being planned. We couldn't absorb everything. On the drive home from the airport John and Debbie explained things a little more slowly. Before Shannon arrived at the small Wiley Post Airport the next day, a limousine would pick us up and take us to a reception at the airport. Ron's head and mine were spinning. Tessa and Troy were asleep again. Debbie continued to give us an itinerary.

Shannon was being flown in on a private jet from Washington, D.C., where U.S. senators and representatives, led by Oklahoma senators Don Nickles and David Boren, had held a reception for her. Shannon would land at about 11:00 A.M. We would go home for a while and then, about 4:00 P.M., another limousine would pick us all up to take us to the parade to be held in downtown Edmond at 5:00 P.M.

Neighbors were scheduled to bring us meals for the rest of the week, since they assumed we would be too busy to cook. I couldn't comprehend it all. My vacation was over. I was scheduled to be back at work at the bank the next morning. I hoped my boss would understand. It turned out that my boss and most of the bank officers were part of the plot. The reception at the airport was delightful, and it was thrilling to hear people from Oklahoma City and Edmond give their version of what had been occurring.

We had not called home from Barcelona because we left

the hotel early in the morning and returned long after midnight. We hadn't had access to any American newspapers, except a rare *USA Today,* and we had been having so much fun we hadn't thought to seek them out. There were so many outstanding athletes in the 1992 Olympics that we didn't expect anyone to take special notice of Shannon. She had not been the object of great media attention before. We had no reason to think anything had changed.

Even as we looked around the room at the airport reception and were so proud to see so many people who cared, we still wondered what they were expecting to happen when Shannon arrived. Everyone kept talking about the big crowds. This was a workday. What big crowds were going to come all the way out to this little airport to see Shannon? We saw that we had underestimated our friends back home, the people who so generously sent us to Barcelona. They had a vested interest in the Millers in more ways than one. Oklahoma had been following Shannon's career closely since the 1989 Sports Festival and avidly since 1991 World Championships. Oklahoma was ready for another hero, and just might have found one in Shannon.

When Shannon's plane landed and she stepped out, reporters and cameras emerged from everywhere. We could not get close to her. She finally came inside and we got to hug her for an instant before she was whisked away for interviews. When she rejoined us we were told a crowd was waiting to see her outside. We wondered what the definition of a crowd was.

Shannon, Steve, and Peggy led the way outside to a platform, and Ron, Tessa, Troy, and I followed. We all stopped dead in our tracks. None of us was prepared for the five thousand people waiting patiently to hear a few words from Shannon. Some brought flowers. Many carried signs with 10s to tell her she was perfect in their sight, or "pure gold" even though she didn't get a gold medal. Some had drawn gold medals on posters because they thought she deserved gold in the all-around. For months afterward we got gold medals in the mail made out of every conceivable substance.

Shannon was overwhelmed. She greeted everyone, thanked them for coming, and let them know how happy she was to be home. She was so small that Steve picked her up to give everyone a better look. She let him get away with it but later confessed she had been terribly embarrassed. After all, she was fifteen.

Soon after she spoke to the gathering, Shannon was whisked away again for more interviews and to meet other dignitaries. Ron went with her in case she needed anything while I collected Tessa and Troy, who were still spellbound by the size of the crowd. While they lingered briefly on the stage, swarms of kids came rushing up to ask for their autographs. Tessa, always the bold one, began to sign. Troy figured if she could, so could he.

At long last we climbed into the limousine with Shannon for the drive back home. The Olympics had been an unbelievable experience for her, a real dream come true, but she was ready for home. That's when we explained about the parade. She started giggling and asked, "How can they have a parade just for me?" The more she thought about it, the funnier it got until we were all laughing hysterically. No one had told us any details, and we hadn't had a minute to think what questions we should be asking. The tape had long ago run out on our answering machine and the telephone continued to ring. We knew Peggy and Steve and all of us were supposed to be in the parade too, but we figured that would last about five minutes. Ron pointed out it was a workday and they would be closing the Broadway Extension, the main artery from Oklahoma City to Edmond right at going-home-from-work time. The commuters would not be happy.

More people than we thought possible had already been to the airport. It seemed to us that everybody had seen her already. We couldn't imagine that anyone but our closest friends would leave work early and stand in the hot sun to see us drive by. What had been funny became worrisome. A lot of people had gone to real trouble to arrange this parade. We hoped they would not be disappointed if nobody came to watch it.

Once again we were shocked. People lined the street for about two and a half miles. They carried all kinds of signs, from those reading "10" to those bearing pictures of gold medals. The media estimated a turnout of about fifteen thousand spectators. We didn't even hear of anyone complaining about the Broadway Extension being closed. Shannon rode in a car by herself, followed by a car with Steve and Peggy and then the rest of us in another car. Tessa thoroughly enjoyed the parade. She figured she could get used to smiling and waving, and if anyone wanted her to, she'd sign autographs again too. Troy, however, was a little embarrassed by the whole affair.

Ron and I wore the special shirts we had worn to the all-around competition which had been given to us by former Governor George Nigh, president of the University of Central Oklahoma where Ron taught. We had admired the wonderful red, white, and blue shirts he and his wife wore in a Fourth of July parade. A week later we received identical shirts in the mail to wear as we watched Shannon compete in the Olympics. Ron bought a hat to wear with his shirt in Barcelona—white because, he said, we were the good guys, a cowboy hat because we were from Oklahoma, and big so Shannon could spot us.

Ron thought the shirts would be perfect for the parade, but we had a problem: Barcelona had been hot, and we had worn them during the long day of all-around competition. No one would want to be near us.

"Give me those shirts," said our close friend Mike Graham. "I'll get them cleaned."

With the parade a few hours away, we didn't see how he

could. But Mike and a local dry cleaner came through, and we rode in style in our red, white, and blue shirts.

Ron and I were still chuckling inside as we watched three helicopters, one from each network affiliate station, follow the parade from beginning to end. The band from Shannon's high school marched and played. The cheerleaders performed, chanting Shannon's name, and local gymnasts cartwheeled down the street. We later learned that scenes from the parade had been broadcast across the country.

The best was yet to come. At the end of the parade route we mounted a platform to meet numerous local dignitaries who presented Shannon with gifts and honors. By far the most exciting gift was a bright red 1992 Saturn. A representative of the car dealership who called our house to ask our permission to offer Shannon the car had said it would be hers for a year. Of course, during most of that time she wouldn't be old enough to drive, but her dad would be more than happy

19. Shannon with her medals and the Saturn presented to her by Bob Moore after the 1992 Olympics. © Garrison's Photography, 1994.

to drive her to the gym in it. We accepted the proposal, feeling sure Shannon would be delighted.

When the Saturn dealer made the presentation after the parade he did not make it clear that the car was not hers to keep. On our way home we made sure Shannon understood the arrangements. She was happy with the situation.

In interviews soon after the parade questions kept coming up about how Shannon felt about getting a car she would not be able to drive right away. Reporters began to realize that the car was only on loan, and they were not happy. They thought the dealership representative had implied that Shannon was getting the car permanently. Within a few days the local newspapers and TV stations were astir with the story, and the public was up in arms. It seems everyone wanted Shannon to keep the car.

Soon Bob Moore, the owner of the Saturn dealership, called us and said he had reviewed the tapes of the parade and realized it had sounded as if they were giving the car to Shannon. Now that's what they wanted to do. Ron could hardly believe it and suggested that Bob give Shannon the terrific news himself. Shannon asked him whether the person who made the presentation at the parade was in trouble and said she wouldn't accept the car if it cost anyone his job. He assured her that no one was in trouble. Shannon happily thanked him for her new car, then excitedly ran downstairs to tell us about her conversation.

While the car was probably the most exciting homecoming gift, another one made a pretty big impression. The city of Edmond erected a sign at the main entrance to Edmond stating, "Home of Shannon Miller, winner of 5 medals, 1992 Olympics." She was given a replica during the parade ceremonies. Now every time Shannon rode into Edmond in her new car she was reminded of how proud of her her hometown was.

Shannon determined that she would make every effort to give back to her community some of the love and generosity

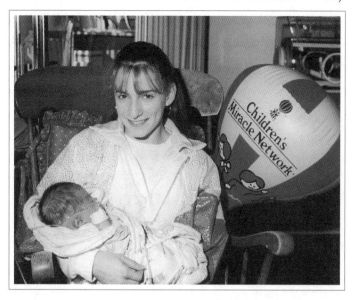

20. *Shannon holds a baby at Children's Hospital in Oklahoma City, one of her favorite charities. Photo courtesy Jake Lowrey for Children's Miracle Network.*

the citizens of Oklahoma had given her and her family. She lends her time and name to as many charitable organizations as possible in Oklahoma and elsewhere.

Soon after the parade she was asked to be the Oklahoma Miracle Balloon Chairman for the Children's Miracle Network Telethon to support a network of children's hospitals. She gladly accepted, and continues to serve in this capacity. She was also asked, in the fall of 1992, to be a spokesperson for the Red Ribbon Campaign (Drug Free Youth), and she still serves in this role. She has supported the American Lung Association, March of Dimes, Feed the Children, Make-A-Wish Foundation, Pediatric AIDS, Henrietta Egleston Hospital for Children in Atlanta, Stay In School (a U.S. Army poster), Kid Care, Muscular Dystrophy Telethon, numerous local school activities (especially reading programs), Kids We Care (an organization that grew out of the Oklahoma City bombing), and many other local and national charitable groups. She occasionally gives talks to civic groups and donates autographed posters and clothing to an average of three or four organizations a week to help with their fund-raising.

Shannon has learned that being a celebrity has its privileges, but it also obligates you to share yourself with your community. When you do share, the feeling is just as good as winning Olympic medals.

After the post-Olympic festivities our family had chores to catch up on and jobs to resume. There were clothes to wash—including Shannon's twenty-seven pairs of white socks from the trip. In a minor miracle, Ron delightedly reported after taking them out of the dryer that every one had a mate.

Our efforts to get back to some semblance of household routine were continually interrupted by the telephone. While trying to cook and do laundry we were taking calls from Shannon's fans from all over the United States and even from other countries. For a while all the attention was fun, but we finally had to set some rules. There was no way Shannon could talk to everyone, so we developed a set of questions to

21. Shannon acts as spokesperson for the Oklahoma Red Ribbon Celebration for Drug Free Youth, 1994. Photo by John Trammell Photography.

22. *Shannon with Olga Korbut at a fall 1991 fund-raiser for victims of Chernobyl.*

determine whether callers were people who actually knew Shannon or gymnastics junkies. At first it was hard to tell adoring children and smitten young men that she would not be able to talk with them. But as the telephone continued to ring, it got easier.

Shannon was frequently asked for autographs and began to get hundreds of fan letters each week, including marriage proposals and heart-wrenching letters from children who were sick, impoverished, or in terrible family situations. Shannon still considers this attention a "perk," and says she is more worried about the time people no longer want to meet her or write to her.

Steve had suggested as soon as Shannon made the Olympic team that we get an agent for her. After 1991 Worlds we had calls from several people who wanted to represent Shannon, but we declined to hire an agent because we did not want to introduce the money element into her life. Shannon said she was not out to make a fortune or become a celebrity, she just wanted to be part of the 1992 Olympic team.

Before he left for Barcelona Steve had asked Ron and me to come to the gym and talk to two agents he had invited from

ProServ, an agency that represents athletes. One was Jerry Solomon, who represented the figure skater Nancy Kerrigan. Steve strongly believed we should have someone looking after Shannon's business and public interests. We were impressed with the men but were still not sure Shannon needed an agent. Maybe if she did wonderfully at the Olympics, we said, then we would consider her signing with an agency. Ironically, about the time Steve finally gave up on us, we decided he was right. Maybe we should have someone working for her. The day before Shannon and Steve were to leave for Florida, we agreed to hire ProServ and quickly got the documents signed. If she didn't do anything at the Olympics, they agreed we would just quietly end the relationship.

ProServ had many clients in the Olympics. We saw Jerry in Barcelona soon after Shannon won the silver in the all-around but before she won any medals in the apparatus finals. He warned us then that life would probably change dramatically for her. At the time we had no idea how much. That was the only interaction we had with anyone from ProServ until a few days after we arrived home.

Right away we learned that Steve had been negotiating with ProServ and with an organization called Bill Graham Presents to stage a gymnastic tour early in the fall of 1992. Shannon would get top billing and would be joined by other U.S. team members as well as Tatiana Gutsu, Svetlana Boginskaya, and members of the men's Olympic gymnastic team.

In the month before the tour Shannon was busy almost daily with appearances, from the "Regis and Kathi Lee" show to shooting a commercial for "Trivial Pursuit" to doing exhibitions and autograph signings at malls and auto shows. She was also trying to work out at the gym five hours a day, although her ankle was still very sore.

She also had to prepare for a tour being conducted by USA Gymnastics. We had not originally wanted to make tour commitments because we were not sure how she would feel after the Olympics. She was ready to do all the tours now. They offered a chance to perform, which she really enjoyed, but with no judges.

With endorsements and payments from appearances and the tour, Shannon began to make some real money. We had always paid her expenses and would continue to do so. We put her money in savings and investments until she was old enough to assume responsibility for her own business dealings. When she wanted something special, we would talk about it and point out the pros and cons. We wanted to counsel her wisely, but she always made the final decision. Probably her biggest purchase was an aboveground pool she really wanted for the backyard. Ron told her that he would build the deck around the pool if she would buy the wood. She accepted his offer.

Shannon's celebrity, her money, and especially her car raised Tessa's hackles a bit. She had spent long hours baby-sitting, working summers at my bank, and doing telemarketing to raise enough money to buy a used car. Shannon was just *given* one—a *new* one. Tessa had helped Shannon whenever she could, had worked hard to make straight A's in school, and had worked at a variety of jobs, but everyone oohed and ahed over Shannon and gave her gifts. Troy was still young and not as competitive as Tessa, so he wasn't too bothered by Shannon's new status, other than getting a little tired of being referred to as "Shannon's brother" at school.

It took a good long talk with Tessa to help her understand that Shannon had worked just as hard as she had for all the "gifts" she appeared to be getting. Tessa had conveniently forgotten all the long hours spent in the gym, the pressure of the numerous competitions, and the physical injuries and pain Shannon had endured for so many years while Tessa had time in the evening and on weekends to enjoy activities with her friends. Fortunately, Tessa has a very logical mind, and when her emotions settled down she coped well with the situation. Shannon also helped by including Tessa in some of her more exciting activities, from enjoying box seats at various athletic events to meeting celebrities at a number of affairs to which she was invited. Tessa would also be grateful that Shannon was making some money, since on several occasions Shannon was able to purchase some relatively expensive items that Tessa needed but could not afford, such as a laptop computer. While Troy much preferred to remain in the background, Shannon made sure he was not forgotten. Troy would never ask for help, but Shannon knew when he had an important need, such as a good microphone for his band. She was there to help.

CHAPTER TEN

Sweet Sixteen

HANNON WAS ENTERING her sophomore year of high school, determined to graduate with her class. When Steve tried to talk her into staying out of school the year before the Olympics, she steadfastly refused and took a full load in the fall of 1991. In the spring, because of longer, harder training, she took only four classes. Now she had a more difficult problem. She would be out of town for stretches of time. Tour organizers agreed to hire a tutor to make sure she stayed on track. Shannon would be required to do all the classwork and take all the tests, but school officials agreed to let the tutor administer them under specified guidelines.

We had to find a tutor who could travel for two and a half months with Shannon. Almost the first person we interviewed seemed to fit the bill perfectly. She was good in mathematics and could help Shannon with algebra. She knew Spanish, the language Shannon was taking, was not married, and had no job that would keep her in Edmond. She had a teaching degree and was willing to travel. And her mother was Shannon's algebra teacher. Shannon was on the quiet side; Terri Thomas was not. The two got along well immediately.

The tour exposed Shannon to a new side of gymnastics.

23. Shannon and her tutor, Terri Thomas, take time to enjoy the beach at Miami during the tour after the 1992 Olympics.

It also brought out a new side of Shannon's personality. Although she was able to perform confidently in front of spectators and judges, she was naturally reserved and did not like to call attention to herself off the gymnastics floor. She did not want to say anything that would be embarrassing, offensive, or hurtful to anyone. She tended to take her time responding to interview questions and to give brief answers. Because Steve enjoyed media attention, she often deferred to him. On the tour Shannon was required to do promotional interviews. Before long, she found it easy to chat with reporters.

Already good at time management, on tour Shannon became even more adept at squeezing schoolwork in whenever she had a few minutes. She had always worked in the car to and from the gym, on airplanes, and in hotel rooms. Now she and Terri did algebra problems between performances and took tests on buses and planes.

Months on a tour, although entertaining, can be trying.

24. *Nadia Comaneci, Tatiana Gutsu, Shannon, and Bart Conner on tour, 1992.*

The stress is different from that during competition. Steve and Shannon now had slightly different roles and had to discover what their relationship would be as they moved forward. Steve, always a dictatorial coach, still felt that he should make all the decisions. Shannon was more mature and self-confident and was ready to make more decisions for herself. At this time she was not sure what she wanted her future to be after the tour ended. She could rest on her laurels, leave gymnastics, and lead the life of a typical high school student, or she could jump back into competition with its long, hard workouts, time-consuming meet preparation and travel, and pressure. Toward the end of the tour Steve began to assert himself. He thought Shannon still had not peaked in her gymnastics career, and he was afraid of losing her.

Shannon was scheduled to catch a 6:00 A.M. flight back to Oklahoma City the morning after the last tour stop in Phoenix, Arizona. She needed to get into the city by 11:00 A.M. to make an appearance with the Olympic gold medal wrestler John Smith for the American Lung Association. Steve had originally agreed to fly back with her. Now he told her he wanted to be her manager as well as her coach, and he thought she needed to skip this event.

Terri was in the room helping Shannon with her homework when Steve made his announcement. Shannon was upset. She had promised to make the appearance and told Steve she couldn't go back on her word and drop out with little notice. He issued an ultimatum: if she flew back to Oklahoma City without his permission, she would have to find another coach. If he couldn't be her manager, he wouldn't be her coach.

After he left Shannon began to cry. She hadn't decided whether to continue competitive gymnastics, but she had planned to keep training until she made a decision. If she continued in gymnastics, she wanted Steve to be her coach. But she had made a commitment and could not break it at the last minute.

Terri realized how distressed Shannon was and called us to report what had happened. By the time Shannon came to the telephone, she had made her decision. She dried her tears and told me she would be on the plane if she could get a ride to the airport. Terri agreed to take Steve's ticket and fly back with her. We were even more distressed than Shannon. I'm not sure which was worse, the anger or the hurt that Steve would put our daughter in such a position unnecessarily.

Ron called Peggy, told her what happened, and invited her to the luncheon in Steve's place. We thought Shannon would be comforted to see Peggy there. Peggy came and assured Shannon that Steve was just feeling pressured and all would be fine. She encouraged Shannon to come to the gym to work out that evening.

Steve let Shannon work out, but he was clearly hurt. He had not expected Shannon to leave without him. For days he ignored Shannon. Peggy put up with this for a while and coached her on all four events until she had had enough. We tried to call Steve, but he wasn't in the mood to talk to us. In addition to his problems with Shannon, Steve was not happy with Ron and me at this time. Money had become an issue.

We had originally decided against getting an agent for Shannon, until Steve persuaded us otherwise, because we did not want to put an emphasis on money. Shannon's primary focus was to make the 1992 Olympic team. However, the year before the 1992 Olympics Shannon had a few chances for earnings, from winning prize money at meets to appearing in advertisements. Since money had not been a subject that had come up previously, neither we nor Steve were fully prepared to handle this development.

When Shannon won money at the 1991 DTB Cup, Steve asked for a share since he felt the money was the result of a team effort. We agreed. The disagreement came over percentages. He felt that as 50 percent of the team, he should receive 50 percent of the winnings. We were naive, but 50 percent seemed to us to be too much. We made a few telephone calls to knowledgeable people and were told he should receive nothing or, at most, if we considered him her "agent," perhaps 10 to 15 percent. We thought it over and finally decided to compromise at 30 percent. Steve had taken Shannon a long way and devoted a lot of time and energy to her career so at the time this figure seemed fair.

Now she had five Olympic medals, still the result of a tremendous team effort. But she also had an agent to whom a percentage of her earnings went. ProServ had expertise in public relations, finance, legal matters, and, of course, the necessary contacts. At the time, Steve did not.

Steve was still the beneficiary of Shannon's success. He had become better known as a result of Shannon's medals, but we certainly didn't expect him to share any of his income with Shannon. His gym was booming, and most of the time, since Shannon needed him when she toured or performed exhibitions, he was paid for accompanying and coaching her. Of course, he was also asked to speak at various events. We felt it best that Steve remain the coach and that an objective third party handle Shannon's appearance fees.

Aside from the money issue, Steve still felt the need to have more control over Shannon's career both inside and outside the gym. After all, he was used to calling all the shots.

Since Shannon had returned from the tour, things were going nowhere. We finally wrote Steve a letter asking for a meeting. Peggy insisted that he take the time to speak with Shannon and us. She knew he cared about Shannon and still wanted to be her coach, but egos were getting in the way. Steve realized Peggy was right. We needed to sit down together and clear the air. We assured Steve that while we did not feel he should be both Shannon's coach and her manager, we would make it clear to ProServ that he should be consulted before scheduling appearances so that no conflicts developed. As for money, Shannon was willing to assist in getting sponsors for the gym and would see that Steve was paid if he had to go with her to an appearance. Steve had a lot of gym

25. *Shannon and Steve, 1992. Photograph by Doug Hoke. © September 23, 1992, The Oklahoma Publishing Company.*

expenses that Shannon did not, but she also did not receive any income from the gym. Steve had been an integral part of Shannon's success and we certainly wanted him to have this recognition, but as her coach, not as her manager.

We had a good discussion. Steve had been hurt by Shannon's actions, and Shannon had been dismayed by Steve's. They were still a good team and wanted that relationship to continue. We had our differences with Steve, but in the end he was usually reasonable. We hoped we were too. Life was getting back to normal—sort of.

On Veteran's Day Shannon was in the living room doing homework with Terri Thomas. Troy and I were in the back room cleaning and organizing when we noticed a strange squealing noise. Troy asked me to go outside and check it out. It was very cold outdoors and pouring down rain, so I put on a jacket and headed out to the backyard. Sprawled against the back of the house was an animal covered in mud. My first thought was that our dog Ebony, a female Labrador retriever, had maimed something that invaded her territory. I dreaded looking but knew I needed to see what had happened. To my surprise, as I got closer, I realized it was a puppy, newborn but large. I quickly picked it up, ran inside, and dashed to the bathroom to wash the puppy and wrap him in a soft towel. Shannon ran next door to borrow an eye dropper, warmed some milk, and took the puppy.

Now Troy and I went outside to find Ebony. She was not spayed, but she had never left the fenced yard and had not looked pregnant. Was this her baby? We walked around the backyard and could not find her, so we drove around the neighborhood calling her. By the time we gave up and came home, the puppy was contentedly full and fast asleep in Shannon's lap. Troy went back out to the backyard to look once more and returned quickly. He had found Ebony in her doghouse, the one place we had failed to look. Ebony always came quickly when we called her, so we had assumed that when she didn't come, she had dug under the fence. She had a reason for not coming this time. She had two more puppies in the doghouse with her.

By the time Ron came home Shannon had claimed the abandoned puppy as hers. Ebony had graciously accepted the puppy into the fold with the others but not before Shannon declared that she and the puppy had bonded. Ron tried unsuccessfully over the next six weeks to convince her it would not be wise for her to keep the puppy, but she was determined. She promised to assume all responsibility, even to pay for food and veterinary bills. Troy eagerly agreed to take care of him in her absence. What could Ron say? Once we found homes for the other two puppies, we would only have two cats, two dogs, a couple of turtles, and a horse.

Shannon mulled over the name of her puppy for quite a while. He was golden, with soft wavy hair. Almost the perfect image of a golden retriever. She finally decided on Dusty. He joined his mother, Ebony, Gizmo the cat, and assorted creatures of Troy's as part of the Miller household.

26. *Shannon and her dog, Dusty. Courtesy Keith Ball Photography, Oklahoma City.*

27. Shannon and Bonnie Blair at the Babe Zaharias Awards.

Dusty adores Shannon, and Shannon feels the same. She's done a remarkably good job of training him. He's intelligent, good-natured, and assumes everyone loves him—including photographers. He often shows up in publications with Shannon. Recently they did a commercial together. As for Ron, let's just say Dusty has him securely wrapped around his fuzzy wagging tail.

The year 1992 drew to a close. It had been fantastic. After the Olympics Shannon had garnered some outstanding awards. She was selected as the U.S. Olympic Committee's Female Gymnast of the Year, won the Sudafed Amateur Sports Woman of the Year honor, was the first woman to win the Steve Reeves Fitness Award, earned the Nuprin Comeback Award and the Jim Thorpe Award, was a finalist for the Babe Zaharias Female Amateur Athlete Award, and claimed the March of Dimes Sports Headliner of the Year for Oklahoma. Shannon was not planning to rest on her laurels, however. She had decided to continue to compete at least through the next World Championships. She settled back into school and training. Her hectic schedule eased up considerably, although she still made some public appearances.

One evening Steve excitedly cornered Shannon and me as we were getting ready to leave the gym after Shannon's evening workout. He had some wonderful news: Kerri Strug was moving to Dynamo to train.

I still remembered what had happened with Erica, but I knew it would be nice for Shannon to train and travel with Kerri. Shannon liked Kerri and had gotten to know her pretty well over the last few years. Shannon was stimulated at the thought of a real training partner, someone who had to prepare for and travel to the same competitions she did. But while Shannon knew Steve considered it a real coup to have attracted a gymnast of Kerri's caliber, she wondered how this would affect her. On the one hand, with competition in the gym Steve might work her harder than ever. On the other hand, Shannon was used to being the favored child in the gym and this might change. She may have been a little spoiled in that respect.

Kerri arrived in late December, so she and Shannon didn't begin training together until after our family vacation. Shannon was rested from Christmas break and challenged by Kerri's presence, eager to work out. Steve had recently started teaching Shannon a double twisting Yurchenko vault. Shannon wanted to learn the vault but had not attacked it vigorously. Now Kerri was also learning the skill, and Shannon was determined to perfect it first.

As I watched Shannon grow more aggressive in workouts, I began to think Kerri's arrival might be just the stimulus Shannon needed. They competed hard against each other every day in the gym, but they were also friends and sympathized with each other. Things were working out better than I could have imagined.

The annual Dynamo Classic was planned for late January. Steve entered both Shannon and Kerri. Shannon would have the hometown crowd cheering her on, which would

28. Troy, Ron, Tessa, Shannon, and Claudia Miller, Christmas 1993. Courtesy David Allen, Oklahoma City.

provide both inspiration and pressure. Kerri had never competed in the Dynamo Classic and would be in Shannon's territory. Both girls trained exceptionally hard for the meet. It seemed more like an international competition than an invitational.

Both Shannon and Kerri performed outstanding routines, but Shannon took a fall off the beam on a new skill. Kerri captured the gold in the all-around; Shannon finished second and was not pleased. As the hometown favorite, she felt humiliated.

Both she and Kerri had been experiencing some back pain beginning a day or two before the Dynamo Classic. We attributed it to the long, hard workouts. Their trainer, Mark Cranston, provided daily therapy. He thought perhaps a new skill or type of conditioning had caused the problem and encouraged Steve to review their workouts. After the meet Steve eased up on the workouts and Kerri's back immediately responded. Shannon's, however, got progressively worse.

Mark wanted Steve to ease up even more on Shannon, but both Shannon and Steve knew this was not possible. The American Cup was at the beginning of March. Twice Shannon had missed qualifying for the finals, and when she had at last qualified she had been suffering from a pulled hamstring and had not performed at what Steve thought was her full potential. This year he planned for her to win this prestigious meet. Kerri was equally capable of winning the meet, but he wanted to demonstrate to the world he had the top two gymnasts. If the girls finished first and second they would both be considered top contenders at the World Championships in April.

Shannon continued to train diligently, and her back continued to get worse. Steve tried to work around the skills that hurt most. Finally, the week before the American Cup, Mark suggested a cortisone shot. Shannon was horrified. She had not had a shot since she was a baby and didn't want one now. Steve and Mark urged her to try it. If she didn't get some relief, Steve feared she might miss Worlds as well as the American Cup. Shannon had the shot. After a few days she felt better. Soon after that she, Kerri, Steve, and Peggy left for Orlando.

Kerri and Shannon battled it out during the preliminaries, with Kerri emerging in first place and Shannon in second after a fall on the beam. She did not want a repeat of the Dynamo Classic and came back with a vengeance in finals. She performed solidly on all four events and claimed the all-around and every event title.

Shannon was now looking toward Birmingham, England, and World Championships. Steve told her he believed she could win the all-around, and she wanted to prove him right. With her Olympic medals, Shannon was assured a berth on the World Championship team. Kerri, however, had to compete at the American Classic, which doubled as trials for World Championships. Only two team members would be chosen from tough competition.

Steve wanted to take it a little easier on Shannon to allow her back time to heal, but her full-twisting Yurchenko vault from the Olympics had been devalued and was now worth a maximum of 9.8. She needed a new, more difficult vault.

Steve wanted Shannon to try a double twisting Yurchenko—the vault she performed in 1992 with an additional twist—before Worlds, but he didn't want her to have to compete through an entire meet with her back bothering her. He entered her in Trials, but she only competed on bars and vault. She made the double twisting Yurchenko but with a weak landing. Shannon still had a few more weeks to improve if her back cooperated.

Kerri had a great competition and just squeaked by Dominique Dawes, who qualified along with Kerri for the World Championship team. Shannon was happy that Kerri had made the team. She had a friend to travel and to room with, a new experience for her.

On March 10, between the 1993 American Cup and Worlds, Shannon turned sixteen. As was the case for almost as long as Shannon could remember, she was not home for her birthday.

We had given up birthday parties when she started to travel so much. This year would be different. A local jewelry store, B. C. Clark's, had asked permission to give Shannon a Sweet Sixteen party at the place of her choice when she got home. Shannon was thrilled. She chose Celebration Station, a local fun center with a variety of entertainment, including miniature golf. During the party the jewelers presented Shannon with a beautiful diamond pendant on a gold chain. Shannon was temporarily subdued by such a fabulous gift but soon rejoined the fray, working hard to win a giant stuffed pink flamingo. She finally succeeded, and Ron and I had to figure out how to get it home and where to keep it.

After the party Shannon and her friends went to a local hotel to eat snacks and watch movies all night. I helped chaperone. The girls all lasted until about 3:00 A.M., when they began to drop off swiftly. Morning came entirely too soon for all of us. Shannon was sad the affair was over. She had not been able to relax with friends in a very long time and it had felt good. Now she had to get refocused. World Championships were on the horizon.

In the meantime something else exciting was in the works for Shannon. At the American Cup, Lon Monk, Jerry Solomon's assistant at ProServ, had introduced Shannon and Ron to Sallie Weaver, president and owner of Elite GK, a gymnastics sportswear company. Sallie was very interested in having Shannon represent Elite GK. Furthermore, she and Lon were discussing the possibility of developing a sportswear line to be marketed under Shannon's name.

As negotiations continued over the next several weeks Shannon was enthusiastic about the project. She had worn GK leotards almost exclusively for her competitive career. This line seemed to fit her better than other lines, and she liked the design of both the leotards and the warm-up suits. Promoting the GK line would be easy for Shannon. She liked the idea of having her own signature line of leotards, biker shorts, and warm-ups, but she made it clear that if a Shannon Miller line was introduced, she expected to have active involvement in the fabric and design. She understood what was comfortable and moved well in workouts and competition. She also wanted to be involved in choosing the logo. Sallie agreed.

Sallie had developed her company into a profitable and growing enterprise because she listened to her customers. Now she understood the value of listening to an expert in gymnastic workout wear. Sallie said Shannon would need to trust her decisions about marketing styles to different age groups. Both realized they would make a good team. The deal was closed.

Sallie hired a marketing person to design a logo and sent about fifteen possibilities to Shannon, who immediately rejected them all. She described to Sallie what she had in mind, and soon another group of about fifteen proposals arrived. Shannon picked out one or two she could live with but told Sallie these still were not to her liking. Sallie had not been particularly happy with them either.

Shannon then suggested that Sallie let Tessa help her design her own logo. After a few tries Tessa had a version Shannon liked. She sent it off to Sallie, who called to congratulate her. She said the logo was better than any of the previous proposals.

Next Sallie sent Shannon some fabric choices for the leotards. Shannon looked them over and sent her response. When sample leotards were made Sallie hired a model about Shannon's size to demonstrate each one, videotaped the session, and sent the tape to Shannon.

Sallie had been a little surprised at how seriously Shannon took the logo. She was even more surprised when she got the telephone call after Shannon's review of the video. Shannon had spent an entire Sunday afternoon poring over the video, listing each garment, rerunning the tape, and making meticulous notes. She called Sallie and carefully went over each leotard, pointing out the advantages and disadvantages of each. Shannon noticed details only an experienced gymnast with years of competition would take into consideration.

Sallie and Shannon continued to function as effective partners. When Shannon thought of a new design for a leotard or a new product that they hadn't sold before, she didn't hesitate to call Sallie. Sallie was always willing to listen and evaluate the proposal. If she saw an inherent problem, she explained it carefully to Shannon. Sometimes they discarded ideas, sometimes they reworked them, and sometimes Shannon's ideas ended up in finished garments.

Shannon's own catalog of clothing is produced four times a year. Shannon models all the clothing in her catalog and in the annual GK catalog. A modeling session usually lasts six to

1. Shannon on the balance beam, around age 12.

2. Shannon, Steve, Peggy, Claudia, and Ron (in our patriotic shirts) during the 1992 parade.

3. Shannon competing in the uneven bars during the 1992 Olympic games. Courtesy David Fischer, M.D.

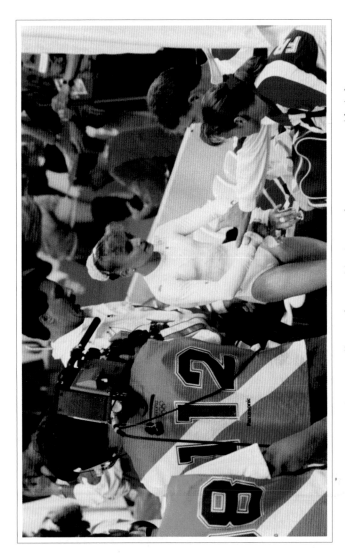

4. Steve and Shannon during the all-around competition in Barcelona. Courtesy David Fischer, M.D.

5. The 1992 Olympic Team on the awards podium: Kim Zmeskal, Kerri Strug, Shannon, Dominique Dawes, Wendy Bruce, and Betty Okino. Photo courtesy Jerry Butler.

6. *Shannon performing the Geinger release move on the uneven bars in the 1996 Olympics. Photo courtesy Steve Lange.*

7. Gina Gogean, Shannon, and Lilia Podkopayeva accepting the beam awards at the 1996 Olympic Games. Photo courtesy Steve Lange.

8. *Shannon Miller with her two gold medals from the 1996 Olympics.*
© *Garrison's Photography, 1996.*

CHAPTER ELEVEN

1993: Miller Time

THE ONLY PROBLEM still nagging Shannon as 1992 ended was her back. I was massaging it every night to give her a little relief, and we still believed that with less intense training after the meet season it would mend itself. When the pain continued to get worse, we realized it was time for more prayerful work.

With only a couple of weeks until Worlds, Shannon would not agree to another cortisone shot. She wanted to place her trust firmly in God and work through Christian Science. I have learned that healings sometimes come almost instantaneously and sometimes take longer. Shannon had experienced both. Now Kittie directed her thoughts to two inspiring messages, one from the Bible and one from *Science and Health*.

From the Bible, Shannon studied the guiding words from Proverbs, "Trust in the Lord with all thine heart and lean not unto thine own understanding. In all ways acknowledge him, and he shall direct thy paths." Shannon knew God had been directing her path all her life and that she could always trust Him to help her make the right choices. Sometimes it was hard to get her own ideas and wants out of the way and to remember "thy will be done," but with Kittie's guidance and our support, she could follow God's direction. From *Science and Health*, Shannon studied the words, "Hold thought stead- fastly to the enduring, the good, and the true and you will bring these into your experience proportionably to their occupancy of your thoughts." It was so tempting to give in to frustration, anger, fear, and disillusionment when the pain was almost intolerable. Steve was pushing hard, time was running out, and Shannon's body wasn't cooperating. At these times, though, Shannon did cling to Mrs. Eddy's words. She struggled to keep her thought in line with all the good she knew God was daily providing to her.

Steve recognized that he could not continue to press Shannon vigorously until Worlds, so he arranged workouts that would avoid to the extent possible the moves that most aggravated her back. A week before the American Cup Steve had realized he did not have an adequate middle tumbling pass in Shannon's floor routine. Many of the rules had changed after the 1992 Olympics. Now the gymnasts had to have even more difficulty in individual skills and put more emphasis on connecting moves with each other. Shannon needed more "series" bonus and at least one more "C" level skill in her floor routine.

Steve settled on a double twisting back layout, a move she had performed with ease when she was ten years old but had not worked in five years. To relearn it Steve started her out on the trampoline, and within a couple of days she was able to hit it consistently on the floor. He added two whip backs (a flip- flop without putting the hands on the floor) through to the double full for series bonus points, then, when this went well, he tacked on another whip back. Again Shannon seemed to do the series with ease, so Steve added a punch front (a front somersault performed immediately after the previous skill) out of the double full. Shannon had it down fairly well by the

American Cup. Steve hoped she would have it more polished for Worlds—that she would not have regressed with less training.

Between the American Cup and Worlds Peggy had decided that on beam Shannon would attempt a back handspring to her hands with a quarter turn in the air, as she had in the Olympics, but immediately on landing on her hands she would do a hop half-again landing in a handstand. This innovative move came to be known as the Miller. When Shannon demonstrated it to judges, they rated it an E—one of the most difficult moves in gymnastics.

I watched the last workout before the girls, Steve, and Peggy left for Birmingham. Shannon had eased off bars and some of the tumbling skills on beam. She had worked on the double twisting Yurchenko only occasionally. Steve had thrown so much relatively new tumbling into her floor routine that by the time he asked her to perform full routines on all of the apparatus the morning before they were to leave, she found herself struggling. I was disturbed. I wondered whether my daughter really needed to go to this World Championship competition if her back was still so sore and she was not fully prepared.

When I voiced my concerns to Steve he firmly reminded me that he was the coach and made the meet decisions. I confess that I wondered whether Steve's apparent lack of concern was because Kerri had an international reputation and was looking very good in all four events. If Shannon did not do well, Dynamo could still have a good showing. I started to question myself—was I worried that Shannon was not completely ready for this meet, or was I worried that she wasn't looking as good as Kerri?

Shannon emerged from the gym confident and happy. One look at her eager face told me I had been seriously falling down in where I put my faith. Each night we studied and prayed together, and I did my best to keep Shannon's spirits up, but my own priorities were out of line. This time I was the one who needed Kittie's help.

I was at work, my thoughts far from World Championships, when my telephone rang. Shannon's voice was on the other end of the line. I had not calculated the time difference between Oklahoma City and Birmingham, so I did not know what time she would be competing. Once I made the decision to place her in God's care, I felt as if a weight had been lifted and I could think about my other children, my husband, and my job. Now Shannon was excitedly telling me that not only had she qualified for the final all-around competition and for all four event finals but she had completed preliminary competition in first place in every event. Of course, when the final all-around began the previous scores would be dropped and all the gymnasts would start from scratch. Only two gymnasts per country advanced to finals in this world competition. Shannon and Dominique Dawes had made the final cut for the United States. Kerri had finished a very respectable fifth in the world, but Dominique had edged her out in the all-around competition. Kerri had qualified for floor finals.

While Shannon still faced the all-around competition, she did not dwell on it. She was missing a lot of school and she didn't want any more B's. On tour the previous fall, Shannon had learned to concentrate almost anywhere at the meet. She and Kerri had been in different sessions and she wanted to cheer Kerri on, so she carried *Animal Farm* with her to read during breaks in activities. At Steve's insistence, the girls took a short nap every afternoon. Nevertheless, Shannon set aside some time each day to do homework.

As Shannon prepared for finals, workouts were going well but her back was still giving her some trouble. Steve asked the American trainer who had traveled to Birmingham with the team to give Shannon appropriate therapy. The trainer told Steve she needed to take some medicine to reduce the inflammation. Shannon knew Steve was counting on her.

She was afraid that if she refused the medicine and performed poorly, Steve would say she should have taken it.

Shannon did not realize that some medicines should be taken with food. She was suffering from nausea but did not realize what the problem was. She usually just prayed quietly until the uncomfortable feeling left. Steve and Peggy knew she didn't feel particularly well but assumed the problem was back pain.

The day of the all-around arrived. Shannon felt ready in spite of some pain and a little nausea. She started on bars, did a good routine, took a small step on the landing, but still earned a good score. On beam she was a bit shaky but held on until she overrotated on the full twisting double back dismount and had to take a few steps. This was a costly error in a competition with gymnasts of such high caliber.

Shannon was now in third place. Steve saw World Championships slipping away, but he knew Shannon was a fighter and a win was still possible if he could get her motivated again. All she had to do was hit a fantastic floor routine and two outstanding vaults!

Steve reassured Shannon of his confidence and reminded her she was there to do her best, regardless of the outcome. She told me later that a phrase from our Sunday School lesson flitted through her mind as she thought about what he said: if everything we do expresses all the good qualities God has bestowed on us, we cannot feel burdened.

Shannon executed her floor routine with precision and elegance and earned a high enough score to boost her into second. She felt eager to charge down the vault runway. Steve now faced a crucial decision. Because of her back Shannon had not been able to work on the double twisting Yurchenko as diligently as he had hoped. She needed the more difficult vault to have any chance of moving into first place, but if she attempted it and failed, she could drop out of the medals altogether. Dominique Dawes was in first by less than a tenth of

29. Shannon in the floor exercise at the Birmingham World Championships, 1993. Photo courtesy Jerry Butler.

a point, but Gina Gogean of Romania was just a hair behind Shannon.

Steve made his decision. He would not chance the more difficult vault. Shannon responded with two excellent Yurchenko twists. In the final competition scores for both vaults counted. She had great repulsion and landed her first vault perfectly. The judges scored it at 9.775 out of 9.8, almost perfect. The second one was even better. This one earned the full 9.8.

Steve was carefully watching the numbers. When Dominique suffered a small problem on her first vault, she left the door open a little for Shannon. Then she fell on her second vault—and out of first place.

Steve turned his attention to the floor and to the only other gymnast who could unseat Shannon. Gina performed a nice floor routine but not as elegant or difficult as Shannon's. Her score was 9.8. Steve knew this would be close. Was it enough? Someone ran up to tell him Shannon had eked out the win by only 0.007, the closest World Championship ever. Shannon was immediately surrounded by reporters and cameras and couldn't escape to call home.

I had been invited to judge the Level 10 Regional Championships in Dallas and was gathering my things to leave my office early when the telephone rang. It was a friend calling to congratulate me on Shannon's victory. I was confused. He said he had just heard on the radio that Shannon had won World Championships.

Of course, I knew she had done well in preliminaries. But World Champion! I was flabbergasted. I knew that Shannon was a very happy girl and that Steve and Peggy must be shouting the news from the rooftops. I hung up and tried to call Ron to tell him the big news, but he had already left work to drive Troy to a gym class. By the time I reached him, he already knew. He had heard it on the car radio and confessed he could not remember how he had gotten home.

Shannon's career seemed to be complete. Steve had convinced her she had the potential to be a world champion. Now she was. While we called everyone we knew to tell them the news, Ron and I wondered whether she would quit gymnastics now. Shannon, however, was thinking only as far ahead as the event finals she still had to go through. Her back was still painful, so she kept taking the medicine the trainer had given her and the nausea continued.

Vaulting again posed a dilemma. She had hardly had time to work on the vault, as evidenced by the fact that she did not attempt the double twisting Yurchenko in the all-around competition even though she had successfully thrown it a few weeks before at Trials. She did not have a second vault ready.

Steve weighed all the options and decided that since she was nauseated and in pain, there was no need to put her through the vault competition. He withdrew her, leaving her only bars to concentrate on during the first day of event finals. She did not disappoint him. She hit a perfect routine, outdistancing the rest of the field to easily capture the gold.

On the day of beam and floor finals she was even more nauseous than usual and finally told Peggy how bad she felt. Peggy suggested that they pull her out of all events that day since she already had two World Championship medals. Steve was willing. Shannon was not. She had not been happy about withdrawing from the vault competition, and now she especially wanted to redeem herself from a less than stellar performance on beam in the all-around competition.

It was not to be. She competed, but her first tumbling pass took her out of contention. She fell on a layout flip to two feet, hitting hard on the side of the beam. She was embarrassed but not about to quit. She climbed back up on the beam and fell again, this time on the Miller, her signature move. Once again she hopped onto the beam and finished her routine. Later she said it never crossed her mind to leave out any of her skills, such as the three layout back flips in a row (which she successfully completed) or to water down a skill to something easier. She could have performed a double back for her dismount but went for the full twisting double back and ended up sitting on the floor.

Later, when as a senior in high school Shannon had to give a presentation in English class about the most embarrassing moment in her life she talked about this beam routine. In the same meet that she became the honored world champion she fell three times on an apparatus she had always regarded as her best event.

Steve realized that Shannon might not be eating enough while she took her medication. He scrounged up a banana. Commentator and former Olympic gymnast Kathy Johnson, who knew of Shannon's back problem, also guessed her nausea might be from the medicine. She offered Shannon Power Bars. Shannon ate some and declared herself ready for floor. While she was eating she had missed part of her warm-up time for floor, but she forged ahead.

I admit to being a prejudiced parent, but I have enough experience to know that anyone can have a single great day. A true champion rises to every occasion and never accepts defeat. Shannon may have been tremendously embarrassed by the turn of events, but with a real champion's heart she blamed no one and no circumstances—not her coaches, not her illness—and she did not give in to feeling sorry for herself. She shed some tears, but once the emotions were under control and Steve was again giving her directions for floor finals, she was back in the game.

She hit a beautiful floor routine and was rewarded with the high score of the day, another gold medal and another record. No American gymnast had ever won three gold medals at World Championships.

Karen Rosen, sports writer for the *Atlanta Journal-Constitution*, wrote, "If this is what Shannon Miller can do when she's sick—reel off three World Championship gold medals while her stomach is turning flip-flops—what can she do when she's healthy?"

When Shannon arrived home at Will Rogers Airport, we were not the only people there to greet her. So were a bevy of reporters and photographers and some Oklahomans who were eager to tell her how proud they were. Shannon was all smiles, obviously pleased at the turnout and glad to be home.

We knew Shannon, Peggy, Steve, and Kerri had taken an extra day to do some sightseeing in London, see the play *Joseph and the Technicolor Dreamcoat*, and shop at world-famous Harrods. Ron and I expected to hear news of the trip on our way home, but we had barely gotten past the airport parking attendant when we heard some sniffles from the backseat.

It took a few minutes for Shannon to tell us the problem. Steve was worrying about Kerri because although she was an exceptional gymnast, she had not won a major competition. He knew Kerri's time would come but was afraid she would quit gymnastics if she did not take a major title soon. He told Shannon he might pull her out of Nationals to give Kerri a better chance. Shannon was crushed. It seemed to be the Erica situation all over again.

Ron and I were astonished. We vacillated between feeling angry at Steve and thinking surely Shannon must be wrong. We did not see how, after all their time and work together, she could have misunderstood Steve completely, but we thought he had learned his lesson with Erica. We promised Shannon we would talk to Steve and Peggy, and she calmed down.

Ron and I were direct when we met with Steve and Peggy. We had two major points to clear up: Why had Shannon been eating so little that the medication made her ill? And what was the real story on his plans for National Championships?

Steve and Peggy said the girls had breakfast, lunch, and dinner daily, but they did not know whether Shannon liked the food that was served. The coaches said they had not been concerned because they kept a basket of fruit in the room Shannon and Kerri shared and thought the girls would nibble on it if they got hungry. They had not noticed that much of it was exotic fruit that the girls were not used to eating. We asked that they watch Shannon's diet a little closer in the future or allow her to bring food with her.

Now to the really sticky issue: Championships. When we broached the subject, Peggy was aghast. She said she could not believe Steve would have considered such a thing. Steve insisted that Shannon had completely misunderstood. He had been angry because reporters began questioning him as soon as Shannon left the victory stand about whether she would be able to win the National Championships with Dominique and Kerri both looking strong. In frustration he had declared he just might not have her compete at the National Championships so that no one could claim to have beaten the world champion. Shannon remembered these things differently but had trusted Steve for years and accepted his explanation. The issue appeared to be closed.

It was now May. The girls had no more major meets scheduled until the Olympic Sports Festival in July. Steve had debated long and hard about whether to enter the girls because it was so close to U.S. Championships and he didn't want them to be worn out. Both the U.S. Olympic Committee and the San Antonio committee hosting the meet wanted both girls to compete. Because of all the relatives who lived there, San Antonio was a second hometown to Shannon. She wanted to compete in that meet and told Steve so. San Antonio was only an eight-hour drive, so Ron, Tessa, Troy, and I could go too. Steve decided to enter them. The U.S. Olympic Committee asked Shannon to join weightlifter Mark Henry in lighting the Olympic Festival torch on top of Pikes Peak in Colorado in June. Shannon happily accepted, and we were invited to accompany her.

In mid-May Kerri and Shannon were invited to Los Angeles to compete on an American team against Belarus and Ukraine in the Hilton Challenge. When Steve accepted the invitation, neither girl was thrilled. They were still tired from World Championships and had the Olympic Sports Festival and U.S. Championships coming up. Shannon was still nursing her back, and Kerri had aches and pains too. Other demands for Shannon's time, such as exhibitions, autograph signings, and charitable events, increased after she won World Championships. Now Steve had committed her to another meet.

Steve began immediately to prepare them for the competition in June. Less than a week before they were to leave for Los Angeles, I dropped by the gym after work to watch the end of the workout. When I walked in a group of parents were gathered at one end of the viewing room talking excitedly. I looked through the window into the gym and saw

Shannon curled up on the floor with Peggy bending over her. No one seemed to know what had happened.

I rushed downstairs and into the office to go onto the gym floor the back way. By the time I got halfway through the office, Peggy was coming inside with Shannon, who was barely walking. Peggy had sent for the trainer, Mark Cranston. While we waited Shannon gloomily explained that her back had seemed to seize up. She couldn't do anything.

Shannon had continued to work in spite of the pain, and therapy had provided only partial relief. Mark arrived and confirmed what she described. Her muscles, in rebellion, had contracted and seized. Massage and ice took care of the situation for the present. However, Mark felt that only resting her back altogether would provide long-term relief. Steve reluctantly acceded to Mark's recommendation. Shannon would not have to officially withdraw from the Hilton Challenge since USA Gymnastics was sending an alternate.

Shannon had been invited to a USOC function in Atlanta, but we had turned it down because she could not afford to miss training so close to a meet. We asked Steve whether, now that she was not going to the meet, she could miss a day of workout to go to Atlanta. He granted permission.

Ron was invited to fly to Atlanta also. Shannon was especially excited, because Charles Barkley would be there. She had met him briefly in Barcelona but hoped to talk to him again and get a photograph. Shannon and Ron had a good time and Shannon kept her eye on Charles, who was whisked away immediately after the event. Back in the hotel room Ron asked Shannon whether she had talked to Charles. She told him Charles had left too quickly. Ron said he had seen Charles being taken to another room as they were leaving and perhaps he had not yet left the building. If they hurried, they might still catch him. Shannon had now changed into an old pair of jeans, but she rushed to the elevator with Ron trailing behind her. As she arrived downstairs Charles was at the door. Someone noticed Shannon coming and pointed her out to Charles, who graciously waited for her. He hugged her, told her he was glad to see her again, and took time for Ron to take some photographs. For Shannon, seeing Charles was really exciting. The year 1993 was turning out to be very good, even with the back problem.

When Shannon returned from Atlanta Steve told her he wanted her to go to Los Angeles even if she didn't compete. I was not happy about the plan, and neither was Peggy. We both thought Shannon would benefit more from staying at home, resting, and doing some mild workouts with Peggy. Steve asked Shannon to try a complete bar set. When she made the bar set, he asked her to do a beam routine. When she did that relatively cleanly, he suggested the day before they were scheduled to leave for Los Angeles that maybe she could compete in bars and beam at the meet and forgo the other events.

Shannon was skeptical. She didn't feel she was in condition to compete, but she trusted Steve. She wanted to go and didn't seem to be worried. I was not so trusting and was now even less enthusiastic about her going, but I decided to leave the decision up to her and the outcome up to God.

We did not hear from her while she was in Los Angeles, which was not unusual when she was out of town. At the more important meets in the United States Ron or I was usually there and we called home. Now we assumed she had not competed or had done only one or two events.

When we picked her up at the airport Steve was in good spirits but didn't say much. Shannon was tired and hungry and wanted to stop at Pepe's, her favorite Mexican restaurant in Edmond. While we munched tortilla chips and waited for our order she talked about the meet. After the food arrived one phrase that came up was, "When I won . . . " Ron and I both almost dropped our forks.

"How could you win without competing in all the events?" one of us asked her.

"Oh," she said, "I did compete in everything."

"But how could that be?" I asked. Shannon hadn't worked on a floor routine since World Championships, and she hadn't even tumbled in at least a week.

She described the scenario to us. She had started on vault. The team had been weak in this area, and although she was still doing only a 9.8 vault, Steve felt she could pull off a good score. She had two tries to land a good vault, and she did. He had planned for her to compete in bars. She had done a couple of routines over the last few days and had done well. He told her to warm up on the beam and see how it went. One move was giving her problems, so he pulled it out. Even without it she had plenty of difficulty, so she had scored well in competition. After three events she was in first place by a good margin. Steve said it would be a shame to quit now.

Since she had not planned to compete floor, Shannon had not even taken a turn during the warm-up period before the meet. Steve told her to take her thirty-second precompetition warm-up and make a decision. He thought she could water down the routine a little and still get a good score.

She decided to give it a try. She hit the routine well, earning a more than respectable score, and brought home the gold medal from a meet in which she wasn't even supposed to compete. We shook our heads in amazement.

Next on Steve's agenda for Shannon was the Olympic Sports Festival in late July. Next on Shannon's schedule for herself were a quick trip to Colorado to light the Olympic Festival torch and registration for Driver's Education. She would finally learn to drive the Saturn she had been given.

Former Governor Nigh had promised Shannon after the 1992 Olympics that he would give her a "scholarship" for a Driver's Education class at the university where he was president. Shannon took him up on his offer in June. She went each day for about an hour between morning and afternoon workouts at the gym. In a week the instructor declared her ready to take her test.

Shannon had only had the opportunity to practice parallel parking once and was a little worried about this particular driving skill, especially since Tessa had encountered some difficulties with it on her test. When the examiner instructed her to parallel park, Shannon was even more dismayed to discover a pole at one end of the parking space and a boat on the other. However, she carefully followed the directions in the driving manual and parked almost perfectly. It was obvious when she arrived home that she was not only excited to have her driver's license, she was quite pleased with herself for mastering the art of parallel parking. Of course, she doesn't like me to mention that soon after getting her license she was mortified when she drove the wrong way down a one-way street, discovering her mistake only when motorists began honking and waving at her.

CHAPTER TWELVE

Battling Burnout

By now it was July, and Steve's priorities became Shannon's. The Olympic Sports Festival was next on the agenda. As time for the competition neared, Shannon became irritable. We attributed the mood to concern about having so many family members in the audience in San Antonio. Later we decided it was caused by too many orders in the gym. The 1993 season had already been a tough one, and yet she still had the Sports Festival and U.S. Championships. Shannon appreciated having Kerri as a friend but found that daily workouts felt more competitive with another top gymnast on the premises.

Shannon was getting tired of being on the receiving end of all the orders. She had always understood that life and limb could depend on paying attention to what Steve told her. She did not argue with him and rarely questioned his instructions or decisions. Steve had high expectations for both upcoming competitions and bore down on Shannon to get ready.

At the gym Steve drilled perfection into the girls every day. At home Tessa set high academic standards Shannon strived to meet. The victim of Shannon's built-up pressure was her younger brother. Shannon obviously loved Troy. She would go to bat for him, helped him with his homework, and willingly hauled him around in her car, but she decided that if she had to work so hard, so should he. Troy was the most laidback of our three children. He didn't like losing in sports but didn't consider it a tragedy if he didn't win. He preferred to make good grades, but B's were fine.

Shannon certainly didn't give orders at the gym, although she took plenty of them, and she wasn't about to order Tessa around. Troy was another story. When he brought home his report card, Shannon usually grabbed it first and lectured him. When she had time (which, fortunately for him, was not too often) she gave him discourses on everything from how he dressed to the sloppiness of their shared bathroom. One day I got the benefit of her counsel. Shannon decided I needed to be a stronger disciplinarian. I tried to explain that Ron and I did discipline Troy but only for major infractions, which, fortunately, were rare. I reminded him to clean his room and pick up his clothes, and if his grades really slipped there were always repercussions.

Just before leaving for San Antonio Shannon was badgering Troy. This time he had enough and let her know it. I felt she was out of line and told her so—not what she wanted to hear. She went to her room and refused to talk to anyone until she left for San Antonio the next day. We received a curt good-bye.

Now I felt bad. I knew I was justified in standing up for Troy, but I thought I should have handled the situation better. As we drove to San Antonio, I worried. Shannon had an important meet and wanted very much to do well. I hoped her frustration would not affect her performance. I think it might have, but not in the way I feared. She was fired up, led her team to an easy victory, and then returned the next day to effortlessly capture the all-around medal. On the next day she won three of the four event finals and took silver on the fourth.

After the meet we went down to the floor. She came over

to us, trying to be stern. But in a few minutes we were all apologizing and hugging. Troy and I were "forgiven."

While in San Antonio Shannon was invited to make an appearance at Sea World and to bring her family and team with her. We enjoyed ourselves immensely. Shamu the whale gave Shannon a big kiss, and she, her teammates, Tessa, and Troy got to pet him and the other whales. Shannon was able to take one set of grandparents to Sea World and go out to dinner with the other set. She visited with aunts, uncles, and cousins too numerous to count. All too soon the fun was a pleasant memory and she was back in the hot, non-air-conditioned gym training for U.S. Championships.

The Olympic Sports Festival had helped to boost her confidence. To rest her back she had eased up on the difficulty in some of her routines and still won the gold easily in a field with such great gymnasts as Kerri Strug and Amanda Borden. Championships would be a much tougher competition, and she would need all her most difficult moves. She could not afford to take it easy on her back much longer.

Shannon knew she had the ability to win Nationals, a meet in which she had not previously excelled. The year before she had an excellent beginning and finished compulsories in first place but had to withdraw from optionals when Steve determined she was not yet ready for full routines. So far Shannon had had a phenomenal 1993 season. She desperately wanted to cap it by winning Championships.

She felt good about compulsories, even though she was now performing a completely different set of compulsory routines from those she competed at the Olympics. She knew the new routines were far from perfection, but Steve had periodically invited judges in to evaluate the girls' routines and they were usually impressed.

After the first day of competition Shannon was in first place with a nice lead in the compulsory session. Optionals were harder on her back. Back tumbling on beam and floor was the most difficult. Mark Cranston had tried everything he could to help her with her back, but Shannon believed the ultimate answer was not physical. She still worked regularly with Kittie, who reminded her gently that when things seemed the bleakest, she most needed to rely on God.

Shannon started optionals on bars. Both Kerri and Dominique Dawes had gone before her and scored very well on this event, but Shannon managed to top their scores.

On beam Dominique was superb, but Kerri fell. Shannon performed on beam flawlessly, making the Miller look simple and again bettering Dominique's score.

Floor would be Shannon's biggest challenge. She had not practiced much back tumbling, having had to take some difficulty out for the Sports Festival, but now it was again in her routine. She wobbled slightly once but still earned a good score and retained her lead over Dominique.

Shannon was a good vaulter, but so was Kerri. About two weeks before Championships Kerri had complained to Shannon that she was having to stay an additional hour in the hot gym. When Shannon asked why, she learned that Steve had been privately coaching Kerri on a new vault, a Yurchenko Arabian with a start value of 10. Shannon marched in to Steve's office to let him know she would also be staying for a "private" vault lesson. He told her Peggy would be coaching that day but he did not approve because he was concerned about her back. The trainer had warned him to take it easy on her or she might not be competing at all. He planned to give her a well-deserved rest after Championships. When Shannon's back improved, he told her, they would worry about vault again.

Shannon was undeterred. She asked Peggy to work with her, and Peggy gladly agreed. Shannon surprised Peggy by immediately hitting some of the double twists. Peggy called Steve over to watch, and he admitted that he was impressed but was not prepared to say Shannon could go with the harder vault in competition. "We'll see," he said.

Vault was Shannon's last event. As at Worlds, Steve had

to decide whether to let Shannon go for a harder vault with a value of 10 or stay with a safer 9.8 vault. He knew Shannon would want to do the more difficult one. He also knew that if she hit a reasonable full twist, she would win the meet. Once again he decided not to take the extra risk. He directed her to compete the full twist, the easier vault. She performed a great vault and earned a good score. Even if Dominique scored a 10, she couldn't catch Shannon. As Shannon walked back from vault, Steve promised, "You can throw the double twist in vault finals."

At that moment Shannon was no longer thinking about vault, nor was she thinking about event finals. With no falls this time she had actually won U.S. Championships. After she had taken the Olympics by storm and won World Championships, she was finally national champion. Steve teased her about working backward. As they walked back down the vaulting runway after Shannon had completed her last vault, he laughingly told her, "You're the president!"

Shannon qualified for all four event finals. She performed a spectacular bar set and easily captured gold. She fell on beam, got back up, and finished her routine with full difficulty and hardly any additional deductions. She had learned long ago the importance of going all-out after a fall. Now, even with the fall, she took the bronze medal. She came back on floor with a great routine and won another gold.

Dominique, who had won beam, hit two great vaults for the gold, but Shannon took home silver. At the last instant Steve had decided it wasn't worth risking injury to Shannon to have her try the double twist. Shannon was not dismayed. She was quite happy with her medal take from event finals.

We all breathed a big sigh of relief. A very long, difficult competitive season was over. Steve promised her no more meets until after the first of the year. She was glad—at the time.

With Olympic, World, and National titles, it seemed Shannon had done it all. What challenges were left? This would become a critical issue in the next two months.

Steve now had three juniors, Jennie Thompson, Tanya Meiers, and Soni Meduna, who had finished one, two, and three in their division at Nationals, and he had to prepare them for a big international meet in Australia late in the fall. At about the same time Peggy would be taking Kerri to the DTB Cup in Germany. Shannon would get to rest.

She was eager to have fun away from gymnastics. As was our tradition, we scheduled a week off from work, piled our luggage in the car a day or so after Shannon got home from Championships, and set out on a vacation. This year we decided to go to Branson, Missouri. The kids enjoyed the fun park, riding go-carts, browsing through the gift shops, and most of all renting a boat and going out on the lake. While Tessa, Troy, Ron, and I loved tubing behind the boat, Shannon preferred driving the boat. Tessa and I did a little cliff diving, but Shannon decided bar dismounts satisfied that feeling for her.

Although Shannon did not have a heavy gymnastic schedule, she had a short tour coming up. This one was primarily on weekends, so Shannon would be home most of the week. School and gym training would not be so disrupted. Shannon could now drive her own car to and from school and gym and could even take friends out to lunch during their break at school.

She expected life at the gym to be relatively easy for a while, but things weren't working out that way. During the first two weeks Steve had been easy on her, but her back was feeling better and he feared she would get lazy. She needed to learn a new vault or get the double twist down to perfection. He thought she should add a new skill on bars. And she needed a new tumbling pass. Steve wanted her to work a double back in a layout position, as well as to improve her front tumbling. The other girls at the gym had been working on front tumbling for a while, but because she had hardly been able to tumble at all with her painful back, Shannon had been forced to stick to the skills she needed for her floor routine.

Shannon's meet season would begin again after the first of the year, and Steve and Peggy would be gone for several weeks in late November and early December. Shannon needed to get going again.

A few weeks after Nationals I stopped by after work to watch the last part of her workout, only to find she had been kicked out of the gym. (Steve was still using this method to show dissatisfaction with his gymnasts.) While Shannon gathered items from her locker I stepped into Steve's office to ask what was wrong. He insisted she had not been tumbling well, that her double layouts were not coming along as they should have. She was making them but not using the technique he wanted, and he felt that if she didn't use the prescribed technique she would never have a good double layout. He was angry at her, and as we headed for the car I could see she was angry with him.

This was not their first spat, and I figured that, just as before, they would get over their differences by the next day. I told her, "You can go home and get your homework done in time to get to bed at a decent hour. Then you'll be ready for whatever Steve throws at you tomorrow." She agreed that was probably true.

The next day Steve was still unhappy. Shannon was again kicked out and arrived home from gym before I got home from work. Steve had told her she would not be working on double layouts anymore. Shannon had wanted to work on double layouts before the 1992 Olympics, but there had been too many competitions, and then the elbow injury. Steve knew she wanted very much to get this skill.

In the next few weeks he decided he would work her hard on front tumbling. She picked up a front layout quickly and gradually was able to do a front with a full twist, but it was not consistent. When he tried to teach her a front with a one-and-a-half twist, she had a lot of trouble.

For about two weeks she was kicked out of the gym every day when it was time to tumble. Steve was really angry now. Kicking Shannon out in the past had always quickly brought her around to his way of thinking, but it didn't seem to be working now. He usually let the gymnast stew for a while in the lobby, then he would go out, lecture her, and bring her back in for the next event. That was what he expected to be able to do now. He had completely forgotten that Shannon was now driving herself to gym. When Steve kicked her out she just climbed in her car and left.

The first time she pulled this stunt she came home smiling and said, "I bet Steve forgot I could leave." She giggled on the way up to her room. She knew Steve would be livid— and he was—but that one delicious moment was worth the wrath to come. Pulling a fast one on Steve was fun the first time, but getting kicked out almost every day was not fun. Shannon realized something had to change.

We talked over her alternatives and assumed the difficulty was centered on front tumbling skills. She needed to learn the front full and front one-and-a-half twist Steve was counting on. Except for the brief time working on vaults with Kerri, Shannon had never had or wanted private lessons. We feared long-term private lessons would soon burn her out. Now, however, we decided that since Peggy had seemed sympathetic to Shannon's situation, it might be a good idea to ask her to work with Shannon on these skills.

Peggy agreed this might be the solution and thought a few half-hour lessons would do the trick. In fact, after only two lessons Peggy thought Shannon did not need any more. But once Shannon began working again with Steve, she seemed to fall apart. With the end of October approaching, Shannon was disheartened and Steve seemed to have absolutely no patience with her.

Around this time Steve held the annual gym picnic. Shannon always enjoyed these affairs. It was a time to forget about gymnastics and have fun like a normal teenager. This year she especially enjoyed the volleyball game. However, it began to get late. Shannon had homework to do, and we had scheduled a meeting with Steve and Peggy that evening to try to iron out the problems Shannon and they seemed to be having. When Ron went to pick up Shannon, she was not happy to see him. She had enjoyed getting out and forgetting about everything except having fun and was not ready for the experience to end. She was an angry girl when she arrived home. She declared vehemently that she was tired of gym and the life it forced her to lead. She thought she might like to quit gymnastics.

We had encountered these feelings once before and were not too surprised. Shannon had accomplished most of her goals in gymnastics and had just finished a long, tiring, but very successful year of competition. Where was she to go? Steve wasn't helping matters by humiliating her with being kicked out of the gym frequently, and we weren't helping by reminding her she still had to devote a significant amount of time to schoolwork. Not much time for fun. Nevertheless, we asked her to at least sit down with us and Steve and Peggy and talk things over. She could wait one more day to decide if her gymnastics career was over. She complied.

We had a good discussion covering what seemed like all the bases—Shannon's frustrations, our concerns, and Peggy's and Steve's feelings about the current situation. What we failed to cover is what anyone thought about where Shannon's gymnastics career might be going. However, at the end of the meeting everyone was feeling better. Shannon's feathers were not so ruffled, and she had decided she wasn't ready to call it quits.

For a few days it seemed that we had cleared the air and made some progress, but in just over a week the scenario started again. We were not sure how much was Steve's impatience and how much might be Shannon getting tired of gymnastics. We suspected there were also other factors involved.

Shannon and Peggy drove to Kansas for an appearance. Peggy used the opportunity to try to get Shannon to open up. When she brought Shannon home, Peggy came in to talk. She said Shannon had not said a lot, but she thought Shannon might be missing her sister.

Tessa had left in late September for California, where she started college at Caltech. Shannon and Tessa had not gotten to spend a lot of time together the last few years because both had busy schedules, but Shannon liked having the family living together. She knew that Tessa's departure meant things would never again be quite the same. I was feeling some of the same emotions but had not realized how much Tessa's leaving had disturbed Shannon. Tessa's departure was another sign of the changing times Shannon was trying so hard to cope with.

I called Mark Cranston to ask for his assessment of Shannon's back. She rarely complained about physical pain to us, and I thought that might be a source of Steve's and Shannon's frustration. But Mark indicated that Shannon's back seemed to be doing better—probably because she was doing so little tumbling these days. I felt our prayers were also making a difference.

Mark commented that with the frequency of open conflict between Shannon and Steve, the gym was beginning to seem like a war zone. He did not think Shannon was going to accept Steve's impatience much longer. He said he had expressed concern to Steve, but Steve didn't think Shannon cared about gymnastics anymore.

I could see we had two immovable objects—Shannon and Steve. An idea began to form, and I discussed it with Mark. It occurred to me that with Steve training Kerri and the three juniors for important upcoming meets, he did not have time to indulge Shannon in any way. He needed her to do exactly as he said and not demand additional attention. Shannon, however, was used to being the one he was getting ready for a meet. She had no goals right now and was not sure why she was still training.

The solution I proposed would require sacrifices from both Steve and Shannon, and I was not sure either of them would go for it. I thought Steve needed to work one-on-one with Shannon for a while. If he could devote all his attention to her for a brief time each day, he might be more patient, explain things better, and rebuild the bond they had before he had so many gymnasts to train. We would be asking Steve to give up two to three hours of his time each day for at least a few weeks. For her part, in a one-on-one situation Shannon would not need to spend so many hours in the gym; however, she would have to be tutored so that she could spend some time away from school working with Steve. She liked going to school and having other gymnasts around for training. I didn't know whether Shannon would react favorably to this idea either.

Steve was unhappy with our whole family at the time, so I hesitated to make the suggestion. Mark offered to present the idea to Steve. If Steve agreed, I would talk to Shannon.

Steve knew he was on the verge of losing Shannon. He was frustrated with her, but he didn't want her to quit. He was willing to take the time to try to get her back on track. Shannon also readily agreed to the arrangement. She seemed to be impressed that Steve was willing to spend extra time with her. She would come in for three hours in the morning by herself to train with Steve for two hours and Peggy for an hour. While Shannon was frustrated in the gym, she was not sure quitting would make her happy. If this new plan was not the solution, then maybe she would consider retiring from gymnastics.

In their first session Steve made an important discovery. He had been instructing Shannon to twist in the wrong direction in front tumbling. He had forgotten she was a left twister, and since she was moving forward, Shannon had not understood it would be easier for her to twist in the other direction. In no time she was consistently hitting her front fulls and making rapid progress on the front one-and-a-half.

Steve started her on a new vault, the Yurchenko Arabian. Since it was already November, he was afraid she could not get the double full vault solidly by the competitive season. Within two weeks she was throwing the new vault and almost had a new move on bars.

By Thanksgiving Shannon was ready to get back to evening gym, her friends, and school. She was excited about gymnastics again, and Steve was recognizing her needs. One of these needs, he realized, was to give her some goals. He wanted her to go to World Championships again. No American had ever won two World Championships, but with the progress she was making he told her he thought she could do it. He told her he did not think her career had peaked, that she could learn much more. He wanted her to make a commitment to remaining in gymnastics until 1996. Shannon was a little overwhelmed at first, but by the end of the year she realized she was only two and a half years from the 1996 Olympics. That didn't seem so long.

The fall hadn't been completely gloomy. While working with the American Floral Society Shannon met the legendary Paul Harvey, whom she had been listening to on her way to the gym for years. Ted Turner was preparing to stage the 1994 Goodwill Games and wanted Shannon to participate, so she and Steve traveled to New York for a kickoff reception. Not only did Shannon get to meet Ted Turner, but even more exciting for her, she met his wife, Jane Fonda. Shannon said Jane looked every bit the movie star she is but was easy to talk to and did not seem at all conceited. Jackie Joyner Kersee and other great athletes were also there.

With our assistance Shannon did a spot on "I Witness Video," a weekly TV show that demonstrates the various ways in which people use home video. Of course, we had been filming Shannon's meets for a long time. As Ron and I were rarely able to attend a meet together, whoever went filmed for the other. Also, Steve filmed workouts, especially when the girls were trying to learn a new skill or were having trouble with a move.

While Shannon was working out her troubles with Steve, Kerri was developing some of her own problems. It was difficult to train for a meet when her training partner was spending less time in the gym. Even worse, as Kerri put in long, hard workouts, she pulled a stomach muscle. Steve and Peggy tried to work around it, giving her some time off, but the meet was coming up fast and she had to begin routines. Some days she seemed better, but then the pain would come back. Her parents wondered if she should be going to the meet in Germany, but Peggy and Steve were confident she would do well. Steve left with the juniors for Australia. Peggy left with Kerri for Europe. Shannon continued to work out with one of the other coaches in the gym.

The problem with Kerri's stomach muscle grew worse, and she could hardly perform in Germany. Peggy withdrew her from some of the events. Kerri was in pain and worn out. She had had a longer season than Shannon, and she needed some time off. When she and Peggy returned to Oklahoma, Kerri arranged to go home for a while. Later she decided to train in Arizona. She had been living away from home for years and missed her family.

Shannon was sorry to see Kerri go. Other good gymnasts were training at Steve's gym, but most were juniors. They would not be competing in the same meets as Shannon would. She would miss her traveling partner.

Christmas was an exciting affair as always. Shannon begged to wrap Tessa's and Troy's gifts so that she could see what I had gotten them. I loved having her take care of that chore and valued her opinion. More than once I returned items to the store on her advice and never regretted it.

Christmas had a special allure this year. Tessa was coming home from college. Our budget did not allow for her to fly home often, and she had chosen Christmas, spring break, and summer break. It had been about three and a half months since we had seen her. Shannon was starting to think about college herself and was eager to hear about Tessa's experiences. She was not certain where she wanted to go to college, but she didn't think she wanted to go as far as California. She was considering the University of Oklahoma in Norman. Like Tessa, she wanted to live in the dorm, even though Norman was within commuting distance.

Tessa admitted to being very homesick the first month or two, but now she loved living in the dorm and enjoyed the freedom and activities on campus. Shannon had always known she was college bound. Listening to Tessa, she could hardly wait.

Christmas and New Year's Day flew by. We had taken another short vacation, and Shannon was ready to begin rigorous training for the approaching competitive season. As the reigning World Champion, she again did not have to attend Trials to qualify for the World Championship team. However, according to the rules, she had to demonstrate readiness by finishing in the top six on any one event at the American Cup. Neither she nor Steve were worried about this rule. Steve wanted her to repeat as the American Cup champion.

CHAPTER THIRTEEN

Victory Down Under

SHANNON HAD A few other events before the American Cup. She and Dominique Dawes represented the United States in the Reese's Cup, a new and unique meet that involved costumes and different routines. Steve had turned it down because he didn't want to waste Shannon's time when she needed to be getting serious about the American Cup and World Championships. When meet promoters assured him that she did not have to participate in all events or wear a costume, he decided the Reese's Cup might be a good season warm-up and entered her on bars and beam only.

Shannon was a little dismayed that most of the other gymnasts wore costumes, but Dominique had also been told costumes were not necessary, and she did not wear one. Also, Shannon was later criticized for leaving the meet early, even though Steve had told organizers he wanted to get her back to Oklahoma City for school the next day. On the positive side, both Shannon and Dominique performed good routines and tied for second on both bars and beam. The meet introduced Shannon to a whole new format and foreshadowed events of the future. It also provided an opportunity to try out her new bar skill, a one-and-a-half twist to a handstand on the low bar.

Since Shannon had this meet added to her schedule, Steve chose to have Shannon perform an exhibition rather than compete at the Dynamo Classic in 1994. Shannon thoroughly enjoyed being a part of the Dynamo Classic because it gave her friends a chance to see what she spent so much time doing. She was glad not to have the pressure of competition, but she still put plenty of pressure on herself because she knew people had paid money to come and she thought they deserved her best. She decided to try out the Yurchenko Arabian vault.

Next came the Peachtree Classic in Atlanta. With new skills on almost every event, Shannon did not feel fully prepared for the Peachtree. Floor was giving her the most trouble. She had gotten far behind in tumbling the previous fall, and although she had been making rapid gains since November, it was now only early February and she had done hardly any full floor sets.

Steve contemplated having her compete in only three events. At least she would get a taste of competition and try out her new vault and bar skills. Peggy had also done some rearranging of her beam routine, and Shannon was working on a new mount on beam.

Ron and I were not too concerned about the Peachtree. We knew Shannon was not fully prepared but hoped she would be happy with her performance. Although it may be hard to believe, medals were not the most important thing to Shannon. Mastering a new skill or a new routine was equally gratifying.

The team began on vault. Shannon hit a nice Arabian. She performed a good bar set, hitting her new skill. Beam also went well. Shannon found herself in first place after three events.

True to form, Steve suggested that she compete on floor and eliminate some of the more difficult moves. By now Shannon had Steve figured out. She complied without surprise. She performed a nice routine and scored well enough to take the all-around title. Shannon called home to tell us. After all these years her father and I still wondered how she managed to pull off these things.

The American Cup was a much more important meet, not only because Steve put a great deal of importance on it but also because Shannon would be using this meet as her qualifier for World Championships. Less than two weeks before the meet Shannon's stomach began to hurt quite a bit. On bars she could hardly do a kip—a jump into a full body extension, pulling the feet back toward the bar, and then pulling the bar up the legs as if putting on pants. Beam and floor tumbling were becoming more painful. After a day or two she was forced to tell Steve. He immediately recognized the symptoms. Kerri Strug had suffered from the same complaint, a pulled stomach muscle. Mark Cranston confirmed Steve's diagnosis.

Shannon was not worried. She thought that if she rested the stomach muscle for a day or two she would feel better. Steve agreed and then eased her back into tumbling and bars, but as soon as she resumed hard workouts the pain returned, worse than ever. Shannon called Kittie. She knew getting anxious and worried would not solve the problem. God had a plan for her. She would do her best to listen to it.

Mark cautioned that continuing to force her to work on the muscle could result in an injury so severe that surgery might be necessary. Steve evaluated the situation. As much as he wanted her to defend her American Cup title, World Championships in April were far more important. If Shannon could qualify for Worlds at the American Cup, he could give the stomach muscle some rest before gearing up for Worlds. Shannon remained remarkably calm.

The only thing that didn't seem to aggravate the stomach muscle was vault, so Steve determined they would concentrate on that. She would have to count on scoring well on her new vault to qualify for the World Championship team. The Yurchenko Arabian was a new vault in the Code, the governing book of gymnastics, and some of the coaches were not sure how it should be scored. Shannon executed what Steve thought was a pretty good vault. It received a reasonable score but not what he wanted. Since he did not have a great deal of experience with this vault, he wasn't sure how the judges were looking at it. He hoped the next vault would score better. It did not.

Now Steve was really worried. He had thought Shannon would not have any trouble placing in the top six, but when vault was over, she was in eighth place. He realized she might have to attempt beam.

In the meantime information on the vault was starting to filter down to him. The judges had taken 0.3 off each of Shannon's vaults because he had posted the wrong vault number. One of the judges pointed out that two vaults in the Code were very similar and it was easy to confuse them. In fact, in this meet a Romanian coach had done the same thing, and the judges had pointed out his mistake to him after the gymnast's first vault so that he could correct it on her second vault.

Steve was furious. If the Romanian coach had been able to save the 0.3 deduction on his gymnast's second vault, Shannon was entitled to the same treatment. The judges discussed the matter and agreed that Steve had a valid point. They would give back the 0.3 on Shannon's second vault. Both vaults are averaged at the American Cup to obtain the gymnast's score, so her score was not raised a full 0.3, but the increase did move her into fourth place and onto the World Championship team. Steve, Peggy, and Shannon breathed a sigh of relief.

Since Shannon competed only in vault in the preliminaries, by the time she flew back home and was back in the gym for her workout, her stomach was beginning to feel better. Steve took advantage of her lack of pain and started strenuous workouts. In a day or two the pain was back. Mark once again explained that she absolutely had to rest that muscle for seven or eight days, after which she could gradually increase the level of skills. Steve did a rough calculation and figured that if all went well, Shannon could start routines about two weeks before leaving for Worlds.

Steve adhered to Mark's advice and Shannon's stomach began to mend. After what seemed like an eternity, Shannon was ready to begin routines. More than three weeks had elapsed since Shannon had been able to work on all of her skills. At least one skill on every event was relatively new. Steve and Peggy were pushing hard because there was so little time.

Shannon had had a stellar competitive season in 1993 and had seemed unbeatable. Steve had been sure she would repeat as world champion. This seemed like a distant dream now. Shannon was frustrated and not performing well. The harder she tried, the worse she seemed to perform. Steve was exasperated with her. He called USA Gymnastics to tell them he didn't think he could have her ready for the meet. Federation officials pointed out that this was not a team competition so if he could just have her in medal contention on one or two events, it would be worth her while to go. Steve was not so sure.

Peggy did not want to give up. She agreed Shannon wasn't looking very good, but they had a few days left in Oklahoma and almost a week in Australia before the competition. When Steve became too angry to coach Shannon on floor, a problem since late last year, Peggy took over coaching that event. They had to keep pushing.

While I watched Shannon perform her floor routine the day before she was scheduled to leave for Australia, the judge in me automatically went to work. Every Saturday from fall through early spring I was away from home judging a meet somewhere. Many of these were Level 9 and 10 optional meets. One of a judge's primary responsibilities at this level is to make sure the gymnast has all the required difficulty in her routine. If she is missing a lower-level skill, the judge is required to substitute a higher-level skill for it, thereby possibly leaving the gymnast short of full difficulty. Analyzing Shannon's routine, I could not find all of the C-level requirements. If she was short a C, one of her D's would be utilized and she would not be starting from a maximum score of 10. I was afraid that in their anxiety to help Shannon regain the major skills in her routines, her coaches had not taken a close look to make sure she had all the required lesser skills.

After the workout the gym hosted a going away party for Shannon. Just before the party was over I asked Shannon about the C's in her routine. She could recite all the skills contained in her routine but wasn't sure of the value of each skill. I had her talk me through her routine and then assured her she was missing a C. She asked me to talk to Steve or Peggy.

I was afraid to question the coaches about a gymnastics routine, but I knew somebody had to raise the issue. I tried to talk to Steve first, but he sent me to Peggy, who at times could be even more intimidating than Steve. I did not expect her to listen to me, but, to my relief, Peggy was receptive. She went over Shannon's routine and agreed she couldn't recall enough C's but thought surely we were overlooking something. She said she would have Shannon run through a routine before they left the next day.

On the way to the airport the next afternoon Shannon brought up the subject. She now had a switch side leap (switching her leg in the air while doing a quarter turn in the leap) in her routine, the additional C-level skill she needed. Shannon was proud of me for catching this problem. I was proud of myself for having the courage to tell Steve and Peggy.

In the few weeks before Shannon left for World Championships she was under even more stress than usual. She had not only decided to attempt to be the first American to win two World Championship titles but she had also announced her intention to try for a spot on the 1996 Olympic team.

The pulled stomach muscle had come at an especially bad time. Steve was frustrated with her even though he knew her routines suffered because of the injury. She was hurt that he was so impatient with her, and at the same time upset with herself. As at so many other times over the past few years, she realized she must place her direction in God's hands. She never prayed to win a meet but to understand God has a purpose and a place for each of us if we are willing to be still and listen. Shannon struggled each day to remain calm and confident that all would be well. We talked frequently about a passage from *Science and Health* in which Mrs. Eddy writes, "You can do whatever it is right for you to do, without harm to yourself." Shannon worked hard at reminding herself, when the temptation to despair threatened, that she did not have to be afraid of a physical problem, of Steve's anger, of embarrassment, or of failure.

As a parent and a judge, I have learned that fear can be a competitor's greatest foe. It can be completely debilitating. A gymnast can have such a great fear of falling that she is bound to fall. Or she might start out relatively confident, fall or wobble, and allow the rest of her routine—or even her performance in the rest of the meet—to disintegrate. Shannon understood the need not to let those fears incapacitate or inhibit her. Her greatest fear is of disappointing her coaches, her family, her friends, her fans, and herself. Shannon has been criticized for crying frequently. She has a high pain tolerance, so her tears are seldom because of physical injury. More frequently they flow because she thinks she has failed to live up to her own high standards.

One of Shannon's favorite Bible verses, which she read daily during this time and which she has used many times since, is from Isaiah: "Fear thou not; for I am with thee: be not dismayed; for I am thy God: I will strengthen thee; yea, I will uphold thee with the right hand of my righteousness." Together we looked at this passage almost nightly and considered its import. Shannon became more relaxed. She would do what was right for her; God would take care of the rest.

In Australia daily workouts were trying. Shannon was still struggling to regain the skills she had let slide while recuperating from the stomach problem and to improve those new skills she had added to her routines. It was obvious that Shannon was not fully prepared for the meet. Bart Conner, working as a television commentator, even told the broadcast audience that things did not look good when Shannon and her

30. Shannon competing in the World's in Australia. Courtesy Felipe Monsivais.

coaches arrived. But Steve does not believe in doing things halfway. He refuses to tolerate excuses, and Shannon doesn't like to make them. So she, Steve, and Peggy set out to get her in top shape by the time the competition began a week later.

The preliminary competition would determine which gymnasts advanced to the all-around and which gymnasts made event finals. Shannon had a good meet but not a great one. Her lack of training showed, especially on bars. She missed a hand when landing on the low bar out of her new one-and-a-half twist on the high bar and took a deduction that placed her ninth overall in the uneven bars competition. Only the top eight made event finals. She performed good but not great routines in the other events and managed to qualify for three event finals.

The day of the all-around competition Shannon began on bars. Steve was glad because he wanted her to get them out of the way early. Shannon put everything she had into the routine to redeem herself from her previous mistake and earned a top score. She advanced to beam where she also did a beautiful routine. After two events she had a slight lead over Livinia Milosovici, who had also done very well on her first two events and was proving to be Shannon's toughest competitor. Dominique Dawes had been having a fantastic meet until she took a fall on vault in an earlier session. Gina Gogean also had a good meet, but her scores were not quite up to Livinia's and Shannon's.

Shannon competed a good floor routine but had a small problem in one of her tumbling passes. She received a reasonable score, 9.75, leaving the door open for Livinia. However, Livinia's bar set was not as difficult as Shannon's, and she scored only a 9.775. The two were still neck and neck going into the last event.

Shannon was performing the new Yurchenko Arabian vault. After her first vault she took a big step on landing. The score was decent, but she would need a very good score on

31. Dina Kotchetkova, Shannon, and Livinia Milosovici on the awards podium at the 1994 World Championships. Courtesy Felipe Monsivais.

her second vault to have any hope of winning. Livinia was on beam. She had a wobble on her side somersault but still earned a big score. Shannon took her second vault, performing more explosively but still taking a step. The score came up 9.812—enough to take the lead from Livinia. Steve literally jumped with joy. Shannon's face was luminous for the first time in a long while. Another dream had come true.

Ron and I were fast asleep when the telephone rang. It was Peggy, yelling into the phone "We won! We won!" It took a minute to absorb what she was saying. We knew how hard the last month had been for Shannon. Back-to-back World Championship titles would have seemed miraculous under wonderful conditions, but with the recent injury and other stressful conditions, Shannon's achievement was even more amazing. It was clear we had more proof of God's care.

Shannon was elated with her all-around title but, as always, was taking event finals very seriously. On the first day of event competition she had only vault. In vault finals the gymnast is required to perform vaults from two different families. The Yurchenko Arabian was still a relatively new vault for Shannon. A few weeks before she pulled the stomach muscle Steve had begun to teach her a completely new vault of his own creation, a Tsukahara Arabian, which involved a forward approach to the springboard and a half-twist off the horse with a laid-out front somersault. Although she had had very little opportunity to practice this second vault, she tried it. She executed a good Yurchenko but fell to her seat on the Tsukahara Arabian. She was unhappy with the fall but glad to have had the opportunity to attempt the new vault. She now knew she could master it.

Shannon was looking forward to beam finals. At World Championships the previous year this event had been trouble in the all-around and a disaster in event finals. She knew she was a good beam worker and wanted a chance to prove her prowess. During warm-ups she wobbled or fell on almost everything. Peggy was exasperated and contemplated scratching her. Shannon had the all-around medal and did not need to embarrass herself again in event finals. Shannon, however, was adamant that she could do this event. She had added a new front somersault mount to her routine but had not performed it in the all-around competition because her routine had contained plenty of difficulty under the rules. Event finals required additional points from high-level skills.

Shannon was second in the rotation, not a good place for top scores. She hit a flawless routine full of difficulty and concluded with the most difficult dismount, a full twisting double back, rated an E. Then she waited and watched, but no one else even came close. Shannon had her redemption and another World Championship gold medal.

In floor competition Shannon stepped out of bounds on a tumbling pass and finished fourth, just out of the medals. But she had now earned five gold medals in World Championships, placing her in an elite group of international gymnasts and making her the most decorated American gymnast. Successfully completing each routine throughout the competition had been an achievement. Bringing home medals was icing.

Steve and Peggy always tried to provide some time to see the country in which Shannon was competing. Following the competition they drove to a park where Shannon and Peggy petted kangaroos and held cuddly koalas. Shannon thoroughly enjoyed Australia. The spectators were enthusiastic and supportive, and the local people were outgoing and friendly. Peggy had such a good time that she returned several times to give gymnastic clinics. She now serves as a coach for the Australian women's gymnastics team and is engaged to marry an Australian.

Shannon's flight home had a brief layover in Los Angeles. Her practitioner, Kittie, her sister, Tessa, and Tessa's new boyfriend, Morgan, greeted her. Shannon had not previously met Morgan and had a full report for us when she arrived home. The report was good. Morgan had passed Shannon's critical evaluation. We were relieved. If Shannon approved, he must be okay.

Shannon had taken homework with her, but she still had tests to make up and reports to turn in. She was glad to be home and happy not to have to work routines for a while. She loved learning new skills and found meets fun, but working routines daily could be tedious.

With no impending meets Shannon was able to travel to Tulsa in May to receive the newly created Henry Iba Award given by the Rotary Club of Tulsa. Shannon was the first female recipient of the award, and she was proud to be so honored by her home state. Although our house is full of certificates, bowls, trophies, and plaques that Shannon has received, she is genuinely grateful each time she is given another one. She is especially happy when people respect her as a person as well as an athlete.

Shannon's break was short-lived. Steve soon accepted another meet invitation for her. Sponsored by Budget Rent-A-Car, it was a dual meet against Romania in Worcester, Massachusetts. At first he hesitated to have her go head-to-head with Livinia Milosovici and Gina Gogean immediately after her triumph in Australia but soon was convinced that the U.S. team needed her. Her Dynamo teammate Mariana Webster had also been invited, and this made training and traveling much more palatable for Shannon.

Since she had not planned on any competition for a while, Shannon had been concentrating on her new skills and had not had much time to prepare for the meet. She started on bars, missed a move, and had to improvise. Although she did not take a fall, her score suffered. She came back strong on beam and hit a nice floor routine and a clean Yurchenko Arabian vault. The Romanians were strong and won the team medal, but both Livinia and Gina had problems on beam. Shannon found herself on the podium again to accept the gold medal for the all-around.

CHAPTER FOURTEEN

Mountains to Climb

T HE 1994 SEASON was starting out almost as well as the fantastic 1993 season had. Even before the meet with Romania Shannon had been slated to compete in the Goodwill Games in late July at the invitation of Ted Turner, founder of the games. In fact, she had gotten up early the day after getting home from World Championships in Australia to fly to New York and film a commercial for the games.

Since Steve and Shannon were already going to the Goodwill Games, and since most of the other coaches were not enthusiastic about having their gymnasts compete just a few weeks before U.S. Championships, Steve had all four members of the U.S. women's gymnastics team for the games. Shannon, another senior elite, and two top juniors would be going.

Competing overseas for a week could be very tiring and stressful with another major competition on the horizon. Steve knew he was taking the chance of wearing his girls out before the most important American meet of the year at which gymnasts' rankings for the year—and thus their training funds and meet invitations—would be determined. But he realized that doing well at the Goodwill Games could enhance a gymnast's reputation internationally.

The four-girl team of Shannon, Soni Meduna, Jennie Thompson, and Mariana Webster, with Mina Kim as the alternate, boarded a plane with Steve, Peggy, and Mark for St. Petersburg. Shannon still had memories of her trip to Moscow but found that Russia had changed in her absence. It was not the clean, safe place she remembered. On our earlier trip I felt comfortable walking alone at night. I once left my briefcase containing our airline tickets and other valuables on a bus and it had been quickly returned. My aunt had a similar experience when she lost a beautiful sweater.

In St. Petersburg Shannon frequently saw what seemed to be gangs. She was surprised to discover litter when she walked along the beach. The Americans had been told beforehand to beware of water contamination. They brought bottled water with them, but found that showering without taking in any water was difficult and shaving their legs was even riskier. Because they were wary of fruits and vegetables washed in local water, they mostly ate canned goods they had brought with them.

Competition had its own difficulties. Midsummer temperatures were very high and there was no air-conditioning. Buses scheduled to pick up the American gymnasts and coaches were often late or sometimes did not show up at all. The vault runway was not regulation length, and problems in the scoring system resulted in long delays.

The crowds, however, were enthusiastic. Shannon was chosen one of the most popular athletes of the games. The team was excited and had prepared thoroughly for the meet, but they did not perform up to Steve's expectations. All the girls, including Shannon, suffered mishaps during team competition. Although Shannon did not fall, her performances on bars and beam were not up to her usual standards. The team ended up in fourth place, just out of the medals, and Shannon was very disappointed. She felt she had let down her team. Steve was disillusioned too but didn't stay down for long. The all-around and event finals were still to come.

Shannon was determined to be more aggressive in the all-around. She had seen how well the Russian gymnasts Dina Kotchetkova and Svetlana Chorkina competed in the team competition and knew the all-around would be a tough battle. She began with a good score on vault after a very good first vault and a slightly weaker second one. Bars went much better than in the team competition, and she scored well again. Beam was terrific, with a perfect landing that earned a great score. On floor she performed a lovely routine with only a step on one tumbling pass.

Meanwhile, Dina Kotchetkova, the floor gold medalist from 1994 Worlds, was turning in exceptional routines. Shannon waited while Dina executed a perfect floor set loaded with difficulty. Her score showed that she had edged out Shannon for the gold all-around medal.

Some reporters quickly proclaimed the demise of Shannon's career. After a year and a half someone had beaten the two-time world champion. Surely she must be in decline. Shannon was surprised at the reaction as no other gymnast had stayed on top so long at the international level. When commentators asked her how it felt to lose, Shannon boldly replied that she did not see winning second place at the Goodwill Games as a loss.

In event finals, Shannon went on to set more records, taking the most medals any American had ever won in the Goodwill Games. Shannon, who seemed to get better with each day's competition, had qualified for all four event finals. She captured the silver on vault and bars and the gold on beam and floor, outdoing Dina and Svetlana in event finals.

One meet still remained—the mixed team competition, in which two American men were paired with two American women to compete as a team against similar pairings from other countries. Shannon hit her routines well, but the team as a whole, consisting of Shannon, Jennie Thompson, Chainey Umphrey, and Scott Keswick, ended up in fourth place. The Americans took a day to do some sightseeing. The team left for home tired but content.

Shannon remembered her sightseeing a few years later when she took a geography course at the University of Oklahoma. While the class watched slides of the beautiful cathedrals and other historic sites, she vividly recalled seeing the real thing up close.

Shannon felt that she had had another successful competition, but some writers and commentators continued to predict her decline. Shannon usually dismissed their predictions, but sometimes she became frustrated. Ron and I agonized inside, feeling she had been treated unfairly, and insisted to Shannon that she was as good as ever. She was an awesome gymnast. We knew it, and we wanted her to remember it. We asked her to name anyone else who hadn't finished in less than second place in any meet, U.S. or international, in a year and a half. What she knew inside about her God-given talent was true. The media saying otherwise could not change the truth. She trooped back to the gym every day with this knowledge in mind.

Shannon was relieved to be back in the United States, with "real" food and good water, and she didn't hesitate to say so. In more than one interview she acknowledged the benefits of living in the United States.

The days of competition had taken their toll on the girls, especially those who had competed in several days' events. Jennie and Mariana had not had Shannon's rigorous schedule, but they had worked out daily preparing vigorously for the competitions for which they had qualified. Mariana's knee was bothering her, and Jennie's ankle was hurting.

Shannon had competed in four full meets within a week without the luxuries of American gymnastics, such as crash mats. While her back had improved tremendously and her stomach was fine, she now had severe shin splints and found walking painful and landings on dismounts excruciating. She had complained since she arrived home from St. Petersburg that her legs felt like Jell-O. Steve cut back on her vaulting and floor tumbling, but he could only ease up so much. Championships were so close.

By now Shannon was very used to working with some pain. Emotionally and spiritually she was getting much stronger. She never considered giving up or giving in. Championships were approaching. She planned to be there and be ready.

At National Championships Shannon's routines were becoming more finely tuned, and her compulsories continued to improve. At the end of the first round of competition she was in first place. However, her competitors had spent the last year working hard on compulsories too and had narrowed the gap. Dominique Dawes was breathing down her neck.

Shannon's only problem came on beam. After a routine executed with precision, she leaned too far forward and put her hands down for an instant on her dismount, a mistake that counted as a fall. She pulled her hands up quickly, as though this error could not possibly have happened.

Shannon attributed the slip to scaling back on practicing dismounts to protect her legs. Steve thought there might be another cause. He looked up into the stands and spotted a familiar and unsettling face—someone who had first approached Shannon on her tour following the 1992 Olympics when she was fifteen. In Las Vegas this young man had followed her up to her hotel room. At first Shannon, being naive, had paid little attention to him, but as she reached her door and he was almost on top of her, reaching into his jacket, she was terrified. He pulled out a stuffed fox and handed it to her with a shy comment that she was a foxy lady.

Although he left quietly, the incident made Shannon realize for the first time that she needed to be more observant and more cautious. The uncomfortable feeling stayed with her for a long time. Later the same man sent her long letters, often writing fervently about religion and criticizing the Christian Science faith. He frequently sent her other stuffed foxes. Shannon always sent him a card thanking him for the stuffed animals and gently expressing her right to believe as she chose. After a while, though, his letters became more aggressive. Reporters who learned of him characterized him as a stalker.

Just before National Championships Shannon had come out of the athletes' rest room and found him standing near the door. She spotted him immediately because he had recently unnerved her by showing up to watch one of her workouts at the gym and appearing at a private autograph session in Oklahoma City. Steve's extreme concern made Shannon even more jittery.

Now, at the meet, the young man was sitting in one of the first rows right in front of the beam. Steve was angry and felt his presence contributed to Shannon's lack of concentration on her beam dismount. Steve went up into the stands to confront the man, who promptly moved farther back.

Later that evening the man called Steve to ask whether he could attend event finals. Steve said it might be best if he stayed away. We never found out whether he heeded Steve's advice. Shannon didn't blame her performance on his presence. She later wrote to the man to express her regrets over the incident. Shannon did not publicly reveal her concerns about the man until late 1995 when the issue of security came up at a coaches' meeting.

Whatever the cause, Steve was not going to indulge any lack of focus. He wanted Shannon back on track. She had two events left, and he wanted her to place as high as possible. She rose to the occasion. Adhering to her longtime philosophy, she forgot about what she couldn't change and concentrated on that over which she still had control—floor. She hit a great routine for a great score. Dominique was also hitting outstanding routines and passed Shannon for the lead.

Shannon then moved to vault where she hit two exceptionally good vaults and earned another terrific score. But Dominique ended up with a slightly higher score. Once again some commentators characterized Shannon's placement as a "loss," but after a snafu on beam she felt lucky to be holding a silver medal. And even with the fall she had qualified for all four apparatus finals.

If the media had seemed ready to end her career after the Goodwill Games, they were more eager to predict her downfall now.

Shannon was by no means pleased about not placing first in the all-around. She knew that without the fall on her dismount she would have walked away with another U.S. Championship title. She was determined to prove she still had the ability to be the best.

In event finals Shannon hit two great vaults, but with a hop on the landing of her new Tsukahara Arabian. She finished a close second to Dominique Dawes again. On bars Shannon hit a superb routine full of difficulty, including four release moves and a double layout dismount, but the judges awarded Dominique, who followed her, a slightly higher score and Shannon received her third silver of the meet. Rather than become frustrated, Shannon simply became more determined. She hit an excellent beam routine with only a slight mistake. Again Dominique followed Shannon. And again, although television announcers said it appeared to them that Shannon had the better routine and predicted she would take the gold, she came in second to Dominique.

Shannon was still confident. She knew she was hitting fantastic routines. She had an exceptional performance on floor. Dominique hit a good floor routine but clearly had a few mistakes. The announcers pointed this out and said that Shannon would finally get her gold—but it was not to be. Again the judges awarded Dominique the gold and Shannon the silver. Television commentator Tim Dagget stated on the air that he disagreed with the call.

Media reports after the meet were harsher on Shannon than ever. While reporters raved about Dominique Dawes's historic achievement, capturing the all-around and all four event finals, Shannon was not ashamed. Winning the silver in all five of these events was very good and she knew it. She did not mention in interviews that she had just come off another rigorous meet season, including the very recent and tiring Goodwill Games. She did not make any excuses.

We were immensely proud of Shannon's sportsmanship, discipline, dedication, and fortitude. And we still thought she was the most talented gymnast ever. We worried a little that she might be disheartened or depressed and sought to console her. We quickly realized that she needed no consolation. When I picked her up at the airport, hugged her, and told her I thought she deserved the gold on more than one event in apparatus finals, she nonchalantly replied, "It doesn't really matter. I see next year's Championship meet as more important since it will be a lot closer to Olympic Trials. Dominique can have this meet. I intend to have it next year."

With that the discussion was over and we could move on to more exciting things like vacation. We had agreed Colorado would be nice this year. Tessa was in California where she had a summer job at Caltech and would not be able to go on vacation with us, which was disappointing, but we were all still looking forward to the trip. We planned to see the sights around Colorado Springs and to climb Pikes Peak. I had been running about two miles three times a week for the last six weeks to get in shape for the big climb.

As we planned to be in Colorado Springs only four days, we jumped right into our activities. We arrived in the evening and rented bicycles the next morning to ride through the mountains all day. By the time we got back, at about 8:00 P.M., it was dark and raining. We had a great time anyway.

The following day we had scheduled our hike up Pikes Peak, which rose 14,000 feet. It sounded like a piece of cake to us. We were a little concerned about Shannon's legs because of the shin splints, but walking didn't bother her too much when she wore her trusty high-top Reeboks. Troy worked out hard at Tae Kwan Do three times a week and also ran with me occasionally, so he was not worried either. Ron had opted not to hike but to take the car to the top to drive us back down. It all sounded so good.

We started our ascent, waving vigorously to Ron who smiled indulgently and watched us go. The scenery was breathtaking, and we stopped frequently to take pictures. We each had a backpack in which we had a couple of bottles of water and some food snacks, a light jacket, Kleenex, and other miscellaneous items. For a while we felt invigorated. It was crisp outdoors but not at all cold. Shannon's legs were bothering her a little more than she had anticipated, but she was still enthusiastic. After what seemed like a long time, we began seeing signs noting how far it was to the halfway mark. Time passed. The halfway mark didn't seem to be getting much closer. Shannon, Troy, and I were beginning to tire. When we finally arrived at the campsite that marked the halfway point, I wondered whether I could make it to the top. We rested for about half an hour (I would have preferred longer, but Shannon and Troy had quickly recovered and were eager to move on). It was now much cooler. We donned our jackets and headed out. Once we got going again, I felt somewhat rejuvenated and determined I could certainly do this.

You can't walk straight up Pikes Peak, so you do a lot of zigzagging, making the total climb up the 14,000-foot mountain some thirteen miles. By three miles from the top I was really dragging. Shannon and Troy were now having to stop and wait for me to catch up. By two miles from the top I started to wonder how they rescued people off the mountain. Troy was now beginning to suffer too, becoming quite nauseated. Shannon was getting impatient. She had long ago gotten her second wind and was eager to get to the top and take a look around the souvenir shop. I was contemplating sending her for help when we came to a sign that told about a woman who had climbed Pikes Peak a number of times, most recently when she was eighty years old! I determined to make it to the top on my own if I had to crawl. I did, however, give Shannon permission to go on ahead. By now we had taken a few hours longer than I had expected, and Ron would be wondering what in the world had happened to us. Shannon bounced out of sight. Troy and I struggled miserably on. At about a quarter of a mile to go, I realized we had spent more time traversing the last two miles than it took us to climb the first six to the campsite. With despair looming, Ron appeared. He had spotted us with the binoculars and descended to us. He took our backpacks and kept telling us how close the end was. We continued to place one foot in front of the other until we crested the top of the peak and spotted the most beautiful sight—the restaurant and souvenir shop. Shannon had already had a snack, done her shopping, and been out numerous times to look for us with binoculars.

I collapsed at one of the tables inside. Before long Ron went out and heated up the car. I dragged myself to it and had never felt so good as when I curled up in the warm car. In no time I was asleep and we were at the bottom of the mountain driving up to our hotel. Troy and Shannon wanted to see a movie, so we decided to get food, bring it to our room, and watch a movie in the room while we ate. I took a few bites, said goodnight, and was out cold until the next morning. Shannon and Troy said the movie was great. I'm sure it was.

We had a big day of sightseeing planned following our hike. We were also going to take a horseback ride through the Garden of the Gods. I was almost afraid to step out of bed the next morning. Every inch of my body had ached the night before, especially my legs, but by the next morning I felt terrific. Soon Troy and I were discussing what we would do differently the next time we climbed Pikes Peak.

CHAPTER FIFTEEN

Competition Controversy

SHANNON SURVIVED Pikes Peak quite well, but she was still tired physically and mentally. Steve promised her a break from competition and she was glad to get it, even though she would be missing team World Championships. She needed to let the shin splints heal. According to the rules, since she was injured, she could miss World Trials. Her scores from the U.S. Championships were entered into the computer after Trials, and she still qualified in second place to be on the World Championship team.

Steve had told U.S. gymnastic officials even before U.S. Championships, however, that Shannon would not be going to Worlds. One person high in the gymnastics hierarchy had warned Ron that the announcement might affect Shannon's scores at Nationals. At the time Ron found this hard to believe, but later he wondered.

About two weeks before the American team was to leave for Worlds, Jackie Fie, the highest-ranked American judge and a very renowned judge internationally, contacted Steve to discuss Shannon's possible participation on this team. Steve explained that even if he wanted her to go, she wouldn't be the best person for the team since she had not been training optional routines since Nationals (about two months) and had not been training dismounts and other skills that were hard on her legs. Even if he felt that she was physically able to start training hard again, which he did not, she could not be ready in time. Jackie offered a compromise. Could Shannon compete in compulsories only? The team could use her scores. Preliminary competition in both compulsories and optionals would determine whether the team made it to the next round. After the first round the team would compete only in optionals, in which the Americans felt stronger. Steve hesitated but said he would talk with Shannon and with us.

The next evening we all sat down in Steve's office to make a decision. In the meantime Jackie Fie had also called our house and talked with Ron, who would make no commitment. Jackie made it clear that she thought it was very important that Shannon be a part of this team. Steve was concerned. Shannon had always been a team player; he did not want it said that she let the team down, nor did he want to displease U.S. gymnastics officials. But he also didn't want to throw Shannon into a situation for which she was unprepared. That would benefit neither Shannon nor the team. Furthermore, he had made Shannon a promise and felt guilty about breaking it. He wanted her healed so that she could be fully prepared for the next meet season.

We fully understood the dilemma. In the end we all agreed the best we could do was lay out everything for Shannon and let her decide. She took a few minutes to evaluate the situation and then told Steve she would try to get ready for the compulsory competition. Steve contacted USA Gymnastics the next day to tell them that Shannon would join the team but would compete only in compulsories. Federation officials expressed delight. Steve also explained that Shannon was now a senior in high school and needed more than ever to be in school as much as possible and that she needed to continue therapy on her shin splints. He told them he and Shannon would probably come home after compulsories, although Peggy could stay on to assist the team.

Steve told us that there was the remote possibility that if the team was desperate, he might ask Shannon to do a beam routine in optional competition. We understood but thought the scenario was unlikely. The United States was sending a very strong team: Shannon, two former Olympians, Kerri Strug and Dominique Dawes, and two girls who had been in World Championships, Amanda Borden and Larissa Fontaine. There were also two relative newcomers: Amy Chow, who was sixteen and had been a senior for a while, and Jaycie Phelps, who was fifteen.

Shannon worked hard for the next two weeks. Her compulsory routines came around quickly, but just before she left, she pulled an Achilles tendon. Steve was disturbed about this new injury. He had declined the meet to get her body healed, succumbed to a request to enter it, and now, getting ready for it, she had incurred another problem. As for Shannon, when fear crept in, she read her note cards with inspirational messages and her Sunday School lesson. There were days when it seemed as though she would never be physically sound again. She could not get over one injury before another cropped up. Critics speculated that her age was catching up with her, but Shannon would not accept that. She continued to remember the teaching from *Science and Health* that "trials are proofs of God's care"—not that God sends trials to us, but that when we do experience problems in our lives, we can always turn to God for protection and solution. Adversity can help us to grow stronger. As she overcame each difficulty, Shannon was gaining strength and confidence.

The American team began the compulsory session of the meet on beam. Shannon's almost flawless routine earned the high score of the day. She did a good vault and a beautiful floor set. The United States was struggling on bars, and, as the strongest American in the event traditionally, Shannon was last. Just before she began Steve reminded her not to put her feet on the bar too soon before the dismount. Some gymnasts put their feet on the bar when they are still almost over the top of the bar, curtailing the height of their dismounts. In response to his warning, Shannon delayed too long and her feet slipped off the bar. She never missed a beat, kipping right back up and repeating the action so that she could complete the dismount. She hit a beautiful dismount, solidly landed, and ended up with a respectable score, 9.525. She was embarrassed at her mistake and a little surprised that she still scored so high. Steve, however, clearly understood the score. The routine had been almost flawless, except for the foot slip. Since Shannon had continued with the routine, the most the judges could take off for this error was 0.3 for an extra swing and a little in execution for the mishap. A 9.5 seemed logical to Steve and to me. Being a judge, I knew exactly how and why the judges had arrived at this score. So I was dismayed and surprised when Shannon called home that evening and described the controversy that ensued.

As the Americans left the arena after the meet, some in the crowd booed them. Shannon was confused. She wasn't sure if they were booing her; if they were, she didn't understand why. She asked me whether it was considered a fall for her feet to miss the bar. I assured her it wasn't. There was only one American judge on the panel; if she had scored Shannon's performance too high, her score would have been tossed out, so Shannon's score was the average of the other judges. I explained how this worked to Shannon and why the judges must have taken off only 0.3 instead of 0.5. Shannon felt better. We tried to look at the situation objectively and understand the feelings of the Europeans in the stands who perhaps did not understand how the scoring worked. Shannon harbored no ill feelings for the spectators. Even she had not really understood her score.

Steve was dismayed at the hubbub and disturbed that U.S.

officials made what seemed to be only a half-hearted attempt to explain and justify her score. He had already planned that he and Shannon would leave shortly after the compulsory meet. Shannon was limping more than ever, and after the fuss over Shannon's bar score and what he perceived as lack of support from USA Gymnastics, he saw no need to stay any longer. Steve's big mistake, we all realized too late, was slipping away quickly and quietly. If he had let reporters know his plans, the innuendos that followed would have been avoided.

As it was, reporters didn't know they had left until they were long gone. When reporters caught up with them in Chicago, Shannon had no idea there was a problem. She did not realize she and Steve had left without telling anyone of their immediate plans and did not understand why anyone would mind. She, after all, had only been following her coach's instructions. By the time Shannon arrived in Oklahoma City, she knew something was up but was too tired to worry about it. We were happy to have her home, and although we knew some strange things were going on, we still had little knowledge of what had transpired.

In the weeks that followed some sports writers and television reporters seemed to delight in raking Shannon over the coals. Not only had her missed foot on the high bar given them more fuel to support their theory that she was over the hill and out the door, but her decision to leave led them to believe that she didn't care about her team. No one bothered to note that if she hadn't cared about the team or USA Gymnastics she would not have gone to Worlds at all but would have stayed home, nursed her injury, and avoided the ensuing controversy. Even with the mistake on bars, she was the top scorer for the American team and finished fourth in the world in compulsories.

Furthermore, criticism of Shannon, a seventeen-year-old gymnast, seemed unfair as Steve, the coach, made the decision to leave. Steve had made it clear to officials that she was going to Germany only to compete in compulsory routines. It would have been rude and unsportsmanlike for her to usurp the position of another team member so that she could perform what would likely be inferior optional routines. The gymnast who was prepared deserved to compete.

As time passed and the criticism continued, Ron and I decided we needed to come to Shannon's defense. We wrote a letter to Kathy Scanlan, president of USA Gymnastics, laying out the situation and requesting a show of support from the organization. At their behest Shannon had set aside her plans, worked with injuries, and competed for her country. In return she was ridiculed.

Kathy responded that she understood our feelings, but little was done to support Shannon's position. We had long been teaching Shannon and our other children to work at expressing love for everyone, even those who seemed to exhibit the opposite feelings. We needed to take our own advice. So we put the issue to rest and hoped the critics would do the same.

Shannon, as usual, took things in stride. We had asked her if she minded that we wrote to Kathy Scanlan, and we insisted she review the letter before we mailed it. She was pleased that we wanted to go to bat for her and glad the letter was relatively subdued. (We had toned down our first draft, which had been written in the heat of frustration.)

The rest of the year was quiet, although we did receive some upsetting news. The bank for which I was working and which had been so supportive of Shannon and our family as we worked to get to the Olympics was bought by another bank. My job and those of my staff were in jeopardy. Many of the functions we performed would be handled out of the main office of the new bank, located in another state.

Our family had been through pressures before, however, and we had endured and grown in our faith in God and each other. After the initial shock we regrouped and determined to look at this new experience as a window of opportunity, a time to turn to God for continued guidance.

Shannon was wonderfully supportive during this time. We teach our children, and in turn, they teach us. Her inner peace and joy made it much easier to go to work each day and express the same confidence to my fellow employees who also had fears to overcome. By late the following spring I learned that five of my six employees and I had jobs with the new bank. The sixth employee was already planning to retire.

After returning from Germany Shannon again had to take it easy in workouts while her Achilles tendon healed. With an easier gym schedule she was able to accept a few more appearance requests and to enjoy Christmas preparations. Tessa arrived home from Caltech with her boyfriend, Morgan (Mo), in tow. Troy took an instant liking to Mo, as did the rest of us. He accompanied us on our trip to San Antonio. The car would have been a bit too crowded with the addition of another body, except for Steve's master plan. He had long ago given up trying to talk us out of pulling Shannon out of gym for vacation, but her tendon was healed and her shin splints were improving. He needed her on the Pan-American Games team, and she was again invited to the American Cup, where she had competed only in vault in 1994. This meet and then Trials for the Pan-American Games were in February—not much time to get ready.

Steve proposed that Shannon work out in the gym on the morning we left for San Antonio, then catch a plane to arrive about the same time we did. When we left San Antonio we would send her off on a plane to Oklahoma City, he would pick her up to work out, and she would be finished about the time we made it home. I was hesitant, but the idea appealed to Shannon. Going directly from a vacation trip to the gym would be hard on her, but she agreed with Steve that she needed to make sure she was ready for the upcoming season. With those arrangements made we enjoyed a great holiday season and Shannon had no guilt about her workouts.

CHAPTER SIXTEEN

Argentina Adventure

I N JANUARY TRAINING got really serious. Shannon was scheduled to do an exhibition in front of a hometown crowd in the Dynamo Classic at the end of the month. She performed exciting routines and initiated a few new skills. This exhibition was a good warm-up for the Peachtree Classic coming up very soon.

As Shannon worked to get into competitive shape, she had some thrilling news. She had won the coveted Dial Award, an honor bestowed by the Dial Corporation each year on an outstanding female and male senior in high school. The award is based on athletics, academics, and citizenship. Shannon was immensely proud to be given this great honor and took time out to fly to Washington, D.C., to receive the award.

In early February Shannon and her teammates went to Atlanta for the Peachtree. This was always a big and exciting meet, packed with good competitors. It would serve as excellent practice for the upcoming American Classic. Shannon easily captured the all-around. Steve Hummer of the *Atlanta Journal-Constitution* described the crowd's reaction: "Every

32. Shannon accepting the 1994 Dial Award for National High School Athlete of the Year.

time Shannon Miller appeared, the youthful squeals were the kind usually only conferred upon recording artists and some stars of the Fox network. . . . She was bun and hair ribbons above the rest Saturday. She finished a full six-tenths of a point ahead of her nearest rival, the gymnastic equivalent of a super bowl spread."

Next on Shannon's busy schedule was the American Classic. Steve was determined that Shannon would be on the Pan-American Games team, and this was the qualifying meet. Many of the talented juniors were now eligible to move up to the senior ranks. Furthermore, the rules specified that the Pan-American Games team would be composed of both true seniors (age fifteen and over) and some juniors (under fifteen). This did not leave a lot of room for the senior competitors. Shannon would have to place at the very top to earn a spot on the team. Steve, however, understood the real significance of this meet: for the first time Shannon would be competing against the upcoming juniors who would later be vying with her for a spot on the Olympic team. They were fresh, talented, energetic, enthusiastic, and just as determined as Shannon.

The American Classic was hard-fought. Dominique Dawes and Kerri Strug did not compete, but all the other seniors including Amanda Borden, Amy Chow, and Jaycie Phelps were there. Among the most notable juniors were Dominique Moceanu, Kristy Powell, Doni Thompson, Katie Teft, and Mary Beth Arnold. They were an impressive field. Jennie Thompson, also an outstanding junior, was still out as a result of an ankle injury. Steve pressed Shannon hard to concentrate and stay focused.

Compulsories went very well. Shannon was off to a good start, but Dominique Moceanu and Amanda Borden were close on her heels. In optionals Shannon was adding back her third layout on beam and some additional difficulty on floor. She hit all her routines with exceptional execution and grace and surprised herself by easily winning the all-around. Dominique and Amanda tied for second.

Shannon had been a little worried about this meet. Her shin splints had become aggravated when she began to work out hard again in January, and she hadn't competed optional routines with full difficulty since August. In neither the Dynamo Classic nor the Peachtree had she needed to put in all her difficult moves. She also wondered how the juniors would handle things. She had watched them more than once and knew how good they were. She was relieved and happy to have this meet under her belt.

In no time, however, she had the American Cup. She would not come home from this meet but would go directly to Argentina for the Pan-American Games. She would be away from home for three weeks.

After the glow of winning the American Classic began to wear off, Shannon gave in to a few feelings of depression. One night, fighting tears, she told me she wished she was not going to the American Cup. Steve had told her if she did well at the Classic and qualified for the Pan-American Games, he would decline the American Cup to give her a brief respite before Argentina. Katie Teft had decided on the same course of action. It was hard on body and mind to stay continually in a competition mode. Steve, however, recognized how well Shannon had competed at the Classic and was positive she could win the American Cup. After having to withdraw from all events but vault the previous year, he was hungry for the win. So they were now scheduled for this meet.

The media continued to keep up the pressure. NBC sent reporters and a camera crew to gather background information for the American Cup; however, the majority of the questions in the interview dealt with Shannon's exit from Germany the previous October. Shannon handled the grilling admirably. When asked if she felt guilty about leaving because she was the leader of the team, the oldest and most experienced gymnast, Shannon corrected them. Actually Dominique Dawes was the oldest, and both Kerri and Dominique had been in the Olympics and at World Championships; Amanda and Larissa had World Championship experience. The reporter suggested that Shannon should have felt obligated to give the other girls guidance. With surprise in her voice, she replied politely that coaches would not appreciate her taking over their roles and giving their gymnasts advice. She told the interviewer that the team and the coaches had all known she was coming only to compete in compulsories and that she and Steve would probably leave immediately afterward.

Ron and I had been in the kitchen but could hear most of the interview. We wanted to cheer out loud but decided not to embarrass Shannon. Her answers had been truthful and direct, cutting right to the crux of the matter.

Things seemed to be piling up on Shannon. Her legs were really hurting after the two days of competition at the Classic, she was a senior in high school and felt pressed to keep up in her classes, Steve and Peggy had been fighting a lot lately, and the thought of being away from home for three weeks already made her lonely. I knew we couldn't send her off in this emotional state, so I sat down with her on her bed so we could talk things through.

We decided to get all of the fears out in the open so we could expose them and boot them out with God's help one by one. We would talk to her teachers and get as much of her homework as we could to take with her. Spring break would be coming up soon after she got back from Argentina, and that would give her an additional opportunity to get caught up. She had to see Steve and Peggy in the correct light, as reflections of God, not silly squabbling humans. Each time she was tempted to be exasperated with one of them, she had to think of at least one good quality they exhibited daily. When you're thinking good things about people, the bad seems to fade away. She should give Kittie a call and ask her to work for her regarding the pain in her legs. Last was loneliness. She could never be lonely as long as God was with her.

Shannon was feeling much better but said it certainly would be nice if I could go to this meet. I wanted to go, not just to see my daughter compete, but to be there to support her, whether helping with homework or just talking to her when she was feeling down. She was leaving for the American Cup in less than a week and then a few days later for Argentina. We didn't have the money in our family budget for me to go, I didn't know whether I could get off work, and I didn't know whether I could get airline tickets and accommodations and transportation while there. But I told Shannon I would see what could be done. We agreed that if it was right for me to be with her, then things would work out; if not, she would have the strength she needed to handle these events without me.

Kathy Kelley at USA Gymnastics was eager to help when I called her office the next morning. She had traveled with the girls enough to know that having Mom around was sometimes a big morale booster. She immediately set about finding me an airline ticket and a place to stay. She ended up getting me on a relatively inexpensive USOC flight directly to the site of the competition in Mar del Plata and arranging for me to stay in a suite with some USA Gymnastic officials. We would have to figure out ground transportation when I got there. My boss agreed to some time off.

I wouldn't make it in time for the compulsory competition. That didn't bother Shannon. Knowing I would be there for team optionals, the all-around, and event finals was good enough for her. I could bring more homework with me too. Shannon offered to help with expenses as I was doing this for her. We decided to share the cost.

Life was in fast motion. Ron was going to the American Cup in Seattle, but because he couldn't get off work until later in the week, he would not be there in time to watch the preliminary competition. He would make it for finals. Shannon left for Seattle feeling much more enthusiastic. We were already asleep when the telephone rang. It was Shannon, sounding as though she was on the verge of tears. I asked if everything was all right.

"No," she replied.

I was wide awake now, worried something had happened to her. "What's wrong?" I asked.

"I didn't make finals."

I was so relieved that I wanted to laugh, but I had a feeling Shannon didn't see this as a laughing matter. "Do you want to tell me what happened?" I asked.

She poured out her sad story. Steve had begun working her on a full twisting Yurchenko again to teach her a one-and-a-half twisting Yurchenko. She had this vault down pretty good, but it was not spectacular and its start value was only 9.8, so her vault score had not been tremendous. Bars had gone fine. Disaster had struck on beam. She had fallen on her back handspring quarter turn. She had rebounded to do a good floor routine, but in the all-around Amanda Borden and

Kristy Powell had outscored her. She ended up fourth overall and third for the Americans, but as we well knew only the top two Americans advance to finals. She was calling in the middle of the night because Peggy knew Ron was scheduled to fly out the next morning to watch the finals. Peggy felt Shannon should let him know right away that there was no need for him to come.

That was crazy, I told Shannon. Of course her dad would still want to come. Now he would have some company in the stands. Maybe they would even get to do a little sightseeing before she had to leave for Argentina. Besides, since Ron wouldn't see her for several weeks, he wanted this opportunity before she left. When I handed the telephone to Ron and he again assured her nothing could keep him away, Shannon was relieved.

The Classic had boosted Shannon's competitive morale. Now it had plummeted again. She knew she needed to get her thinking straightened out. Having Ron there for a couple of days would help. Now I was really glad things had worked out for me to go to Argentina.

Mar del Plata was beautiful. While I waited in line to check into the hotel, I casually picked up a paper and immediately saw my daughter's picture in it. I couldn't read Spanish, but there was a list of names and scores and it appeared to me that Shannon had placed first in the compulsory competition held the day before. This was a pleasant way to arrive!

I located my assigned quarters in the USA Gymnastics suite and then set about trying to figure out how to get out to the athletes' village and the competition site. The competition arena was only about a mile from the village, but the village was a half-hour drive from my hotel. I learned that a USOC van would be leaving in the morning to make a delivery at the village, and there would be room for me if I wanted to come. I did. I arrived at the designated spot the next morning and was soon on my way to see Shannon. The team optional meet was that night, so I would need to stay at the village until that evening, find a ride (or walk) to the meet, and then find a way back to the hotel. I knew the U.S. officials and other parents would be coming to the meet and figured I'd locate a way to get back.

I was surprised to discover the athletes' village was quite a distance from town, completely off by itself. The competition arena was in the middle of a large field with nothing else nearby. When we arrived at the village I found that I could not go in because I did not have the proper credentials. A village official decided I could wait in an outer room until Shannon returned from her workout. I knew I would probably be on my own a lot, so I decided this was a good time to read *Science and Health* again. About forty-five minutes later Steve, Shannon, and the rest of the team came trooping through.

Shannon was elated to see me and got permission for me to come up to her room for a short time. With four girls to a room, luggage and clothes were everywhere. How they knew what belonged to each, I'll never know, but they seemed to have everything worked out just fine.

In the cafeteria at lunch Shannon filled me in on what had taken place before my arrival. The arena where the girls worked out each day and would be competing in had flooded the first few days because of heavy rains. The lights went out once. Steve had finally decided they had better give up trying to work out that day. The girls had to be sure to wear shoes unless they were on the equipment, because of all the debris on the floor left over from the flood. After lunch Shannon headed down the hallway, with me trailing after her, for therapy on her legs. After therapy she had to take a nap and get ready for the meet that evening. I gave her a kiss and the schoolwork I'd brought and told her I'd try to see her after the meet.

I had the entire afternoon left. There was no way to get back to Mar del Plata, so I decided I'd take a walk along the beach and then find a place to read. The beach was deserted—beautiful and serene with a gentle breeze. I spent a pleasant afternoon reading and walking. As I drifted along the beach picking up seashells, a security officer approached me and indicated in Spanish that he wanted to see my village credentials. I quickly realized that I didn't have anything other than what the USOC had given me to show I was an American, but I confidently (with a big smile) pulled out my USOC badge and showed it to him. He stared at it for a while a little confused and finally smiled, handed it back to me, and left. I breathed a sigh of relief. I had nowhere else to go until that evening.

As time for the meet drew near I began my walk to the arena. When I was about halfway there a van pulled over. The door opened and the driver indicated I should get in. It looked much like the USOC van I had ridden in so I assumed this was another USOC van; however, as soon as I got in, I realized my mistake. The van was full of male gymnasts in warm-up suits on their way to watch the women's meet. I was not sure what country they were from, since I couldn't understand them and they couldn't understand me. I pulled out an autographed postcard of Shannon and tried to explain I was her mother. They patted me on the back and indicated that they each needed a card. Not hiding my pride, I quickly gave each a postcard and they thanked me profusely.

When I got out of the van I was overwhelmed to see how long the line for admission was, and I was almost an hour early. After standing in the heat (there was no longer an ocean breeze) for half an hour, I grew concerned. The line had not moved at all. A man came down the line making some sort of announcement that made everyone really angry. People seemed to be preparing to leave.

I took out another postcard of Shannon and tried to explain to the man behind me that I was her mother and needed to get into the meet. He smiled at me, picked up my backpack and handed it to his wife, and grabbed my hand. We practically ran to the front of the line. He found an official and talked rapidly to him, taking the postcard from me and showing it to him. This gentleman then passed me off to someone else while the first man ran back to get my backpack. I was ushered inside where I was introduced to a gentleman who spoke English. He walked me completely around the packed arena to where other American parents were sitting and found me a seat. I was so relieved. I later learned they had oversold the event and were not able to let everyone inside. I ended up sitting next to Kristy Powell's mother and grandmother with Doni Thompson's parents behind me. We exchanged stories about how we each had finally made it to the arena. I was glad I had brought a lot of postcards. Everyone who helped me get in came sheepishly by to ask for one or more.

Shannon had a good meet. But after completing a phenomenal beam routine, she sat down on her dismount. I hoped this would not be a repeat of the American Cup. She was a resilient child, but to miss qualifying for finals again so soon might be quite a blow.

After the meet I tried to work my way through the crowd to see Shannon or Steve. I wanted to know how she was handling things. I got to Steve first. He was not happy. I soon found out that he was not worried about whether she had made the finals but only about whether she had finished first in the meet. He had no doubt she was still the number one American, and the top three from each country qualified for the all-around. He was worried about her winning the all-around while I was just hoping she would get the chance to compete in it.

As it turned out Shannon was in first place after the team competition. I got to see her briefly after she finished her media interviews and arranged to visit her the next day since there were no meets. She was also relieved she had qualified for the all-around, but being in first place after the team competition was no consolation to her bruised ego. She had fallen again, and on beam, her favorite event. She knew Peggy was especially disappointed. We decided this meet was history and that the all-around would be another great opportunity to express her God-given talents. I knew she would come back tough.

In the meantime she could enjoy wearing the team gold. This American team composed of juniors as well as seniors had not just won the gold but had set a new team record, winning by a landslide. Amanda Borden, Amy Chow, Kristy Powell, Doni Thompson, Katie Teft, Mary Beth Arnold, and Shannon composed this awesome team.

Shannon started on beam in the all-around competition. She had just finished beam warm-ups, and I knew she was eager to show the crowd she could master this event. When she fell on the mount, a front somersault, my heart dropped. I wondered whether she would fall apart or remember God was with her and allow Him to guide her. She needed my prayers, and I prayed not only for Shannon but for myself as well. I had to remember that she was in God's capable hands. I had read a few hours earlier in *Science and Health* that "Divine Love has met and always will meet every human need." This great love would meet Shannon's needs, whatever they were right now. Steve remained very calm. I saw him speak briefly to her, and the cloud that had formed on her face melted away. Kristy Powell's mother was also a wonderful source of inspiration. I knew she also prayed for Kristy during meets and drew strength from her faith. We had discussed some of these things briefly during the team meet. Now she encouraged me and I truly appreciated her understanding.

One of Shannon's note cards says to hold your thought to the enduring, the good, and the true and you will bring these into your experience. Shannon did exactly that. She didn't think God had abandoned her; she just needed to let Him back in. The rest of her routines were outstanding and reflected what I knew was the real Shannon. She smiled as she performed, and it was clear she was feeling good about herself.

When the last routine was completed and the scores tabulated Shannon had pulled this one out of the hat. She accomplished what Steve wanted so much—she led the team to a gold medal and won the all-around. She missed qualifying for beam finals but would be competing on all the other pieces of equipment. Peggy was a little disappointed, but Steve was thrilled.

Shannon was happy but not elated. She didn't like disappointing Peggy, and she never liked to fall. Three falls in a row on optional beam was not something to be joyous about. She was good on beam. She always did so well in workouts. She wondered why she had so much trouble putting it together in a meet. I reminded her how much focus and inner calmness she must have had to climb back up on the beam after falling and give an almost perfect performance. With a fall, she had still earned a 9.4. If she was going to think about the past, she needed to remember the positive, not just the negative. Her strong comeback after the fall was a clear indication that she was a determined competitor.

The all-around had pumped her up for event finals. She had to do two different vaults. She had started working on a one-and-a-half twisting Yurchenko, but it was not yet ready. She would have to throw the full twist, which was only a 9.8 vault. A front somersault was only a 9.7 vault, and she hadn't worked on it for a long time. Steve decided to dredge up the Tsukahara Arabian. She hadn't trained this vault since the previous August when she competed it in vault finals at Championships. Because of the shin splints and the pulled Achilles tendon she had hardly vaulted all fall. When she had started vaulting again, Steve wanted to work a one-and-a-half twist, but to do this she had to first regain the full twist. She tried a few Tsuk Arabians in her workout the day before event finals and didn't make any. Steve contemplated pulling her out of vault finals, but there wasn't anything critical on the line this time. If she fell, they would chalk it up to a learning experience.

Just before Shannon's turn Steve and Peggy patted her on the back and told her to just give it her best try. She hit both vaults exceptionally well, and her best try earned her a silver medal. Steve was jumping up and down. With a vault that came from a maximum 9.8 and another vault she had not tried in seven months, she was walking away with a medal.

Shannon turned in a great bar set and won gold. On floor her routine was smooth, but several other girls had earned high scores. When the scores were posted Shannon had another gold.

The Pan-American Games experience was almost everything Steve had hoped it would be. Shannon made a few mistakes, but he was sure she would be a force at U.S. Championships. Shannon had also set more records, including the most Pan-American gold of any American gymnast in history.

Argentina had been a memorable excursion. Shannon had performed well, learned a lot, and had some fun too. The coaches took all the gymnasts, male and female, and some of the parents on a beach picnic one day. We talked while the gymnasts enjoyed the ocean. We also hiked through the woods until the rains came and we dashed to the buses to return to the village. I was allowed to accompany Shannon to her room and spend a little time with her while she did homework. Then we all went to watch the men compete in their event finals. The girls had to leave before the meet was over so that they could be rested for their workout and event finals the next day. It was usually 2:00 A.M. by the time I got back from a meet, ate something, and got to bed, but I hardly noticed. I was very happy that I had joined Shannon in Argentina.

I called Ron to give him an update on the meet and learned that Stormy Eaton, the coach of gymnasts Sandy Woolsey and Elizabeth Crandall, had died in an airplane accident. Shannon was fond of Stormy, who had been the announcer on several of the tours in which she had participated. He was entertaining and fun to be around. She would be distressed to learn of this tragedy. Shannon later wrote a short article on Stormy for a book his fiancée was putting together.

Shannon and I were on the same flight back to Oklahoma City, which was great. She did homework most of the way, but we had time to talk. She was eager to get home but happy to have participated in the Pan-American Games. She had gotten to know some of the younger gymnasts and enjoyed them all.

CHAPTER SEVENTEEN

Charity Begins at Home

NOW SHANNON WAS planning to concentrate on school for a while, make graduation plans, and think about going to college next year. The Senior Prom was also coming up, but she wasn't planning to go. The previous summer she had begun dating a boy in her English class. He was a gymnast living in Edmond so that he could train at Bart Conner's facility, working toward elite status and a college scholarship. They talked briefly when she ran into him at an airport, and he later called to invite her to a movie.

She had little opportunity to enjoy the simple things in life and going to a movie with a nice boy sounded good. They had a similar training schedule, so dating was limited to weekends. Both wanted to do well in school and in gymnastics, planned to go to college, and cared about family. Sometimes he had a meet on a weekend or was visiting his family near St. Louis and sometimes Shannon was away, so they only saw each other two or three times a month.

By December, however, Shannon felt uncomfortable with what she saw as her boyfriend's increasing possessiveness and declining interest in school. He sometimes admitted to cutting gym or leaving early. Just before Christmas she came home frustrated after a shopping trip. She said he seemed to want to tell everyone who she was and make sure they knew he was her boyfriend. He had done this a little in the past, but she had overlooked it. This time she was really bothered. She was not an attention seeker and much preferred to be as anonymous as possible when out shopping or eating. She finally decided she was exaggerating what had occurred. He was fun to be with and had lots of friends who seemed to appreciate him.

A couple of weeks after Christmas break it was time for midterm exams. Shannon was studying hard, determined to get all A's. She declined an invitation to go out the weekend before exams but told her boyfriend he was welcome to come over and study with her. On Sunday afternoon he dropped by, and Shannon went downstairs to visit with him.

I was busy upstairs and was a little surprised when he left so soon. Shannon came in, plopped on my bed, and announced that she was thinking of breaking up with him. She said when she asked him about studying, he replied he didn't plan to spend much time at it. He figured he could get C's in most of his classes without studying for midterms. Shannon was appalled by his attitude.

Ron and I liked this young man because he was always pleasant and thoughtful, but we also disapproved of his attitude. I wondered if something was bothering him or if perhaps he was just trying to be macho for Shannon. His parents were coming to see him compete in a meet in a couple of weeks and we were supposed to get together. I suggested to Shannon that she give the situation a little more time before deciding to sever all ties.

After another week and a few more indications that school and gymnastics were becoming less important while Shannon's celebrity was becoming more important to him, she came back for another talk. If she ended things now, in late January, he would still have plenty of time to find another date for the prom. She wasn't thinking about the prom for herself. She doubted she would even be in town, so there was no use making plans. She invited him to have a Coke with her and told him they needed to break things off.

I was proud of her. I had dreaded seeing her break up with him right before he had a meet, especially since we were scheduled to meet his parents. After she explained to me that she was doing him no favor by waiting, I realized that she had the more mature attitude and was truly doing what was best for both of them. It would have been easier for her to turn down dates until he got the message. She was going to be out of town a lot and could have made all kinds of excuses, but she wanted to be honest with him. She was forthright, yet gentle.

Shannon was not planning to date until after the 1996 Olympics. There simply wouldn't be time. She had three invitations to the prom but turned them down. Her philosophy was that the prom should be a magical night to share with someone important to you. The boys who asked were all nice, but she hardly knew them and had never had a date with any of them. She preferred to stay home.

One event she did not plan to miss, however, was graduation. She had clearly informed us, her agent, and Steve that nothing should be planned on the day of graduation.

While we flew back from Argentina Shannon thought about graduation but knew she had a lot to do before that big day. She had several appearances scheduled, including an exhibition at an auto show and some gymnastic clinics for children. It was time for the Miracle Balloon drive, and she was scheduled to make a public service announcement and tour the Children's Hospital of Oklahoma. During the long flight Shannon confided to me that something had been preying on her mind and she needed to take some action. Her former geometry teacher, Darrell Allen, had been diagnosed with cancer the previous December, and in January and

February the school had held a number of fund-raisers to help his family with their expenses. Shannon had been so busy and out of town so much that she had had little opportunity to participate. She felt tremendous remorse about this. She used her celebrity status so often to help various charities around Oklahoma and across the nation, and yet she had not been able to do anything to help her teacher. She wanted me to help her think of a way to raise some money for the Allen family.

Unwittingly Shannon had already provided the answer. She often donated autographed items to charitable auctions. We could hold a celebrity auction. Shannon had made many friends in the athletic world over the last few years. We needed to call and write these people to ask them to donate to the Allen auction. We made a master list and divided it up. Shannon's agent, Greg Metzer, also began making contacts.

In no time autographed items were pouring in. They came from athletes everywhere who were willing to help: Bonnie Blair, Oksana Baiul, Tracy Austin, Brian Boitano, Nadia Comaneci, Bart Conner, Janet Evans, Nancy Kerrigan, Steffi Graf, Boomer Esiason, Dan Jansen, Shawn Kemp, Trent Dimas, Tiger Woods, Julie Krone, Tommy Moe, Greg Louganis, Bryant Reeves, Gabriella Sabatini, John and Pat Smith, John Starks, Eddie Sutton, Barry Switzer, the Orlando Magic, Mickey Tettleton, Nolan Ryan, Gil Morgan, the San Jose Sharks, and even Bela Karolyi and Kim Zmeskal. Local TV announcers donated items, as did other local celebrities and businesses. Steve and Peggy gave generously, and Steve allowed us to use the Edmond gym to hold the auction.

Friends who had some experience with this kind of affair offered excellent advice on how to get organized. Mike Reeves, one of my colleagues at the bank, arranged to have a credit card machine and someone to run it. The Allens' church offered to help run the auction. Dynamo gymnasts and their parents and many of my friends at work also offered their services. One of Steve's coaches organized an exhibition to entertain the auction participants as they waited for the high bids to be announced. Mr. Allen's parents also stopped by for a visit. Mr. Allen was still in the hospital and unable to come, but his family was optimistic. The auction went smoothly, and we had a wonderful time putting on the event.

A few days after the auction Shannon received a call telling her Mr. Allen was home from the hospital and would like her to visit him. He was not doing well but wanted to be at home. Shannon later told me that visiting him was one of the hardest things she had ever done. She had not seen Mr. Allen since she had taken his geometry class and argued with him over the B. He had been a very robust man then. Now he was wasted away. Although she didn't want to cry in front of him, her eyes had gotten teary. He died a few days later. She was glad she had made the visit, and even happier that she was able to help his family. We raised more than $5,000 that day. Over the next year people occasionally sent checks to the bank, where we had set up an account for the family.

The auction was held in mid-May. We had originally planned to have it in late April, but an event at 9:02 A.M. on April 19 literally blasted everything else out of Oklahomans' minds: a truck bomb exploded at the nine-story Alfred P. Murrah Federal Building and left 168 people dead and many more injured.

I was preparing to teach a class at one of our branch offices in northwest Oklahoma City on the flight path to the airport. Ron was at work at the university in Edmond. Troy was at school in Edmond. Shannon had just arrived at school after morning gym and was getting out of her car. I, and most of the people in my class, thought the noise and jolt was from an airplane. Troy's pen jerked as he worked in art class ten miles away, and he looked up to see whether someone had bumped the table. Shannon thought the boom was thunder or a plane and looked up, but nothing was in the sky, not even a small cloud.

A few minutes later I received a call saying I needed to get a security guard to our downtown office. There had been some kind of explosion that might have caused damage at our office. As security officer for the bank, I quickly sent a guard and then returned to my class. As I walked in all the participants were staring mutely at the television I had turned on just before I left the room in preparation for showing a video. At first I couldn't comprehend what they were watching. Gradually it hit me.

Most of the Murrah building seemed to be gone. I looked at the class and told them that anyone who had friends or relatives working in or near the building was immediately excused. Two people quickly left, tears in their eyes. The rest of us sat in stunned silence as television reporters told us there was a day care center in the building. So many children missing. So many feared dead. The scene was pandemonium. TV crews were trying to get an estimate of how many people might have been in the building. While they tried to determine how many might be dead in the building, other reports began to filter in. People were dead and seriously injured in nearby buildings as well.

Steve was going with me to my noon Kiwanis meeting that day. When I went by the gym to pick him up he was waiting for his fiancée who worked in the courthouse downtown near the bomb site. She arrived soon, shaken but physically fine. Our Kiwanis meeting was a glum affair. The husband and son of one of our members worked in the federal building, and no one had heard a report on their safety. We would later learn that her son had survived but her husband had not.

Our community was torn apart and yet brought closer together. I spent that day collecting blankets and organizing a sandwich crew. The Homeland grocery store where I did my weekly shopping generously donated all the makings for hundreds of sandwiches for the volunteers at the site who were digging through the rubble in the hope of finding survivors.

Shannon was eager to help too. A local TV station asked her if she would prepare a comforting message for the children of our community. She readily agreed. She also wrote a $1,000 check for the victims' fund. She had heard the volunteers would like fresh fruit, so we drove to the market, loaded up a basket of fruit, and drove it down to the volunteer site. Still she felt restless.

She asked fellow gymnast and friend Soni Meduna to go with her to take a basket of flowers to the firefighters. Soni's mother and I drove them downtown. At the gate Shannon asked the officer on duty to give the flowers and cards to the firefighters. When he realized who she was he asked Shannon and Soni to give the flowers to the firemen themselves. Shannon was very touched by what she saw in the huge room at the Myriad set aside for the volunteers. There were donations of clothing, food, medicines, everything a volunteer could possibly need. There was a place to get a massage, to exercise, to watch TV, to call home. And while a great deal of it came from Oklahoma, there were donations from every state in the Union and even from foreign countries. People were rushing everywhere to help, giving of their time, their energy, and their money. People actually gave the clothes off their backs or in one case the boots off his feet. They donated little things like gloves and hats and big things like cranes and generators. If the volunteer crews needed it, they would have it.

Shannon was always proud to say she was from Oklahoma, but now she felt even more pride. We noticed something else too. During this time people seemed to appreciate each other more. They went out of their way to provide little courtesies. Drivers in traffic were more patient. The crime rate in the city dropped. The situation was difficult to accept, and we knew our city would never be the same. We had to continue to look for the good, and in the midst of devastation there was still so much good to see.

Shannon graduated from high school on schedule with

33. Shannon beams as she receives her diploma at the Edmond North High School commencement ceremony May 18, 1995.

her class of almost five hundred students. She had dinner with her grandparents and us after the ceremony and then went out with friends to a party. Just before 2:00 A.M. the telephone jerked me awake. It was Shannon. She was having so much fun at the party that she wanted to stay another hour or two. This was her night and her dad and I trusted her implicitly. I did ask that she let me know when she got home. Moms just need to know these things.

Shannon spent the summer training in preparation for the U.S. Championships in August, which would also qualify gymnasts for Trials for World Championships. The closer the Olympics drew, the more important this meet became.

Steve was even more determined that all his gymnasts would be in top form for U.S. Championships. He had twice-a-day workouts, training the girls eight hours a day at least three days a week and six hours on the other three days. They usually took Sunday off. Oklahoma summers are extremely hot, and the girls perspired profusely and had to wipe off the beam and chalk the bars frequently. Toward the end of the week everyone was exhausted and tempers sometimes got out of hand.

Steve was planning his fall wedding to Laurie, had committed to a weeklong camp in New York, and was getting calls from reporters who wanted to talk about abuse of gymnasts in the wake of the publication of *Little Girls in Pretty Boxes*. His patience was at zero level.

Enter Mom Miller. I showed up at the gym on a Saturday to watch Shannon work out. Since I worked during the week I might go by once or twice a week to catch the last hour of an after-school workout, but if Shannon was practicing on beam at that time I couldn't see her since the beams were behind a wall. During the summer I was always at work during weekday workout hours. Many Saturdays, Shannon was at a meet or at an appearance.

When I arrived this Saturday I discovered that the upstairs viewing room overlooking the gym was closed. Shannon was the only elite working out that morning, as the other girls had left for the New York camp. Shannon, who had been to this camp for several years, had other obligations and stayed in Oklahoma to train with another coach during the time that Steve, Peggy, and the other girls were gone.

When I looked through a glass door into the gym I saw that Steve, who had not yet left for camp, was working with Shannon, who was on the tumble track. As I talked to a friend who had a child in classes, Steve strode across the gym, opened the door, and told me to leave the lobby. I thought he was joking, so I said, "Open the viewing room, and I'll leave your lobby." My friend and Shannon chuckled too. But Steve suddenly made it clear he was not playing games. In front of several preschool-class parents, he again ordered me out of the gym. I had not done or said anything to warrant this treatment, and now I was embarrassed. Ron and I had been supporting Steve for many years. We had worked at all his meets. Ron had done extensive remodeling of his first gym at no charge. For years we paid him for all Shannon's coaching and meet expenses, while later he waived the fees for some elite gymnasts. My anger flared, and I informed him he would have to bodily remove me. He wheeled around, marched back into the gym, and placed a large mat over the door so no one could see in. Shannon was shocked. Steve said nothing to her but continued the training session.

I called Ron. We had certainly had our disagreements with Steve over the years but had always been able to work things out. Before the 1992 Olympics Steve had welcomed us into the gym and eagerly sought our support. Little by little over the last few years he had grown more controlling of Shannon and made it clear he would be happy if no parents ever came to the gym. At one time he had planned to close the viewing area entirely, but the parents raised a huge fuss and he backed down. The parents were voluntarily sending their kids to this gym and paying the sizable monthly tuition and incidentals such as leotards, warm-up suits, music, choreography, meet fees, transportation, and more. They were also participating, as required, in several fund-raisers a year. Most parents—including the Millers—felt they had a right to come to the gym and watch their children occasionally.

I realize parents can get in the way, and I'm sure I have voiced my opinion at times when Steve really didn't need or want to hear it. I also know there were times when I was upset about a decision he made regarding Shannon which later proved to be a good one. However, I know there were times when we all would have been better off if Steve had listened to Ron and me. And there were even times when Steve did take our advice and when we took his. This incident was an extreme case.

Ron had come into Oklahoma City on business and was not far away. He drove over to see what the problem was. He did not like Steve's rudeness to me, and he was concerned about what Steve might be doing that he did not want us to see. He stepped into the office (even I wouldn't go that far), raised the blinds, and looked into the gym. Steve saw him almost immediately and charged over to tell him vehemently to get out. Ron countered sternly that he wanted to know what was going on.

Steve said we came to the gym too often. Ron pointed out that the girls primarily worked during the day since they were out of school, that he never came to the gym, and that I could come only on Saturdays during the summer. Steve bellowed that we needed to get out. Ron stepped into the gym and told Shannon she needed to leave with us. He did not feel comfortable leaving her with Steve while he was in such a rage.

Shannon felt caught in the middle. She couldn't understand Steve's actions, but she knew he might not let her back in the gym if she walked out with her dad. Championships were less than a month away and Shannon's choreographer was coming to work on a new floor routine for her in about an hour. Shannon had promised her a ride home after she finished the routine.

"Dad, please understand," she pleaded, more with her eyes than her quiet voice. Ron told her we would not force her to leave or punish her for staying. Ron and I both understood the tenuous position she was in, caught between parents and a coach. He told her we'd be back in a few hours to pick her up.

Neither Shannon nor we ever figured out what Steve's problem was. We did later find out that the gym staff had had a birthday party for one of the coaches the previous night and hadn't invited Steve. He was leaving, after training Shannon that morning, to meet his future in-laws for the first time. He wasn't pleased that Shannon would not be attending the New York camp. And one of the networks had been trying to get into the gym, hoping for an exposé. One last possible factor was that I was serving on a USA Gymnastics committee studying ways to avoid eating problems with gymnasts. To the best of my knowledge, and I knew the elite kids and their parents pretty well, none of Steve's competitive gymnasts had ever had an eating disorder, with the possible exception of one or two who had arrived at our gym with a problem and who did not stay very long. The program we were designing was geared to encourage the coaches to watch for eating disorders and to avoid inadvertently promoting the problem. I wondered whether Steve felt that my serving on the committee implied that there was a problem in his gym.

We finally concluded things had piled up on Steve and the last thing he wanted to see was a parent that morning, especially me. I know I stuck my nose into Shannon's gymnastic affairs a lot more than Steve would have liked, but I also know there were times it was a good thing I did. My opinions may have put Shannon in the middle of controversy from time to time, but I always felt I was supporting her. There were many times she begged me to rein Steve in when he called gymnasts names, harped on weight issues, or was on a "kicking out" binge.

We both had our faults and our strengths. In the past we always ended up recognizing this and working out our differences. It took a couple of weeks this time, but things settled back to normal, and then it was time to leave for Championships in Knoxville.

CHAPTER EIGHTEEN

Refusal to Sideline

I WAS AT WORK when the operator asked me to accept a long-distance call from Shannon Miller. I quickly said "Yes" but wondered why Shannon would be calling me at work on the afternoon before the optional competition.

I could hear the stress in her voice as she told me the morning workout had not been good. Her legs hurt and felt weak from the long workouts. Although much improved, the shin splints were still causing her pain. It was difficult to get a good push off with her legs.

She had taken a bad fall on beam and landed hard on her head, dazing her enough to scare Steve. He had declared her beam workout over and taken her to the bars. But she had not fully recovered from the bump on her head and temporarily could not remember her bar routine. Now Steve was really worried. He sent her back to her room to take a nap and told her he would decide that evening whether to scratch her from the meet. He was not optimistic. If he had to, he would petition her to World Team Trials.

Shannon had been working through her problems courageously. As always, she had her note cards with Bible verses and studied one each day, drawing strength from the passages. However, she needed a little reminder that we loved her no matter what and, more important, that God loved and provided for her constantly.

It was easy to see Steve as the culprit, but Shannon knew he really wanted what was best for her. We had to pray that whatever decision he made that evening would be the right one for Shannon, regardless of how the situation might look to us at the moment.

Shannon recovered her composure quickly and was again ready to take on the world (and Steve). That evening Steve decided he would have Shannon warm up her optional routines and see how she was handling things. Her warm-up wasn't the best, but she was performing considerably better than she had that morning. He also knew she was a real competitor. She made it clear that she was fully recovered and that she planned to finish Championships. He did not scratch her.

Optionals were a struggle. Shannon began on beam. Her foot slipped off the beam on her third layout. The fall didn't hurt her physically, but it bruised her pride. She quickly remounted the beam and finished strong.

Floor went very well, as did vault. Not wanting to give up even one hundredth of a point, Shannon worked to hit every handstand in her bar routine perfectly. Out of her reverse hecht on the high bar she landed her handstand on the low bar but was slightly off. Rather than give in and take the fall, she arched her back and used her extraordinary strength to pull her body back to an upright position. She still had a significant deduction but not as severe as a fall would have been. Steve couldn't be upset. He knew she had fought to pull every ounce out of the bar routine.

When the final scores were posted Shannon had not won the meet. Her errors on beam and bars had caused her to drop to second place. Young Dominique Moceanu captured the gold. Shannon was disappointed but not disillusioned. She realized two important facts: had she avoided just one of her errors, she would most likely have won Championships; and, even with the errors, she was still number two in the country, in great position to make the World Championship and Olympic teams. With these thoughts in mind, she charged into event finals.

Shannon had failed to make the beam finals because of the fall and had just missed the bar finals because of the error on the handstand. She would have to give everything she had to her vault and floor. She hit two well-executed vaults, a Yurchenko Arabian and a Tsukahara Arabian and walked away with gold. She performed beautifully in her floor routine but took a step just barely out of bounds on one of her tumbling passes. She still earned the bronze medal. Shannon was ready for World Team Trials. Championships were a good warm-up. She wasn't happy with her mistakes, but overall she had competed well.

Steve was well aware that Shannon was capable of being the national champion once again and was upset that she had just missed this honor. Not one to look back, he was now concentrating on World Championship Trials. He also had two other elite gymnasts who had qualified for this event, Heather Brink and Alecia Ingram. Steve anticipated having more than one gymnast on the World Championship team. He needed to keep all three of the girls in peak condition, so workouts continued to be long and hard. Steve was not particularly patient with mistakes or lack of concentration. When Shannon did not warm up clear hip-to-handstands well, he overreacted by having her do fifty in a row. The next day her shoulders were so sore that she could not perform the compulsory bar dismount well. Steve calmed down and realized he was driving the girls too hard.

Steve, Peggy, Shannon, Heather, and Alecia left for World Team Trials in early October. Problems occurred almost immediately. Heather injured her ankle and had to be scratched from the meet—a huge disappointment. She had finished tenth at Championships and at least one gymnast had declined to come to Trials, so Steve felt Heather had a superb chance to make the team. With Heather out, he focused all his attention on Alecia and Shannon. Both girls had exceptional meets.

Shannon performed beautifully executed compulsory routines and again finished in first. But overall, with the scores from compulsories and optionals combined from Championships, Dominique Moceanu had a slight edge. Shannon was competing well and in an excellent spot going into optionals. She had a slightly rough start on vault, although she hit two reasonably good vaults. She shone on bars, earning the highest score of the meet on this event. Beam was even better. Once again she outdid the field on this apparatus. She concluded with an excellent performance on floor. Although Shannon had the highest scores from the meet, when the scores from U.S. Championships were added, Dominique Moceanu still maintained a slight lead.

Another problem had emerged during Shannon's floor warm-up. She turned her ankle when she landed awkwardly on her full twisting double back. The pain was immediate and intense. This time Shannon was not even tempted to give in to tears or to the pain. She walked to the side of the floor and prayed quietly to herself. She recalled many of the thoughts Kittie had discussed with her in the past as well as the beautiful messages on her note cards. An inspiring thought she always carried with her was "Divine Love has met and always will meet every human need." If she needed to get through a floor routine and to assist her team at World Championships, then nothing could stop her, not even a sore ankle.

The team was scheduled to board the plane for Sabae, Japan, and the World Championships in only two weeks. Although Shannon complained little about her ankle, Steve was aware from her body movements and facial expressions that she was in pain. He knew he had better be careful if he didn't want any problems at the World Championships. The ankle responded quickly, and in the few days before the team left Shannon was hitting solid routines on all four events. She was better prepared for this meet than she had been for any in a long while.

At World Championships Shannon did very well in compulsories. She felt very good about her routines, although Steve and Peggy questioned some of the scores. The Americans had to compete in an early round, which Steve figured cost the team some tenths. Nevertheless, Shannon was first among the Americans and third in the world after compulsories.

When she called home after compulsories, she was in great spirits. The team looked good, and workouts were going well for her. It had been a while since we had such a pleasant telephone call from her when she was away at a meet.

During warm-ups the day before the optional portion of the competition, Shannon landed hard on the sore ankle and twisted it slightly. Beam dismounts had not been going well that day, and Steve was not pleased. He had her do a few more dismounts, and by the time she was done, her ankle was very painful. As she had before at Trials, she tried to pray silently and keep her thoughts properly focused. She completed her workout, but the next morning she could hardly walk. Steve took one look at her and realized she could not perform up to par. He doubted she would be an asset to the team. This was crushing news. Not only did he have high expectations for her at this meet, but the team needed her. Dominique Dawes, Amanda Borden, and Amy Chow had all stayed home with injuries. Jaycie Phelps had recently had knee surgery and was not able to perform on all events. This left the United States with a relatively inexperienced seven-person team. Kerri Strug and Shannon had been to Worlds before, but, with the exception of Jaycie, none of the other gymnasts had.

Shannon called home to tell us what happened and to ask for our prayers. Steve told her he would like her to try bars. Even with the sore ankle he thought she could handle a dismount and felt the team would need her bars score. Shannon was more than ready to do what she could. She didn't want to be a liability to the team.

This World Championships, the year before the Olympics, was the most important one. From this meet the top twelve teams would qualify for the Olympics. Furthermore, the judges would start to formulate opinions about which teams had the capability of winning medals at the Olympics. The Americans needed to demonstrate strength. Shannon remained calm. She would follow God's lead.

The team started on bars, and Shannon hit a solid routine to earn a good score. She was not scheduled to do beam, but as the rotation drew to a close Steve felt that even with her injured ankle she could earn a good score. He pulled out the skill that would be the most painful and told her to do a single full twisting dismount instead of a double if her ankle hurt too much. Shannon completed a good routine and was not about to end it with only a full twist. She threw the full twisting double back and earned another top score for the United States but was limping severely afterward.

The team moved to floor. Again Shannon was not anticipating doing this event. As the conclusion of the event approached, however, Steve and Peggy decided Shannon could score higher than most of the gymnasts so far if they rearranged her routine. They decided to take out the whip back, leaving just the full in as her opening tumbling pass, and add a more difficult leap to regain the lost series bonus. They presented the idea to Shannon. She agreed to do it. She did not earn the score she would have liked, but it was still the highest of the American team.

Only vault, the American team's weakest event, was left. The team was in contention for a bronze medal, but Steve doubted they could get it without a good score from Shannon. He asked Shannon if she could perform just one more time. Since only the best score of two vaults was taken, she could do one vault and accept that score. Shannon readily agreed.

She did a reasonable vault but not good enough to guarantee that the Americans would win the close battle for third. Steve thought the team needed a better score. Would she try again?

Shannon did. Her second vault earned a better score, much closer to what Steve had been looking for. The American team eased into third place and a bronze medal by 0.16 of a point. Shannon silently expressed her gratitude, not just that the team had done well, but that God had directed her throughout the experience and she had been able to help.

We were in San Antonio to celebrate Ron's parents fiftieth wedding anniversary. The call from Shannon came in early one morning while we were visiting my parents. Shannon was ecstatic that the team had won a bronze medal and that her scores had contributed significantly but admitted that after competing in the whole meet her ankle was not doing well. She said Steve was planning to withdraw her from the all-around competition, although she was not sure that was necessary. She fully expected her prayers to be answered. Only three gymnasts, including Shannon, had qualified for all four event finals. Shannon loved to compete. Could she sit these events out?

At home, Ron and I could not keep up with events as they happened. The World Championships were being taped to be shown in parts over several weeks. We didn't hear from Shannon again while she was on the trip. We did read the newspapers every day, and they described her injury in great detail. One day we picked up the Sports section and saw Shannon's name in a list of gymnasts in the all-around competition. We couldn't help but smile.

We were not really surprised. Shannon felt a duty to her coaches, her family, her fans, and herself. She realized competing might mean watering down her routines and taking the risk of damaging her international reputation, but politics don't mean a lot to Shannon. She was the reigning world champion going into what was probably her last World

Championship meet. She could claim injury (everyone could see for themselves she had a problem) and insist she had not yet been defeated, or she could compete as she had been working hard to do for a long time.

Shannon finished in twelfth place that day out of a field of thirty-six all-around finalists but never regretted her decision to compete. She knew she was much happier having tried than she would have been sitting on the sidelines.

Steve convinced her that there was no reason to compete all four events in finals. She would have to do two different vaults for vault finals and she had been struggling just to make the Yurchenko Arabian. Likewise, he did not want her tumbling and doing even more damage to her ankle. He understood her desire to perform in the all-around and could see she was still hungry to win a medal, so he agreed to bars and beam.

Shannon hit a good but not exceptional bar set in event finals and earned a decent score, out of medal range. She gave an even more valiant effort on beam but finished in fourth place. Although she returned home with only the team medal, she was proud of having demonstrated true dedication to her country, her team, and her sport. She understood a little better the value of perseverance. She was continuing to learn the importance of putting her trust in the right place. Shannon was adding to her repertoire of skills, not just in the gymnasium, but in life.

With Championships, Trials, and Worlds all lined up in the fall, Shannon had been through a heavy competitive schedule, and with the sore ankle, she needed rest. Workouts were a little lighter for a while, if not any shorter.

Shannon was registered for two classes at the University of Oklahoma and now had homework and tests to make up. Steve had tried to persuade her to forgo school the year before the Olympics, but Shannon had balked. School was very important to her. She didn't plan to give up gymnastics completely after the Olympics, but she did want to have a real career.

Shannon also had a few appearances to make, including the Christmas Parade for the Henrietta Egleston Hospital for Children in Atlanta. On a previous trip to Atlanta Shannon had visited the hospital. Now she was invited to be the grand marshal for the parade, a notable annual affair in Atlanta. Ron and I were invited to Atlanta with her.

The parade was truly delightful. The many Atlanta children who lined the streets were thrilled to see not only the array of floats but also one of their role models, Shannon Miller. After the parade Shannon gave a brief talk to the crowds shopping and viewing the hospital's Festival of Trees. This was one of the most enjoyable parades Shannon participated in.

The Christmas holidays were almost upon us by the time we returned from Atlanta. Shannon's ankle was already doing much better so she was beginning to train aggressively. Steve and Laurie had married in November and had been away for almost two weeks for their wedding and honeymoon. Shannon had hoped to fly to Hawaii for their wedding, but with school and other commitments, she had not been able to go. Steve returned from Hawaii more relaxed, but after a few weeks Shannon's honeymoon was over too, and it was back to long, hard workouts in the gym. Shannon was in good shape physically and mentally. The Olympics were less than eight months away.

Rather than disillusion Shannon, World Championships stimulated her to train harder than ever. She learned that everyone's difficulty level was increasing and thought she needed to do more to keep up. She wanted a new skill on beam, a new dismount on bars, a new tumbling pass on floor, and a new vault. Not only did she want to be part of the American team, but she wanted to lead it. It felt good at World Championships to be a real factor in the team medal, and she hoped the next time the medal would be Olympic gold. After their admirable performance at World Championships without some of the country's top gymnasts, Shannon firmly believed the Americans could win in the summer of 1996. She intended to help make that happen.

Shannon's top priority was to learn a new, more difficult vault. The Tsukahara was rated at a maximum score of 10, but it never seemed to score that well for any gymnast. Shannon needed a difficult Yurchenko. Steve wanted her to learn a one-and-a-half twist. Shannon had a slightly different idea. She clearly remembered working on and performing the Yurchenko double twist in 1993. She thought she could revive this vault and learn it much better this time. She wanted to try. While Steve was in Hawaii Shannon suggested the idea to Peggy and Rick Newman, the two coaches supervising her training in Steve's absence. They were enthusiastic about her suggestion, and Rick began her training immediately. Picking up the double full was harder than Shannon had thought it would be, but she made good progres. Both Rick and Peggy were pleased.

As the day of Steve's return approached Shannon became a little nervous. Steve had wanted her to work on a one-and-a-half. He would be very surprised that she was getting close to a double full. Rick was amazed at her progress, but he and Peggy were also wary of Steve's reaction. They were still discussing how to break the news to Steve when he slipped into the gym a day earlier than expected and watched Shannon perform a couple of vaults. He was surprised—not pleasantly. He let them know in no uncertain terms that he made the coaching decisions and was not happy about having his authority usurped. He allowed Shannon to continue the vault but pounced on any small mistake.

Shannon found it more difficult to work on the new vault with Steve's constant criticism. Her progress slowed considerably. By early December Steve gave her an ultimatum:

either get the vault on a mat at competition height (or very close) by the end of December or start working on a one-and-a-half twist. Shannon was distressed. Some days she couldn't get the twist around at all; other days it worked remarkably well. She believed she could learn the vault in time for Nationals, but she would need Steve's support.

One evening she came home depressed and angry at Steve. We talked about the situation, and then I asked what she wanted me to do. She said she thought this might be one of those times when a parent talk with Steve would do some good.

Steve was not happy to hear from me. But I knew—and was sure he would understand—that if Shannon was really interested in working on a particular skill, she was much more likely to acquire it. If he eased up on the criticism, she might progress more rapidly. The time frame he set seemed unnecessarily rigid since she would not have to have the vault perfected until Nationals in June. She was prepared to switch to the one-and-a-half twist if she was not making real progress on the double by late January. The change should not be too hard since she used some of the same techniques for both.

Steve disagreed with our logic. He argued that she was wasting valuable time that should be spent working on the one-and-a-half twist. We ended the conversation with his agreement to allow her to continue working on the double until the end of December—but not a minute longer unless she showed some remarkable improvement. The week before Christmas Shannon was hitting the vault better and Steve eased up on his criticism. Shannon was determined to prove she could learn it. Before long, however, the clash of opinions over vaults would be a moot issue.

As usual Shannon was eager to help with Christmas preparations. I don't know how I would have survived if she hadn't wrapped most of the packages for me. This year she had a real challenge: we bought Troy a drum set. Shannon wrapped each drum separately but drew the line at the cymbals. We decided to drape a blanket over the entire drum set. Shannon made a big sign saying the blanket could not be lifted until Mom and Dad were downstairs on Christmas morning.

Troy, fifteen now, was a very happy boy that Christmas, but Shannon soon discovered the disadvantages of living with a drummer. Troy's electric guitar had been bad enough. This was worse. Shannon and Troy finally agreed on a nightly drumming curfew to give her (and us) a little peace.

A few days after Christmas 1995 we left Edmond to drive to Texas. Steve had again proposed that we have Shannon fly to and from San Antonio so she could squeeze in two extra workouts. Shannon agreed with Steve as Olympic Trials were rapidly approaching.

Shannon emerged from the plane happy to be with her family and yet a little subdued. Christmas vacation was always a very exciting time for Shannon, so I suspected a problem in the gym. Before I could ask what was wrong, Shannon told us that her wrist was very sore. In fact, it had been so painful that Steve had decided not to have her vault. Both she and Steve hoped that a few days off the wrist would remedy the problem. In the activity of the next couple of days the wrist was almost forgotten. As Shannon had often trained and competed successfully while injured, we were not alarmed.

CHAPTER NINETEEN

1996: A Dream in Doubt

OON NEW YEAR'S DAY was over. Another week had slipped by. Tessa was back in California, Troy was back in school, and Shannon was preparing for the Dynamo Classic. Although I always enjoyed going to the gym, one Saturday early in the year was not so much fun. I could see that Shannon was really struggling. She could hardly vault, and tumbling was obviously difficult.

On the way home Shannon told me Steve had made an appointment for her to see David Holden, the physician who had treated her elbow when she injured it in 1992. Dr. Holden examined her arm and wrist and said he did not believe the problem was serious, but he advised resting the wrist for at least a week and beginning some intensive therapy. He would then reevaluate the situation.

Shannon eased up on workouts, but with the upcoming Dynamo Classic, neither she nor Steve felt she could completely rest the wrist. The gym trainer was out of town part of this time, so she was unable to begin therapy right away. A week later the wrist and arm were worse instead of better.

Steve and Shannon were now seriously concerned.

Shannon had agreed to do a special promotional meet the day after the Dynamo Classic which would be aired on television. She was scheduled to do beam, floor, and bars. Only a few weeks later she was entered in the Peachtree Classic, followed closely by the American Classic, the qualifying meet for individual event World Championships. There was no time to ease up on workouts, but the wrist continued to grow more painful. Her arm was inflamed up to the elbow. Vaulting and tumbling were now almost out of the question, and bars and beam were getting more difficult each day. Shannon was working closely with Kittie, and we prayed together nightly. Her spirits were still good. She was holding fear at bay, but Steve was beginning to show signs of panic manifested in anger, frustration, and impatience.

Therapy on the wrist intensified. Shannon was able to do a very modified floor and bar routine at the Dynamo Classic, performing an exhibition rather than competing. She was able to do only a bar routine the next day at the televised meet. It was now apparent that the wrist could be a factor in whether Shannon even had an opportunity to try out for the 1996 team. Steve, meanwhile, had decided he preferred to ignore the situation and assume the pain would go away. He was no longer urging medical assistance, but he was pushing her to get ready for the Peachtree, the American Classic, and, especially, the American Cup, which he desperately wanted her to win again.

At this point Shannon was prepared to place her complete trust in God. She had now been to two therapists, a sports doctor, and Dr. Holden. The sports doctor, Carlan Yates, strongly recommended that we take Shannon to Dr. Kenneth Hieke, a specialist in the treatment of hands and wrists. Her father told her it wouldn't hurt to hear what Dr. Hieke had to say. She agreed to the consultation.

What Dr. Hieke said when she visited him in February was no real surprise. There was not much he could do at the time. She needed to stop working on the severely inflamed wrist and arm for two to three weeks and then be examined again. Shannon wouldn't let me tell Steve what the doctor said until several days later, when she realized she desperately needed some relief. At first Steve was resistant to this news, as Shannon knew he would be. After I spoke with him Steve continued to train her on the arm for several more days, but before long Shannon could barely do anything—no tumbling on beam, no release moves or handstands on bars, no vaulting, and very little floor tumbling. Steve and Shannon finally agreed that she would stay off the wrist completely for at least two weeks. Then maybe she would have just enough time to get ready for the American Cup. The Peachtree had already slipped by, and the American Classic was clearly out of the question. The American Cup was three weeks away.

The wrist was soon feeling better, and with the help of Kittie and the rest of us, Shannon's spirits were improving. Steve wanted Shannon to attend the American Classic, even though she couldn't compete. He wanted to keep her competitive spirit fine-tuned by seeing the other gymnasts. This tactic had worked in the past because Shannon always wanted to be part of the action, but this time watching had a different effect. Shannon returned to the gym dismayed. She hadn't given up on God, but she began to wonder whether she was meant to be on the Olympic team. The other competitors had been so prepared for the meet, and she had not been training all-out in more than six weeks. Did God have a different plan for her? And was she strong enough to accept a path different from the one she had chosen?

We had many long talks and decided two things: she needed to take each day as it came, and she needed to do her best to continue to listen for God's direction no matter where it led. It was still hard to go to the gym each day and do conditioning exercises while her teammates worked vigorously at attaining new skills and perfecting old ones. It was even more difficult to think about all the other American and foreign gymnasts training enthusiastically, winning competitions, and otherwise readying themselves for the big event in July.

Shannon has a very logical mind. She always says her favorite subject is mathematics. This problem was not amenable to a logical solution. No one could find a reason for how or why it had occurred or a solution. No one could predict how long she would need to be patient. The only suggestion was to stay off her arm and see if it got better at some future time. This advice was hard for Shannon to accept, but she understood that she couldn't push God. He had a plan for her. His plan never includes pain and misery, but it does require us to be still and listen. She did not think of quitting, or even of not going to the gym faithfully each day. She still looked forward with hope that she would have an opportunity to compete, but she knew she would have true contentment with or without the Olympics.

After two weeks off the wrist Steve began to ease Shannon back into training. Bars came back first, then a few more tricks on beam, some front floor tumbling, a little back tumbling (she used her fist, not bending the wrist), and finally a little compulsory vaulting. In late February, as Shannon improvised in every way possible to work on her skills while avoiding using the arm, overcompensation resulted in a pulled hamstring. The full effects of this would not show up for weeks.

During this stressful period a very timely event occurred. Shannon was scheduled in late March to talk with a group of young Christian Scientists and their parents in Atlanta about her experiences in gymnastics and how she applied Christian Science in her everyday life. Shannon had given many brief talks but never a real speech, as this would be. Bill Merritt, at whose home the event was held, offered to fly Shannon and me out to stay with his family for the weekend.

The occasion was an annual gathering hosted by the

Merritts to let Christian Scientists in the area learn about church programs for children and youth. The Merritts prepared a big barbecue so their guests could relax and socialize.

At first Shannon was hesitant. Sometimes she felt as though she could be a better Christian Scientist: she occasionally went to a doctor and seemed to always be having therapy of some kind. But she did believe sincerely that God was taking care of her, and she also believed strongly in giving back to her church community whenever possible.

Shannon had little time to think about the trip or the speech until just over a week before we were to leave for Atlanta. We sat down together one evening in her room to discuss what she might say. Shannon remembered the many times during stressful periods, including her most recent problems, that she had felt God's presence and the many times God had guided her in the right direction whether the difficulty was fear, a physical problem, or tension in her relationship with her coaches. Shannon realized she needed to express her gratitude for God's guidance to her fellow Christian Scientists who wanted very much to share in her experiences.

This hurdle over, we set out for Atlanta. At the Merritts' house, talking with some of the parents and teens about Christian Science camps, Shannon found herself fitting right in and relaxing visibly. More people than expected showed up for the picnic, but the atmosphere continued to be so relaxed and friendly that Shannon had no trouble delivering her speech and fielding questions.

We flew home that evening. As we drove from the airport to our house, Shannon commented that she was very glad she had met this group. She had found great enjoyment in spending two days with people who really lived their religion, who genuinely saw the good in everyone around them, and who readily expressed their gratitude for the good in their lives. Her trip to Atlanta had been a warm and comforting experience. The trip had provided more than a respite from her hectic training schedule. It had provided additional insight into God's love and protection.

In the gym time passed swiftly, but Shannon's recovery was slow. Even late in March, if she vaulted one day, she had to limit work on the beam and forgo tumbling; if she tumbled, she couldn't vault. At the end of the first week in April her wrist still could not bear up under Yurchenko vaults. She couldn't work on the double or one-and-a-half-twist vault, or even her old Yurchenko Arabian, which had now been devalued to a 9.9 maximum.

Most of the time Shannon contended with the stress wonderfully, but with National Championships only seven weeks away she occasionally succumbed to fear. Although Steve was doing his best to work around her injury, she could see he was starting to give up hope on her prospects of making the Olympic team.

As Shannon's emotional state deteriorated, I sought a way to help her. She was working closely with Kittie and we expected good results, but I felt that as her mother, I should be able to do something more. During this time I frequently listened to a church tape in the car. One day a line from the tape jumped out at me. As soon as I got home I jotted down the inspirational message on a note card and left it for Shannon in her room: "Face each day with the expectancy of achieving good, rather than the dread of falling short." Here was the insight we both needed. We had been dreading what each day would bring, anticipating additional problems instead of looking for all the good that was already available to us. Shannon happily embraced this bit of inspiration, and in no time her attitude and performance improved.

Shannon had been hesitant to return to Dr. Hieke. She still felt her answer was Christian Science, but she also knew time was slipping by and Steve was counting on her. Kittie had helped her to understand that just because she visited a doctor or consented to medical assistance, she was not turning her back on God. We decided that if Shannon did not feel she could resolve her physical problem in the time she had, there was no harm in obtaining other assistance. In the end God is directing all of us, including Dr. Hieke.

This time Dr. Hieke was pleasantly surprised. Her arm was virtually healed, and her wrist was much better. He recommended a cortisone shot, a procedure he would not even try when her tendon was severely inflamed. Shannon knew her prayers were doing some good. She had had very few shots in her life and did not relish one now. But she had come this far. She should not ignore the doctor who was trying his best to help her. Once again she was required to rest the wrist for a few days until the cortisone took effect.

Gradually Shannon was able to add skills back into her daily routine. Her wrist continued to improve, and her spirits soared. Soon she was working on Yurchenko vaults and beginning the one-and-a-half twist. She had lost some precious time, but she found it a real joy to go to the gym and really work out again.

Steve had given up the idea of adding a double layout tumbling pass to Shannon's floor routine. They would have to make do with the tumbling she had, since there simply wasn't enough time to get everything done. Now, however, as Shannon was again doing full workouts, the hamstring she pulled in February made its presence known. Piking—holding the legs straight, bending at the hips, and bringing the legs parallel to the body—was extremely painful, so working a piked full twisting double back, her traditional opening pass, was difficult. In desperation Shannon asked Steve if she could try a double layout. Steve was doubtful. Learning a skill that difficult could easily take a year, and Shannon had less than a month until Championships. The alternative was to work on nothing that required a pike position and to disappoint Shannon, who was now eager to move forward. Steve decided to let her try.

Steve spotted the first few double layouts and was

astonished at how good they were. Shannon came home excited. She had actually done a few of the double layouts by herself, and Steve had called Peggy over to watch, proof that he had been impressed. A few days later, when I stopped by the gym, she tried the double layouts again, and again she did them perfectly. That day the double layout was ordained her opening tumbling pass.

Vaulting had been tough. Getting her timing back while also trying to learn a new, more difficult vault was exhausting. But as mid-May approached the Yurchenko Arabian was looking good and the one-and-a-half was getting better each day.

Shannon was now approaching each day at the gym with fresh vigor, but with less than two weeks to go before the Dynamo group was to leave for Championships, her wrist flared up again. Each day it became a bit more sore. National Championships were now entirely too close for Shannon to lay off the wrist.

She clung steadfastly to the principles she and Kittie had discussed and tried to work through the pain, while Steve daily stressed the importance of the upcoming meet. Tempers flared as the stress became too great. Shannon tried to see the best in Steve and some days was able to remain calm, but other days she allowed things to get out of hand.

Vaulting, especially, was now almost impossible. Just a few days before the girls and the coaches were to leave for Nationals, Shannon could no longer bear the pressure. She wanted to make the team even more than Steve wanted it for her, but her body was not cooperating. Steve was so furious at her poor vaulting that he refused to even set the springboard for her. She was so angry and hurt that she almost convinced herself she no longer cared. She headed for the door to leave the gym.

Steve's booming voice stopped her. "Don't even think it!" He strode over to her and took her firmly over to the locker area. She prepared herself for an angry outburst, but instead Steve was calm. He uttered the words she most needed to hear at that moment: "Peggy and I still believe in you. We know you can make the team." If Steve and Peggy still believed in her, she knew she couldn't let them down. Shannon determined to give all she had and to continue to pray that it would be enough to satisfy everyone, including herself.

For the next few days Shannon skipped vaulting and did only essential tumbling, using her fist. Steve knew she was an extraordinary athlete and was counting on her years of training, her ability to focus, and her desire to compete to get her through. Shannon was counting on God.

At the end of the compulsory competition at Championships Shannon was in first place. Since compulsories count for 60 percent of the overall score in U.S. competition, this was an auspicious start, but the real test was yet to come.

Shannon began optional competition on beam. As she dived backward onto her hands to complete a back handspring in preparation for the two layout flips to follow, the injured wrist gave slightly and threw her off balance. She was able to pull out the first back flip but slipped off the beam unable to complete the second one. Standing on the floor ready to remount the beam, she realized that winning Nationals was probably out of the question but that she needed to fight back and finish as high in the standings as possible to pave the way for Olympic Trials. She finished her beam set with a minimum of other errors and received a decent score. She dreaded facing Steve and Peggy, but they handled the mishap well. Steve greeted her with, "Okay, beam is behind you. You have more new skills to try out today. Let's get focused on your next event." Shannon knew that was exactly what she had to do. Beam was history, but she still had to compete in three more events.

Floor was next. Shannon had been very busy during

April and May adding new skills, but now, to avoid overusing her wrist, she had not even warmed up a double layout without Steve spotting her. The opening tumbling pass would be her most challenging, but she also had another new pass, a front full twist into an immediate front layout. She hit the double layout beautifully and was charged up for the rest of her routine. She nailed all three of her other tumbling passes and was rewarded with a 9.9 from the judges. Things were starting to look up.

Next on the agenda was vault. Since the episode in the gym several days before, Shannon had not vaulted. Steve's strategy was to rely on her experience to get her through a Yurchenko Arabian, a vault she had used in competition for several years. If she earned a fairly good score, then he would have her attempt the new one-and-a-half twist to try to improve her score. The Arabian's start value was 9.9, whereas the one-and-a-half's was 10. Shannon hit the Arabian solidly and earned a 9.8, a very good score but not high enough to ensure that she would be a contender in this meet. After some last-minute instructions from Steve, Shannon blasted down the runway and completed the more difficult vault with only a slight hop. She improved her score to a 9.9 and moved into second place. Steve was jubilant. Television cameras showed Shannon trying unsuccessfully to suppress a rare smile.

Shannon's last event was bars. Because of the sore wrist she had had trouble gripping the bar for a long period, so she had been working on her skills in segments. Even when she warmed up for the meet she did not do a complete routine and omitted the dismount. She and her coaches knew she could do every element of the routine—but could she do them all at one time?

The routine went smoothly with no technical errors until the dismount. It was a little low as Shannon struggled to grasp the bar, but she pulled it around and stuck the landing solidly. The judges scored the routine a 9.85. By now the competitors challenging Shannon for the top spot had also finished competing. Shannon's bar score moved her into first place. She had won the meet, even with a fall.

During the spring, as Shannon's wrist and then her hamstring had given her so much trouble, her dad and I had prayed she would have just a chance to try out for the Olympic team. We had not dared to think she might win National Championships. Once again Shannon had shown us we should not place limits on her. She certainly had put none on herself as she worked emotionally and physically to show herself and the world that she had not lost anything but had gained much. All was not perfect, however. Steve pulled her out of event finals—an indication of his continuing concern about her wrist.

There was hardly time to stew over the situation. Officials of the Make-A-Wish Foundation and the Pediatric AIDS benefit had asked Shannon to assist with their events. Make-A-Wish tries to grant wishes of terminally ill children. One little girl's dream was to meet Shannon.

Although Shannon had a very tight schedule, she wanted to continue her involvement with both organizations. Her agent worked diligently with Steve and leaders of the two organizations to schedule times that would work for everyone. The Pediatric AIDS benefit was to be held the Sunday after Championships, and Make-A-Wish officials coordinated with the benefit schedule.

USA Gymnastics generally holds meetings for the gymnasts and the coaches on the day after Championships, but Steve felt Shannon could miss the meetings since she had attended many of them in the past, she had competed in Olympic Trials before, he and Peggy would be there as coaches, and Ron was willing to sit in on her behalf. Federation officials, however, insisted that Shannon attend the majority of the meetings or lose the chance to be on the Olympic team. They said they wanted to foster team spirit.

34. Shannon and Kevin Costner at the 1996 Pediatric AIDS Benefit in Los Angeles.

Ron thought this was a little odd because gymnasts had often previously missed these meetings and the Olympic team had not yet been chosen.

We quickly notified the Pediatric AIDS group and the Make-A-Wish Foundation of the problem. The child from Make-A-Wish had her heart set on seeing Shannon. Could Shannon make it at a later time? The federation agreed that if Shannon attended the morning meetings, her dad could sit in on the afternoon session. Shannon rushed to the airport after the morning session for the next flight to Los Angeles. Pediatric AIDS had also flown me to L.A. from Oklahoma City for the event. We finally arrived at the benefit fifteen minutes before it ended. Shannon spent at least half an hour visiting with the young girl from the Make-A-Wish organization. She was also able to sign autographs and have her picture taken with other children. Shannon was glad to have made the extra effort to get there.

We planned to fly back to Oklahoma City that night. Steve expected Shannon back in the gym the next morning. After the Make-A-Wish event we looked for our limousine to

35. Shannon, Robin Williams, and Claudia at the Pediatric AIDS Benefit.

the airport. It was not there. Fifteen minutes later we asked foundation officials, who had arranged transportation, to check on it. The limousine company assured them that it was on the way. After another fifteen minutes with no limousine, we realized we would have difficulty making our flight. When a benefit volunteer offered to drive us to the airport, we were grateful. Shannon knew Steve would not tolerate her missing a workout with Olympic Trials looming.

The young man did an admirable job of negotiating heavy L.A. traffic and we arrived at the airport with ten minutes to spare, only to be trapped in a long line of immobile cars. I jumped out of the car to run to the gate and try to persuade airline personnel to hold the plane until Shannon could get there with our luggage. As I raced from terminal to terminal I learned that there was a bomb threat. No traffic would be allowed through until the situation was resolved. I ran up to the gate out of breath, only to find that our plane was long gone. By the time Shannon arrived I had spoken with airline attendants and found there were no more flights that would get us to Oklahoma City that night. The best we could do would be to fly to Denver, spend the night there, and get an early flight out the next morning. We scheduled the flight and called home so that Ron could let Steve know Shannon would not be at the gym on time. Troy, who was home alone, told us Ron was not there. His flight home from Championships had been delayed.

The next morning Shannon and I boarded the plane out of Denver, carrying our bags with us. Shannon was in first class. I had a seat in coach with the regular people—who happened to include Ron. He had spent the night in the Chicago airport because of inclement weather. The only way he could get to Oklahoma City at a reasonable time was to go through Denver.

Troy, at fifteen, at first hadn't relished the idea of staying home all night by himself but quickly came to realize this was a great opportunity to demonstrate he could handle anything. He brought Shannon's dog Dusty in for company. The house was still standing when we all got home.

As we rode the crest of Shannon's win at Championships, Ron and I had no idea of the trauma ahead. Shannon had briefly mentioned before Championships that her wrist was sore and then said nothing more. She didn't tell us about the day she almost walked out of the gym until Championships were over. Ron and I had no idea how severe her wrist problem had become. Shannon had felt the need to communicate with God privately to shut out all the other pressures. She knew that although she always had our support, our love, and our prayers, the time had come for her to handle this situation herself.

We had not seen her working out in pain because several years earlier as the number of elite students at his gym increased, Steve had instituted a policy of locking all parents out of the gym, even the viewing area, for about two weeks prior to what he deemed was an important meet. With the various levels of students at the gym, this meant that parents were frequently barred. Parents—including me—complained periodically about this rule, but other than move to another gym, there wasn't much we could do. In the early days (before the 1992 Olympics), Steve had insisted that coaches, parents, and gymnasts work as a team. For much of that time, though, Shannon had been his only elite gymnast. Now he had as many as eleven.

With the increase in the number of elite gymnasts, Steve had also cracked down on gymnasts' weight more than before. He began weighing the girls regularly, which most of the parents objected to. He and Peggy admonished the gymnasts to watch what they ate and indicated that a slim gymnast could perform better and would likely be viewed more favorably by the judges. Although he didn't punish girls for gaining weight, Steve let his displeasure be known. The girls knew better than to be caught with candy bars or other junk food. From time to time Shannon—and others—smuggled extra food on trips, but she always took such foods as dried fruit, crackers, and canned chicken. Shannon rarely complained about the stronger enforcement. Her only complaints were that in a rush to or from an airport to meet a schedule Steve might forget to allow time for a meal or that Peggy sometimes ordered food for the gymnasts without considering their tastes. Shannon understood that eating properly was important for both looking and feeling good.

Right now, going into a critical time, she was feeling anything but good. Ron and I first realized how serious her wrist problem still was when Steve pulled her out of event finals. Shannon prided herself on making event finals and loved to compete on each apparatus individually. She would not readily agree to withdraw. When she arrived home it was with instructions from Steve to go back to the hand specialist immediately. By now he understood that the solution would probably be to rest the wrist again for at least a week or two. If this were the case he would need to try to petition Shannon through Olympic Trials. He would need a doctor's evaluation before proceeding with the petition.

I called Dr. Hieke's office and was able to get Shannon an immediate appointment. I was not especially concerned. Like Steve, I assumed the doctor would recommend giving the wrist some relief and, perhaps, suggest another cortisone shot. Neither would make Shannon happy, but neither was very drastic.

Previously the doctor and we had assumed that something Shannon had done had caused the wrist to get inflamed and that continued use of it had aggravated the inflammation. It had improved significantly after she got off of it in February. The doctor attributed the improvement to rest; Shannon credited her prayers. Despite both, enough pain persisted to keep her from performing to her maximum ability. Now Dr. Hieke began to think there was a more serious problem. After a thorough examination and numerous questions, he gave us his verdict: he feared continued work on the wrist could result in a snapped tendon. If Shannon was vaulting, on the high bar, or in the middle of a complicated move when it happened, the resulting fall could cause a traumatic or even fatal injury. Dr. Hieke strongly recommended that Shannon end her gymnastics career.

I was stunned. I had not expected this reaction from the physician. He was now part of our team, and I assumed he would be eagerly searching for a way to get Shannon ready to compete in Atlanta. Caught off guard by his frank honesty, I said nothing but looked over at Shannon to see how she was absorbing this news. She looked very calm, not at all shocked. The doctor then excused himself so that he could schedule an MRI for her wrist. While he was gone I asked Shannon how she was feeling. Her response was quick, "God and Mind got me through Nationals; they will get me through the next meet." I couldn't help but smile, proud that she had so much faith, and pleased that it was in the right place. Her calm answer inspired me to a sense of peace I hadn't felt in some time. How could I doubt that God would get her through whatever trials she faced?

Shannon called Kittie that night for additional prayerful support. Before bed Shannon and I read from a *Sentinel*, a weekly Christian Science periodical. Shannon never traveled without a *Sentinel*. She enjoyed reading an article or testimony just before going to bed so that she would drift off to sleep with good thoughts in her mind. She also read from a *Sentinel* whenever she was worried, lonely, or in physical pain. The comforting messages always brought some relief.

Peggy had confirmed this one morning after Championships when I dropped by the gym before work to deliver a birthday gift from Shannon. Peggy told me she and Steve believed it was a miracle that Shannon had made it through Championships, much less that she had won the meet, since she had hardly been able to work out because her wrist was in such bad shape a week earlier. Peggy said she had noticed that Shannon often read a "little book" and that she had asked about it. Shannon showed her and explained what it was. "After the meet, I told Shannon I needed one of those little books if they helped perform such miracles," Peggy said. We were about to get even more evidence of the effectiveness of Shannon's faith.

The day after Shannon had the MRI, Ron, Shannon, and I met again with Dr. Hieke to discuss his observations. Mark Cranston, who was still giving Shannon daily therapy on her wrist and hamstring, called to offer his support and ask if he could be there. He had been providing therapy for Shannon's various injuries since long before the 1992 Olympics and was an integral part of our Olympic preparation team. He was assisting Steve with preparing the petition to submit to USA Gymnastics.

Ron drove Shannon to the doctor's office. I came from work and was a little late. By the time I walked into the office Dr. Hieke and Mark were reviewing the numerous MRI pictures for a second time. Shannon had a quiet smile on her face, and I knew from her serene expression all was well.

For the third time both Mark and the doctor examined the pictures. They could not find any of the severe complications Dr. Hieke had anticipated. A buildup of fluid was causing pain, but the tendon looked remarkably good. Dr. Hieke smiled at Shannon and said there might be a chance she could still compete. He was now willing to try another cortisone shot—outside the tendon—to ease the swelling. Shannon knew that no matter what he said she was going to pursue making the team. She had resources other than medical on which she would rely.

Dr. Hieke knew Shannon was not keen on getting another shot, so he suggested we spend a few minutes discussing the issue in his absence. Ron and I strongly believed this decision had to be Shannon's. She had struggled alone before Championships because she had understood then all the choices were hers. Things had not changed.

Mark, however, wanted to help her understand his and the doctor's viewpoint. He, too, knew Shannon did not want another shot, but the news was so much better than anyone had expected that he wanted very much for her to take full advantage of this second chance. Shannon did not deliberate long before agreeing to the shot. She did not believe strongly that it would help her, but neither did she believe it could cause harm. She knew good things were happening without cortisone, as proved by the MRI, but having the shot would please Mark, the doctor, and Steve.

Almost another week had slipped by since Nationals by the time Shannon had the cortisone shot. Then she had to rest the wrist for a few days to allow the medication to take effect. Steve worked hard putting together a petition to exempt Shannon from Olympic Trials. He did not want to overexert the wrist and risk making it so sore that she could not compete in the Olympics. He realized that even when Shannon began to work out again he had to introduce skills gradually. Even if she was able to compete in Trials, she would not be in top form. She might place so low on the team that she would not be considered for team all-around competition, or not make the team at all. Four of the seven girls selected for the team would compete in all four events of the team competition— vault, bars, beam, and floor. Only those four would be eligible to qualify for the individual all-around portion of the Olympic Games.

Steve shared bits and pieces of what he was doing with Shannon, and she passed the information along to us. We were confused about how the petition process worked, so we asked for a meeting with Steve. He explained that USA Gymnastics would normally send a doctor to look at Shannon's wrist and determine her ability to prepare for the meet, but in Shannon's case, the federation doctor knew the sports physician, Dr. Holden, and trusted his evaluations. Dr. Holden was familiar with Dr. Hieke, and Steve had just taken Shannon to Dr. Holden to get a second opinion. He had done so without telling us. While we understood he had good intentions, we objected to his taking our daughter to a doctor without first informing us. Steve apologized and argued time was of the essence, so we let the matter drop.

We had one more issue we wanted to discuss with Steve. The gym had been locked to parents for almost a month now. Only Jennie and Shannon were still working toward a meet. They worked out primarily during the day, so Sam, Jennie's mom (who also had a full-time job), and I could watch only on weekends. There were not too many of those left. Jennie was only fifteen and might well continue to compete, but we were pretty sure Shannon was not planning to compete after this Olympics. Steve explained that he wanted to keep everyone out until Shannon's petition was approved. He didn't want reporters slipping in and harassing him or Shannon. We understood that but asked to watch our daughter, at least on weekends, after that. "Sure," Steve said—at the time.

If Shannon's petition was accepted, she would not compete at Olympic Trials. After Trials the scores of Shannon and Dominique Moceanu (who had already petitioned through Trials because of a stress fracture) would be ranked with those of the gymnasts who did compete. If Shannon's and Dominique's scores still placed them in the top seven, they would be on the team. Steve knew Shannon had accumulated a good score at Championships. Jaycie Phelps had stayed very close to her, but even with a fall Shannon had significantly outdistanced the rest of the field. Dominique was one of the top gymnasts who could have bested Shannon's score, but she was now locked in just under Shannon.

The other side of the coin was that scores tended to escalate at Trials as the judges pumped the girls for the Olympics and Shannon had had a fall at Nationals. Steve believed her scores would place her on the team, but where she would rank was an open question.

Normally Ron would have gone to Olympic Trials since he enjoyed traveling to meets more than I did, but I was scheduled to give a talk on behalf of USA Gymnastics during a Wellness Clinic being held at Congress during Trials. Shannon and I sat out the meet, cheering on Jennie Thompson, Shannon's teammate and good friend, who had qualified from Nationals to Trials. Shannon was restless. She often popped out of her chair and walked around. She wanted to be out on that floor competing, and she wanted even more to be out on the floor in Atlanta.

When the dust settled, despite outstanding routines and excellent scores from other gymnasts at Trials, Shannon's score held firmly in first place. Shannon was actually headed to Atlanta and her second Olympic Games.

Just as in 1992, there was some criticism of the rankings. Some commentators complained that Shannon and Dominique made the team without going through Trials. Steve answered the criticism in an interview with Debbie Becker of *USA*

Today: "Why should the Olympic team hinge on one competition when you've been building up to it for years? If we want healthy kids on the team why should we want to beat them up? Why would you want to keep star athletes off of the team?"

Although we were certainly overjoyed that Shannon was to be a part of the 1996 Olympic team, there were still some doubts and fears, partly because of her injured wrist, but also because in this Olympics Steve would not be one of the two official coaches. Martha Karolyi and Mary Lee Tracy had been selected. In the Olympics only two coaches are allowed on the floor during the team competition, and this time at least one had to be female. As far as Shannon was concerned, this would mean that neither Steve nor Peggy would be spotting her during warm-ups prior to the competition and neither would be on the floor to give her last-minute advice or to set the equipment. All of these duties would fall to Martha and Mary Lee. Of course, Shannon had great respect for both women, but she was more comfortable with Steve. He was used to how she trained and how she reacted to various situations. She would miss his presence during the team competition.

CHAPTER TWENTY

Team Triumph

OR A FEW days we were alternately relieved and elated
that Shannon would be part of the Olympic Games in
Atlanta. One of the primary reasons Shannon had made
the commitment to try for another Olympics was that the
games would be held in her own country. Reality soon set in.
The cortisone shot was helping, but it was not as effective as
the first one. Shannon could not work on all events every day.
With both compulsories and optionals to be fine-tuned, training was difficult. She began to worry about letting the team
down because if her wrist got worse, she couldn't perform up
to par. She was concerned that she might have taken the spot
of another girl who would be of more benefit to the team.
While she had worked hard and endured a lot to make the
team, she had always assumed she would be an asset. Worse
than not making the Olympic team would be for her to be a
liability.

Stress was again building at the gym for both the coaches
and the gymnast. On the Friday two days before Steve,
Peggy, and Shannon were to leave for training camp in North
Carolina, Shannon called me at work. Steve had kicked her

265

out because, he insisted, she was not running hard enough on vault. She was distressed. Her hamstring still bothered her a bit, but she felt she had been running fine. Mark Cranston, who had been at the gym, commented that he didn't know how she could run much harder. Even in her anger Shannon excused Steve. She knew he was devastated that Jennie, an incredibly talented gymnast, had not qualified for the team largely because of a fall on bars. Shannon knew that Steve blamed himself and feared Jennie might quit the sport.

I knew it would not do Shannon any good for me to bash Steve. She might get upset with him, but she still trusted and respected him and would not tolerate anyone else criticizing him. It wasn't too hard to step back and remind Shannon that just as she had placed herself in God's care, she had to put Steve there too. It was more difficult to take my own advice the next morning when I arrived at the gym to watch the last workout I would be able to see before the Olympics only to find the gym locked again. Surely this was a mistake. The other gymnasts were on a summer break. Only the four elite gymnasts were still training.

I peered through the outside window. Steve saw me and came over. He told me sternly that there would be no viewing because he needed Shannon's full concentration and didn't want any distractions. He knew that Shannon never looked up to the viewing area while she was working out, and he knew I hadn't been near the gym the day before when he had kicked her out because he thought she was not performing up to par. Things weren't making sense, but there was no use arguing. Having been through the debacle when he threw me out before the 1995 U.S. Championships, I wanted to handle things differently now. After all, it was his gym and I certainly wasn't going to drag Shannon out. I decided my only option was to leave quietly.

Shannon and I had planned to do some shopping when she finished. I was a little late getting back to pick her up. Ironically, Steve had lost a little of her attention by not letting me in. She had told her teammates I was coming to watch, and, as gym progressed, one of them mentioned I was not there. Shannon had been worried. Steve had not mentioned our conversation to her. Nevertheless, Shannon had a good workout that day. I had prayed not to let frustration over-whelm me, and was grateful all had gone well. Just as before we never found out what Steve's real problem was. Probably just another case of PMS—Pre-Meet Syndrome. That's what parents in the viewing room dubbed Steve's irritability before a big competition.

The women's gymnastics team that had been put together for the Centennial Olympic Games was hailed as the best in U.S. history. The women were different ages and races, had different coaches, and were from different regions of the country. It was a mature, experienced team with six of its seven members seventeen years old or older.

At fourteen, Dominique Moceanu was the youngest. She had never competed in the Olympics or won a World Championship meet, but going into the Atlanta Olympics she was highly touted. She had been featured in magazines ranging from *Cosmopolitan* to *Newsweek* and had even published an autobiography. Dominique Dawes, nineteen, of Silver Spring, Maryland, and Kerri Strug, eighteen, of Tucson, both known for their power, were veterans of the 1992 Olympic Games. Kerri and Dominique Moceanu were both training with Bela Karolyi in Houston. Amy Chow, eighteen, of San Jose, California, was the quiet, intellectual one. Her routines emphasized difficulty. Amanda Borden, nineteen, was from Cincinnati. She was fun-loving and outgoing, which showed in her routines. The hometown of Jaycie Phelps, seventeen, was Greenfield, Indiana, but she was training in Cincinnati with Mary Lee Tracy, who was also Amanda's coach. Jaycie was most like Shannon, with an elegant style in her routines. All had solid credentials to make them champions.

In many ways Shannon was very different from the four-foot, seven-inch, seventy-six-pound, fifteen-year-old who competed in Barcelona four years earlier. She was five inches taller and twenty-five pounds heavier. She had overcome tremendous obstacles. Her maturity showed, but her experience brought added expectations. She says she remembers lying in bed with her stomach in knots.

"For this one, I really felt the pressure," she confessed later. "In 1992 I was an underdog. Whatever I did was good. In 1996 I was supposed to be leading the team. And in the United States everyone would be seeing it firsthand."

Six of the seven girls would compete in each portion of the team competition, and the lowest of the six scores would be dropped. Some of the girls from the team would also qualify to compete for the all-around and individual event titles. The top thirty-six girls from team competition are eligible for the all-around, with the limitation that only three girls from a single country's team can qualify.

Training camp in Greensboro, North Carolina, went smoothly. Shannon was back on track spiritually and physically, and her routines were improving each day. She did not perform her most difficult moves on floor and used an easier bar dismount during the exhibition at the training camp, but she hit her routines solidly and Steve and Peggy were pleased.

The team headed to Atlanta. In no time, podium training was scheduled. During these sessions, just as during the games, the gymnastics equipment is placed on raised platforms. Originally, the tradition of podium training was established for competition organizers to see how things worked, but it has become an important opportunity for athletes to get a sense of how the equipment will feel during competition.

In Atlanta gymnastics fans showed their enthusiasm for the sport by paying to watch podium training. Many had been unable to secure the high-demand and high-priced competition tickets, and they were eager for a look at the gymnasts. When the girls took the floor for the first time they were stunned and moved to see more than 22,000 people in the stands just to watch them practice. At the next session there were even more.

Shannon suffered some during this event. With the competition so close, she was still not doing full difficulty in all of her routines. On the one hand, Shannon wished for more time to prepare; on the other, she was eager for the competition to get under way.

In the meantime, Tessa flew to Oklahoma to drive to the Olympics with the rest of the family. We planned to stay with Bill Merritt's family for most of the first week, then move to a hotel room for a couple of days. After that we'd trust in God to provide for us. With Shannon's wrist problem, we had not tried earlier in the year to find accommodations. We subdued any worry about Shannon and enjoyed the drive. Tessa was optimistic, and her optimism rubbed off on all of us.

We arrived at the Merritts' house on Friday afternoon after spending a night in Birmingham. Shannon had called us just before we left Oklahoma City to say that all the gymnasts' names had been put in a hat and several had won tickets to opening ceremonies. She won two tickets. Tessa wanted very much to go to soak up every minute of the Olympics. Troy had no desire to fight the crowds. That left Ron and me. Ron would be far better at navigating to and from the arena, and since I knew the Merritts and he had just met them, it would be better for me to stay and watch the ceremonies on television with our hosts.

The ceremonies were spectacular, with a mixture of Southern, international, and African-American themes punctuated with classical references to the Olympic tradition. Because the most countries in the history of the modern Olympic movement had sent teams, the parade of athletes into the city's new Olympic stadium seemed to go on forever. The evening was capped with the dramatic lighting of the torch by Muhammad Ali. Erik Brady of *USA Today* described the festivities as "a worldwide Christmas morning."

Ron and Tessa were excited that they had been able to go. They told tales of being jam-packed, body-to-body, for an hour as the crowds were held back to let all of the athletes leave.

The gymnasts did not march in the opening ceremonies since their competition started early. Athletes who participated in the ceremonies spent most of the day at the arena preparing for the march and did not get to bed until 2:00 or 3:00 A.M. The coaches did not like this at all, and the gymnasts reluctantly agreed.

The USOC had given us two tickets to each gymnastic event, so we had to find tickets for Tessa and Troy. This had not been easy since the women's gymnastics events were among those in highest demand. Rod Davis at USA Gymnastics had helped us buy tickets to some events. When we still did not have enough tickets to the sold-out all-around competition, an Olympic sponsor agreed to supply them in exchange for an appearance by Shannon following the games. Shannon was happy to comply.

We wanted to see all of the gymnastics competition, as we had in Barcelona, so we headed off to each compulsory round. We were a little surprised at how low the scores were, no 9.8s or 9.9s. We wondered whether the judges were holding back for the later rounds. The Americans were in the next-to-last round. The highest scores would probably be given in the last round, but if the Americans did their job, they should be among the top four teams and therefore in the last round of the optionals. The Romanians had drawn a very early round and complained that this would hurt them. Throughout the day the scores held pretty steady.

The Americans, dressed in white leotards with stars on their left shoulders, all looked terrific as they began on bars. Each girl hit her routine. Shannon went last and earned the highest score for the team.

Beam was a different story. The Americans made a number of mistakes, which were reflected in the scores. Shannon was fifth in the lineup of six. Just as it appeared that our girls were giving away the meet, she mounted the beam. With her teammates, coaches, and parents anxiously watching, she performed the best compulsory routine of her competitive career and earned the highest score of the day on beam. The *New York Times* described her performance: "Miller, the two-time world all-around champion, promptly stepped up and changed the momentum, gracefully negotiating every potential mine field and scoring 9.737." She told reporters later, "I didn't really have to calm myself down. I was just telling myself I'd done it so many times and I was comfortable with this routine."

The Americans were back in the game and moved on to

36. Shannon in a pose from the 1996 Olympic floor exercise. © *Garrison's Photography, 1996.*

floor, where they were outstanding and definitely back in the hunt for gold. They followed up their dramatic floor performances with great vaults. Shannon was doing her part, hitting each routine just as she had trained daily in the gym. The team took the lead from the Romanians, but the Chinese and Russian teams had yet to perform.

The Chinese seemed to crumble under the weight of numerous problems, but the Russians lived up to their considerable potential. At the end of the day they had edged the Americans by just over twelve hundredths of a point.

The hometown paper, the *Atlanta Journal-Constitution*, described the results: "All that hootin' and hollerin' about inflated scores and it turned out to be a split. The Romanians, who competed in the undesirable first round of Sunday's women's compulsory gymnastics competition, outscored the Americans on uneven bars and vault. The U.S., which competed in the second round, earned higher marks on balance beam and floor exercise. Overall, the U.S. finished a half a point ahead of the third-place Romanians. Russia ended up in first."

In the individual category Shannon was in second, a fraction behind Lilia Podkopayeva of Ukraine, who scored no lower than 9.737 in any event. Shannon had done her part in compulsories for the team, but as at Nationals, her toughest challenge would be optionals.

We were a happy group that night, excited that the team was in such a good position and pleased that Shannon was competing so well. We sat in the stands during the meet and went up to the USA Gymnastics suite afterward to give Shannon a hug when the team came up.

The next day, with no women's competition, we saw a little of Atlanta and visited with the Merritts. The city was like a giant street carnival with crowds of people and vendors everywhere selling T-shirts, pins, hats, food, drinks, and almost everything else imaginable.

Ron's parents, Charles and Mabel Miller, had tickets to

the optional portion of the team competition and flew into town. We picked them up at the airport and took them to the Merritts' for dinner and then to their hotel room.

On the day of optionals we left early for the competition. We now realized the importance of arriving early to find parking and to reduce the long wait in the heat as everyone crowded together to get inside. It was better to get on the grounds, find a shady place to stand, and get into line as soon as the arena was opened. Just as in Barcelona, Tessa and Troy brought books to read. They had this routine figured out. Ron's parents took a taxi over. We planned to meet them again later after the meet.

We watched the earlier rounds of competition and then waited for Shannon's round to begin. The top four teams would be competing in the final round of competition: Russia, Romania, Belarus, and the United States. The Chinese, to our surprise, had not qualified in the top four. Competition would be very tight between the top three teams, Russia, the United States, and Romania. All three were more than capable of walking away with the gold medal.

On the evening of optionals the U.S. team marched confidently into the arena dressed in identical white leotards with a blue field of white stars on their left shoulders and red stripes across their right shoulders. They all smiled broadly as the audience filling the Georgia Dome cheered wildly when they entered. They wanted that gold more than ever, not just for themselves, but for all the cheering fans whose hopes and prayers were with them.

Suspense built as they warmed up. They were only a fraction of a point behind the Russians but also only slightly ahead of the Romanians. Anything could happen.

Once again the Americans started on bars. This had been a good rotation for them in compulsories, and they anticipated the same tonight. Jaycie Phelps started them off, with "Finniculi, Finnicula" from someone's floor routine playing in the background. She set a high standard with a 9.787, and each girl who followed lived up to it. Shannon, next to last, hit a terrific bar set, but after a long wait for a score, the number that flashed up was good but disappointing. We later learned that the judges had given her a higher score but the control panel headed by American judge Jackie Fie, which reevaluated the judges' scores, had instructed that it be lowered. After many inquiries we never learned why, although later we heard rumors of international politics. Shannon refused to be dismayed. She knew she had done a good job, and her score had certainly not hurt the team. Of course, the wildly enthusiastic crowd was unaware of all this.

When the rotation ended, television commentators said, "The Americans are nailing it and the crowd is loving it." The tally showed that in this single rotation the Russians had lost a remarkable 0.599 point to the Americans and were now in second place. But there were still three events to go.

Beam had been a real trial for the Americans during compulsories until Shannon conquered it. Now the American women attacked it aggressively and earned good scores. Once again Shannon, in the fifth position, received the highest beam score of the day.

The Americans were out to win the gold, and their floor performances proved it. Shannon's lack of tumbling practice showed in one big step. The rest of her routine looked perfect, and she concluded with a strong full twisting double back flip. Her score reflected her mistake, but with vault to follow there was no time to dwell on the error.

Going into vault the Americans had a comfortable lead over Russia. They wanted to keep it. Each gymnast had two opportunities to vault, with only the higher score counting. Gold seemed a little more certain as each of the first three American gymnasts hit solid vaults with no errors. Shannon followed in fourth position and performed a Yurchenko Arabian and a one-and-a-half twist. She added a good score to the total.

Next up was Dominique Moceanu. She was recovering

from a stress fracture in her right shin and her vault had suffered, but no one could foresee what happened. Dominique came up short on both vaults. A check of the scoreboard showed the Americans still leading the Russians but by a slimmer margin with one vaulter to go. Kerri Strug, a strong vaulter, was up last. If she performed well, Dominique's score could be dropped. With the crowd and her teammates watching eagerly, Kerri darted down the runway, vaulted—and fell. Whether from nerves or from a sore leg (she had it wrapped throughout the meet), Kerri found herself sitting on the mat just as Dominique had. In the fall she wrenched her left ankle. As she stood, she shook her foot.

Suddenly the Americans were concerned. They still had a comfortable margin over the Russians, but the Russians had not finished their floor routines. A loss at this point was unlikely since the remaining two Russians would have to score perfect 10s to catch the Americans and no scores even as high as 9.9 had yet been given to anyone on any event. While the girls assumed they could still win the gold, no one was breathing easy.

In what became one of the most replayed moments of the 1996 Olympic Games, Kerri vaulted again, landed cleanly, winced in pain, and then collapsed on the mat in tears. As it turned out, Kerri's second vault was unnecessary. The American women had won the gold, even without it. They were now Olympic champions, and they had outscored a record number of teams.

After optional competition as after compulsories, Shannon had the highest score on the team. She had led the American women to the country's first team Olympic gold medal in women's gymnastics. Overall she had the second highest score in the Games. Only Lilia Podkopayeva was ahead of her.

Shannon had overcome doubts, fears, and injury to get to this moment. Now she joined a handful of women gymnasts who won medals in two Olympics. In both she had been lead scorer on her team. In 1992 Shannon had been the top scorer for the American team, leading them to the bronze medal. Now, four years later, when the world thought she was too old even to make a second Olympic team, Shannon had again led her team to their goal—and gold.

We watched our daughter with an arm full of flowers softly singing the "Star Spangled Banner" as a huge American flag made its way toward the ceiling in honor of her and her team. Shannon later remembered the moment as "the coolest thing." "To actually win as a team was great," she said. "To bring it together and be there with your friends and have your flag being raised and have the national anthem being played—Wow!"

In Barcelona Shannon's spectacular feat, finishing first in the world after team competition, had been completely overshadowed by Kim Zmeskal's dramatic comeback and

37. The "Magnificent Seven" meet Chelsea, Hilary, and President Bill Clinton after winning the team medal in the Atlanta 1996 Olympic Games (Shannon is second from the left).

Karolyi's announcement of his short-lived retirement. She had not been bothered. As parents, we had been somewhat frustrated but had kept our feelings between ourselves. We pushed those thoughts aside and were grateful to be able to see our daughter go on to compete in the all-around and event finals. Shannon was ecstatic to have hit her routines so well, to have been a real support to her team, and to have the chance to continue in competition.

Now history seemed to be repeating itself. No one seemed to notice that Shannon had led the team. Reporters and photographers focused on Kerri, making her a heroine for her vault. Kerri had made an important contribution, but so had six other girls. No one girl had won the medal. The whole team had earned it. Shannon did not point to the scoreboard or explain during interviews who had led the team. She let the media's craziness roll off her because she still had the all-around and an event final coming up.

We met Shannon in the USA Gymnastics suite in the

38. Demi Moore and the Olympic team at Planet Hollywood after the team won gold.

Georgia Dome after the competition. All the girls were thrilled. The room was packed with gymnasts, parents, gymnastic officials, reporters, and photographers. Everyone was giddy with excitement. If Shannon's grandparents could get tickets to only one event, they had certainly picked a good one.

Word passed around the room that it was time for the gymnasts to go over to Planet Hollywood for a small party and that families were invited. Tessa and Troy were worn out and hungry after a day of gymnastics. Then somebody mentioned that Demi Moore and Bruce Willis might be there, and suddenly they were interested.

It took a major effort just to get through the huge crowd outside the restaurant. Inside we were hurried into an elevator and taken to the third floor. The gymnasts were already there and eating by the time we made it. We found a table and placed our order. Shannon came over and sat on my lap, happy to have her family there to share in her joy. She passed her medal around for us to see. While we ate Shannon did some interviews. When one reporter asked Tessa and Troy for their thoughts, Troy had little to say. Tessa, however, had never been at a loss for words. She was waxing enthusiastically about her delight when she spotted Demi Moore. Reporter and food were immediately forgotten as she grabbed her camera. A few minutes later she came back glowing. She had talked to both Demi Moore and Bruce Willis, who, she reported, were real people and talked to her as if she were a good friend. Tessa was mightily impressed.

CHAPTER TWENTY-ONE

A Sense of Balance

For shannon, the glow of the team victory soon faded into the necessity to prepare for more competition. She had qualified again in this Olympics for the all-around competition. She had won silver in Barcelona. Four years of hard work later, she had a chance to do even better.

Shannon's performance on bars was beautiful, but once again the score was a little disappointing. As a former judge, I knew that since Shannon's score on bars had been lowered in the team competition the judges were not likely to give her a higher score now. Her routine in the all-around was as good as, if not better than, her routine in team competition and the score was about the same. Shannon was sad but still refused to let this minor setback bother her.

After another outstanding beam set, she earned the highest beam score of the night. At the end of the second rotation, Dominique Dawes was leading the meet and Shannon was close behind in second place. Hopes of a one-two American finish were building. They were quickly dashed. Both Dominique and Shannon faltered on floor.

Shannon's wrist had been so painful she had hardly

tumbled in workouts. In her double layout she had a step forward for a significant deduction. Then, on the last tumbling
pass, she overrotated slightly and took a step out of bounds.
She was crushed. Tears welled up in her eyes and fell down
her cheeks, but Steve would not stand for crying. With a 9.475
she was out of the running for a medal, but the meet was not
over. He expected her to finish as strongly as she could. By
the time Steve finished his speech, Dominique was also in
tears. Following Shannon, she had taken a spill on floor and
dropped even lower than Shannon in the standings.

Shannon knew Steve was right. She pulled herself
together and marched to vault. Her first vault was good, but
her second one was great. Her score moved her into eighth
place, not in the medals but respectable placement in a field of
the world's best.

When she came to the USA Gymnastics suite after team
competition she had been jubilant. Tonight she was disappointed. We found a quiet place to talk and remind her about
her accomplishments. Despite two years of critics' specula-
tion that she was too old, four years after winning the silver
medal in the all-around in Barcelona, she was once again the
number one female American gymnast in the Olympic all-
around competition. She was still the best America had to
offer. She had been seeing the glass half empty. Her dad and
I could clearly see it was more than half full.

Shannon perked up but remained concerned that as the
alternate, she might have to replace Kerri in individual vault
competition. She would have to have two difficult vaults from
different families of vaults. Because of the stress on her wrist
she had avoided vaulting as much as possible. Now she had to
be ready to perform a Tsukahara, a vault she had not worked
on since the previous fall. She was rusty, and her wrist was
still not in top shape.

When she expressed her concern to me, I reminded her of
a Bible passage she had often found comforting: "With God,
all things are possible." She relaxed and smiled.

While Shannon had literally had her ups and downs during the Atlanta Olympics, the spirit of the Games had been contagious. Many of the hundreds of thousands of people cramming into the city for the sports and other attractions were families from the United States who took their vacation time to be a part of a once-in-a-lifetime event. Atlanta's downtown business district was festive.

At 1:19 A.M. on Saturday, July 27, the casual enjoyment of the Games was tragically interrupted. An explosion rocked Centennial Olympic Park when it was full of post-Game revelers listening to music. The park had been the gathering place for these Games, built especially to welcome Atlanta's visitors and intended to be the centerpiece of the city's post-Olympic legacy. An attack on the park seemed to be an attack on the city's hospitality and on the spirit of the Games.

A woman was killed by the blast, and a man died of a heart attack soon afterward. There were rumors of a "suspicious device" at the Georgia Dome, the gymnastics venue. We were terribly saddened that for the second time in our lives we were close to what seemed to be a senseless terrorist act.

We were not terribly worried about Shannon. The gymnasts were staying at a fraternity house on the campus of Emory University several miles away from downtown. We knew security was tight around the athletes. The bomber had chosen the most open and accessible place at the Games to wreak destruction. Although the bomb was a reminder of the dark side of human nature, the Games continued to try to show the positive elements.

"I'm glad we were able to continue the Games," Shannon said later. "What they're about is peace and sportsmanship."

Shannon had also qualified for individual competition on the balance beam. While she prepared for event finals, we moved for the second time. We had stayed with the Merritts until all their other company arrived. Then after Ron's parents left we moved into the hotel room they had occupied. In the meantime we had been seeking other accommodations but had not yet found any. At church on Wednesday night Laurie and Bill Merritt mentioned our plight and asked if anyone knew where we might stay. The next day, just as we had to check out of the hotel, Laurie called to say friends of theirs, Gary and Sandy Blohm, were going out of town for a week and would love for us to stay in their house. We considered this proof that God answers our prayers. The Blohms lived in a beautiful wooded area of Cobb County, about forty-five minutes north of Atlanta. We spent the day moving and getting settled in.

With renewed confidence Shannon attacked vault and beam workouts. After the first day of working on the Tsukahara, she began to look forward to the vault competition. She could and would do the vault. By now Kerri had officially withdrawn. Here was another opportunity to perform in the Olympic Games, and Shannon decided to appreciate it.

On the night of vault finals her warm-up vaults were great. She hit every one without a hitch. Just before the competition began each gymnast was given a chance to get the feel of the apparatus on which she would actually compete. For vault competition, the norm at international competitions was for each gymnast to do two vaults. If she planned to compete with two different vaults, she would usually practice one of each.

Shannon first warmed up a Yurchenko Arabian. To my surprise as a judge sitting in the stands, she then did the same vault again. I had expected her to do a timer, or partial vault, to prepare for the Tsukahara on her second try, since the springboard would be set slightly different for that vault. I assumed she must be allowed three warm-up vaults during Olympic event finals. Shannon later told us she had assumed the same thing when Steve instructed her to repeat her first vault. She got back in line to prepare for the Tsukahara, but just before her turn an official motioned her out of line. She had no time left. Shannon was a little disturbed but figured she could make the adjustment for the different vault when the time came.

In the stands, I was concerned and confused. I knew she usually got only two practice vaults. Why had she done the same vault twice?

In the competition Steve directed her to perform the Yurchenko first. She nodded at him, looked for the signal from the judges, then sprinted down the runway. She completed a powerful vault—maybe too powerful. She had to take a big hop forward. It wasn't perfect, but she still had another vault to go. I knew she had a reasonably good score. If she hit a great second vault, she would still be in medal contention.

Shannon walked back to the beginning of the runway, concentrating on the more difficult vault. The judges raised their flag to signal that they were ready, and she saluted them by raising her right arm. She charged down the runway to do the Tsukahara. This would be her last vault of these Games.

As she neared the springboard Shannon realized her steps were off, making it impossible to take off from the leg to which she was accustomed. There was no choice but to proceed and try to make an appropriate adjustment. She hit the springboard behind the white line that provides a target for the gymnast's feet. With her legs uncharacteristically split in the air, she twisted and stretched for the vaulting horse.

The crowd in the stands gasped as one of her hands missed the apparatus. The next thing she knew, she was sitting on the mat with coaches, judges, fans, and millions of television viewers watching. After the meet, in her misery, she said, "I prayed so hard. I felt so confident God was taking care of me. What happened?"

Shannon was already in the USA Gymnastics suite by the time Ron and I made our way there. Steve saw us as we entered the room and made his way over. He had tried talking to Shannon. Now she needed her family. With beam competition still to go, she seemed to be overwhelmed. As her mother, I wanted to hug her, dry her tears, and assure her everything would be fine. But now she was a young woman of nineteen and she needed more.

We began talking in the hallway outside the gymnastics suite, but almost everyone who passed had a word of support that seemed only to make Shannon feel worse. We asked for a secluded spot. Someone led us to a suite for viewing the basketball court. There Shannon's dad and I tried to ease her distress.

We reviewed how far she had come from the skinny-legged little sprite who had begun competing ten years earlier. We talked soothingly about all the obstacles she had over-come, the injuries she had worked through, the doubts she had conquered. We described how we had watched her seize almost every setback as an opportunity. We reminded her how she had put mistakes behind her at the Pan-American Games and at Championships to go on and win. We told her how proud we were of her, not only for the uniquely talent-ed gymnast she is, but because of the fine woman she had become.

We encouraged her to keep her faith in herself and her faith in God. I reminded her of one of her favorite poems, "Footprints." A copy is hanging on the wall of her bedroom at our house. She uses a bookmark with a version of it. And once she bought me a key ring with a tiny copy of it. It tells of someone who sees God's footprints beside his own except at the toughest times of life when there is only one set. When he asks why God was not walking with him then, God replies, "During those times, I was carrying you."

Shannon could see many times when God walked along-side her. Now, we told her, maybe she needed to let God carry her. She needed to embrace opportunity, climb up on that beam, and express the talent, beauty, grace, and goodness God had given her. Finally, to our relief, her tears dried and her sweet smile appeared. When we left for the long drive back to Cobb County for the night, we felt we had done all we could. We had to leave the rest to God and Shannon.

Many people, including Shannon's coaches, have described her as a tough competitor. They are right, although she is not tough in the hard-as-steel, never-give-an-inch sense. Shannon is tough in the classic dictionary definition: "strong, but pliant." She will bend without tearing or breaking. Her disappointments in vault and all-around may have bent her quite a bit, but they would not break her spirit. Her dad and I were sure of this.

As we entered the Georgia Dome the next night we stopped to divide the tickets. We had four, two we had bought and two we had received as parents of a competitor. We let Shannon's older sister, Tessa, and younger brother, Troy, pick their seats.

"Troy and I have to have these," Tessa said as soon as she realized two were down in front of where the awards podium would be placed. "I have to be able to get a good picture of Shannon accepting her medal."

Ron and I smiled indulgently and handed over the two good tickets. As we began our climb toward the rafters, we heard Troy say, "I sure hope you're right. I don't want Shannon to feel bad any more. I'm so nervous, I'll be glad when it's over." Ron and I chuckled over this. Troy rarely comments on Shannon's gymnastics. We had assumed he regarded this as no big deal. We were wrong.

I could tell as soon as I saw Shannon that the crisis was over. She was up fourth. The capacity crowd in the Georgia Dome cheered wildly as her name was announced. Two of the three gymnasts before her had taken spills: Alexandra Marinescu of Romania had a difficult routine and fell twice, and Dominique Moceanu slipped during a back flip and landed hard on her head. But Shannon appeared unruffled as she approached the beam.

Shannon saluted the judges, then stretched her arms out

to begin. The cheering, whistling, applauding crowd became instantly quiet. She stepped onto the springboard and raised her hands, holding them in front of her just above the surface of the beam. When I see her like this, I always think of a master pianist preparing to draw every possible bit of music out of an instrument. Shannon seemed incredibly calm, but as she placed her hands on the beam to begin her press-to-handstand, I was barely breathing. I knew her routine by heart and counted off each move as she made it. I knew which ones were most difficult and which ones were most likely to give her trouble. The minute-and-a-half routine felt like hours. Her mount was solid. One down.

The whole crowd seemed to be holding its collective breath. It was as if people were afraid they might blow her off the beam if they made a sound. Suddenly, out of the silence, came a man's voice yelling "Cut out the flashes!" to overeager picture takers. I prayed that Shannon wouldn't be startled by the noise but figured she would not even notice since she was used to tuning out all distractions. Later she told me she had heard him, to her surprise. She remembered thinking he was sweet to be concerned that the flashes might bother her. Then it dawned on her that in the past she had been so completely focused on her routines during competition that she never heard or saw anything. If she was this aware of her surroundings, she was *too* relaxed. She made a concerted effort to think about the beam.

In the stands, I certainly was not relaxed.

Next was a switch leg leap into a back handspring, quarter turn to her hands, and on into two back extension rolls, each ending in a handstand. A good combination. Done! I tensed even more for her front somersault, which would be tricky because of its blind landing. Solid!

I couldn't feel any relief because the back handspring layout, layout was coming up. I had seen her perform this series perfectly many times, but she had missed it at U.S. Championships. I felt frozen and could hardly breathe as she pushed backward into the first skill. The crowd cheered, and I realized I could check off another one. The Miller was left. This was a difficult and complicated move, and she had occasionally missed it in competition. Not tonight. Perfect!

Shannon cleanly executed her leap series, including a beautiful piked wolf jump, then charged down the beam for the dismount. Tim Daggett told his audience of millions, "This is just beautiful. Now she's saying, 'Just stick the dismount!'" I was saying, just land that full twisting double back. Land it she did, with only a tiny shuffle of one foot. Ecstasy!

On the beam Shannon was no longer competing for a medal. She was expressing the pure joy of doing a sport she truly loves. She was feeling all the hard work and love so many people had put into that moment in her life. The crowd sensed it. As she landed the spectators nearly blew the roof off the Georgia Dome with their cheering. When her score came up, 9.862, it was the highest of the competition with four girls to go.

39. Shannon performing a wolf jump on the balance beam during the 1996 Olympics. Photo courtesy Steve Lange.

The instant Shannon's feet hit the mat I was out of my seat, jumping up and down, shouting my joy. Ron didn't dare try to hold me back. Down on the floor Shannon was beaming. It didn't matter where she placed. She had demonstrated her mastery of the beam and of herself.

We knew Shannon had done what she set out to do, but we did not yet know whether it would earn her a medal. We calmed down to watch the other gymnasts. Lilia Podkopayeva was up fifth, immediately after Shannon. She had a difficult and elegant routine but with a slight wobble. Sixth was Olga Teslenko of Ukraine. Only fifteen and relatively inexperienced, she came up short. We knew Shannon had at least a bronze medal.

The last two gymnasts could keep it that way. Gina Gogean, rock-solid with years of competition, had won silver in the all-around. She was steady on the beam, but her routine was not as original or as difficult as Shannon's. When her scores were posted we knew Shannon had silver. By now I was going even crazier. People around us had figured out who we were and were shouting with us.

Finally, the last gymnast, Roza Galieva of Russia, mounted the beam. She was reigning European champion and had a routine loaded with difficulty. She was moving smoothly and confidently along when she wobbled, then fell. Shannon had won an individual Olympic gold medal. It took a few seconds to sink in.

Soon the American flag was being raised again as Shannon stood alone on the center podium of the Olympic gymnastics awards platform to receive her medal. It was the first Olympic individual gold medal on beam by an American and the first gold medal in individual competition by any American gymnast in a nonboycotted Olympics. As we watched Ron and I couldn't stop smiling long enough to sing the "Star Spangled Banner." We were so excited we couldn't keep up with the words.

We were having such a great time in the stands that we hated to leave, but we were eager to see Shannon, Tessa, and Troy. I knew Tessa would be going crazy. Troy would be more sedate. We headed to the USA Gymnastics suite.

While we waited for Shannon to arrive Troy confirmed my suspicions about Tessa. He said she was bouncing up and down telling everybody Shannon was her sister. "Mom, those people will never forget the performance Tessa put on," Troy exclaimed. "Well," Tessa sassily replied, "this is a once-in-a-lifetime experience and I wanted to enjoy it."

NBC's cameras took Shannon's medal ceremony to 103 million viewers. Tessa captured her sister's big moment on film for herself, just as she predicted.

In a tribute to Shannon that ran in the *Edmond Evening Sun*, Jack Chance wrote,

> *She kept us on an emotional roller coaster ride and when it came down to her very last event, with so much riding on it, she showed us what a true champion and hero she really is.*
>
> *Suffering from chronic tendinitis in her left wrist and with pressures that most people could not begin to endure, she managed to stay focused on her dream and dazzled the world with some of the most beautiful and pristine gymnastics that one could ever hope to witness. In front of millions of viewers and cameras flashing she worked the beam with such precision and elegance, performing elements with the utmost level of difficulty, such as her signature move "The Miller."*
>
> *She ended her routine with a picture perfect double back with a full twist dismount, that was followed by a deafening roar from the thirty thousand plus fans in the Georgia Dome. At that moment in time, I doubt that this tiny gymnast realized (how completely) she had captivated the world.*

Epilogue

AFTER THE EXCITEMENT of winning a gold medal and the television interviews that followed, Shannon was still on Cloud Nine when Peggy reminded her she still had to perform in the exhibition of gymnastic stars the next day. She was more than happy to perform again; it was doing the Macarena that didn't thrill her. She was a little embarrassed doing this dance, even though Peggy admonished, "But you're such a good dancer." However, when the lights came on and the cameras came out, so did the performer in Shannon. She found she thoroughly enjoyed all the dances, including the Macarena.

Then the gymnastics portion of the Centennial Olympic Games came to a close. "How fitting that the balance beam was Shannon Miller's final event and that it ended in gold," wrote sports reporter Susan Vinella in the *Atlanta Journal-Constitution*. "The four-inch-wide apparatus requires nerves of steel and unwavering dedication. Miller, America's most consistent performer, was made for the event."

Shannon decided not to attend the athlete celebration in Washington, D.C., this time. Edmond wanted to give a parade in her honor. Plans had been in the works even before

40. Shannon with two gold medals. © Garrison's Photography, Edmond, Oklahoma, 1996.

her first competition. Three governors were coming—current Governor Frank Keating, former Governor George Nigh, and former Governor and Senator David Boren, who is president of the University of Oklahoma, where Shannon took classes the previous fall and spring and was planning to resume classes in the spring.

We had been very naive about the parade before. This time we thought we were better prepared. But you're never really prepared to see fifteen thousand people show up in the heat on a workday, standing for hours to get a glimpse of your daughter. Ron and I were still awed.

Tessa proudly waved to the crowds and pointed out the three helicopters (from the three different networks) flying along the parade route again this time. Two of the local stations carried the parade on television. The second parade was every bit as exciting as the first.

City and state officials made speeches and bestowed gifts

*41. This City of Edmond sign reads: "Home of Shannon Miller, Winner of
2 Olympic Gold Medals, Atlanta 1996, 5 Olympic Medals, Barcelona 1992.*
© *David Allen, 1997.*

on Shannon. The mayor, the postmaster, the superintendent
of schools, and the newspaper editor all had their say.
Shannon was grateful for every word and every gift, but once
again one gift stood above all the others.

A local car dealership, Smicklas Chevrolet, had learned
from Steve that Shannon's dream car was a hunter green
Camaro. At the close of the parade ceremony they arrived in
the car and handed her the keys. She was flabbergasted. The
red Saturn had been a marvelous gift. She didn't think anything could top it, yet here before her eyes was the car she had
always wanted in the perfect color. She was too excited to
drive it home and passed the keys to her dad, telling him,
"Take good care of it."

When the Edmond post office offered "Shannon Miller"
cancellations on envelopes right after the Olympics, 78,000

pieces of mail came in from across the United States and around the world for the special marks.

Shannon's life has been a nonstop whirlwind since the Olympic Games. Although she gets a little worn out from time to time, she's enjoying every minute. Her wrist gradually improved, and she was able to participate in some professional meets. For two seasons she toured with her teammates and other world-class gymnasts performing exhibitions. She and her teammates have become a tight-knit group. She has also become good friends with some of her former competitors from other countries.

Shannon is busy making commercials, endorsing products, signing autographs, writing articles, and giving speeches. Sometimes I'm still amazed when I pick up a telephone book with Shannon on the cover or pass a billboard carrying her picture. She takes classes at the University of Oklahoma, assists with the women'ss team when she has time, and has her own apartment. She comes home to spend the night every now and then, but she is learning the joys and difficulties of living on her own, including paying bills and keeping house for herself.

Along with Carl Lewis, Shannon was co–grand marshal of the Tournament of Roses Parade on January 1, 1997. The theme was "Life's Shining Moments," and Shannon has certainly had her share. She still trains and competes at the professional level. Her team won first place in the USA vs. the World meet in Cincinnati in 1996, and she placed first in the all-around in the World Professional Gymnastics Championships, the Women's World Professional Gymnastics Championships, and the World University Games in 1997. She was the first American to ever win the University Games, which were held in Catania, Italy, where she had triumphed as "Queen Yankee" so long ago in her career. Most recently she and Amy Chow placed first in the 1998 Reese's Gymnastics Cup, repeating a 1997 win.

42. A portion of I-35 that passes through Edmond was renamed Shannon Miller Parkway in 1998 (left to right: Mayor Bob Rudkin, Claudia and Ron Miller, Kiwanian Whit Marks, Shannon, Kiwanian Neoma Weiss, Governor Frank Keating, and City Councilman Bob Huggins.

Shannon continues her support of the Children's Miracle Network and Drug Free Youth and plans to continue to lend assistance to the Pediatric AIDS Foundation. She donates regularly to a wide variety of charities. Shannon still gets hundreds of fan letters each week, and several Shannon Miller web sites have been established on the Internet. The city of Edmond commissioned a bronze statue of Shannon to be the centerpiece of a children's park that will be called the Shannon Miller Park. The Oklahoma House and Senate passed a resolution to name the portion of I-35 that runs through Edmond "Shannon Miller Parkway."

Her motivational book, *Winning Every Day*, was published in the spring of 1998. Immediately after final exams at the University of Oklahoma, Shannon left on a month-long book tour.

Of course, we are proud of Shannon, but not just for her gymnastic talent. Our goal was never to raise the country's most decorated gymnast but to produce a really good person who sets goals and sticks to them and who also considers the feelings of other people and keeps a strong faith in God. Shannon has taught us the value of perseverance and dedication, the joy of seeing the good in everyone, and the benefits of looking forward. Today we look forward with her to a wonderful future.